INTEGRATIVE APPROACHES TO QUALITY, DATA ANALYSIS, AND INTERDISCIPLINARY RESEARCH

INTEGRATIVE APPROACHES TO QUALITY, DATA ANALYSIS, AND INTERDISCIPLINARY RESEARCH

Amir Ahmad Dar, PhD
Waseem Z. Lone, PhD
Editors

APPLE ACADEMIC PRESS

First edition published 2026

Apple Academic Press Inc.
1265 Goldenrod Circle, NE,
Palm Bay, FL 32905 USA

760 Laurentian Drive, Unit 19,
Burlington, ON L7N 0A4, Canada

CRC Press
2385 NW Executive Center Drive,
Suite 320, Boca Raton FL 33431

4 Park Square, Milton Park,
Abingdon, Oxon, OX14 4RN, UK

Apple Academic Press exclusively co-publishes with CRC Press, an imprint of Taylor & Francis Group, LLC

Library and Archives Canada Cataloguing in Publication

CIP data on file with Canada Library and Archives

Library of Congress Cataloging-in-Publication Data

CIP data on file with US Library of Congress

ISBN: 978-1-77964-100-7 (hbk)
ISBN: 978-1-77964-101-4 (ebk)
DOI: 10.1201/9781779641014

Dedicated to my Wife, Samiya Jan

—Dr. Amir Ahmad Dar

About the Editors

Amir Ahmad Dar, PhD
Assistant Professor, Department of Statistics, Lovely Professional University, India

Amir Ahmad Dar, PhD, is currently serving as an Assistant Professor in the Department of Statistics at Lovely Professional University in India. Dr. Dar has an impressive academic portfolio, having published over 20 research papers and 10 book chapters. He has presented his work at eight national and international conferences. His research interests include actuarial statistics, experimental design, financial derivatives, and financial mathematics. He completed his BSc in Actuarial and Financial Mathematics at the Islamic University of Science and Technology in Awantipora, India. He pursued his MSc and PhD in Actuarial Science at B S Abdur Rahman University in Chennai, India.

Waseem Z. Lone, PhD
Research Associate, Indian Institute of Technology, Patna, India.

Waseem Z. Lone, PhD, is currently a Research Associate at the Indian Institute of Technology, Patna, India. His research focuses on Fourier and wavelet analysis. He has published over 20 papers in various esteemed international journals. Dr. Waseem has also served as an Assistant Professor at Lovely Professional University, Punjab, India, and has been awarded a prestigious fellowship funded by the Council of Scientific & Industrial Research (CSIR), Government of India. He earned a master's degree from the University of Kashmir, India. He also completed his PhD in Mathematics at the same university.

Contents

Contributors

Olayan Albalawi
Department of Statistics, University of Tabuk, Saudi Arabia

Bashar Suleiman Argungu
Department of General Studies, Adamu Augie College of Education, Argungu, Kebbi State, Nigeria

Geeta Arora
Department of Mathematics, Lovely Professional University, Phagwara, Punjab, India

Imran Azad
University of Technology and Applied Science, Oman

Abbas Yusuf Balarabe
Department of Mathematics, Kebbi State University of Science and Technology, Aliero, Kebbi State, Nigeria

Yakubu Ibrahim Barga
Mathematics Department, Federal University Birnin Kebbi, Kebbi State, Nigeria

Avneet Kaur Chahal
School of Chemical Science and Engineering, Lovely Professional University, Phagwara, India

Ataur Rahman Farooqi
CEBA, University of Technology and Applied Science, Nizwa, Oman

Jatoth Heeraman
Department of Mechanical Engineering, Sridevi Women's Engineering College,
Jawaharlal Nehru Technological University (JNTUH) Hyderabad, Telangana, India

Akshat Jain
School of Chemical Engineering and Physical Sciences, Lovely Professional University, Phagwara, Punjab, India

Prerna Jain
Department of Mathematics, Lovely Professional University, Phagwara, Punjab, India

Preety Kalra
Department of Mathematics, Lovely Professional University, Phagwara, Punjab, India

Navdeep Kaur
Department of Mathematics, Lovely Professional University, Phagwara, Punjab, India

Arshad Ahmad Khan
Department of Mathematics, Guru Nanak University Hyderabad, India

Mohammad Shahfaraz Khan
University of Technology and Applied Sciences, Muscat, Oman

Manzoor Ahmad Khanday
Lovely Professional University, Phagwara, Punjab, India

Anil Kumar
Department of Mathematics, Lovely Professional University, Phagwara, Punjab, India

Krishan Kumar
Department of Psychiatry, Postgraduate Institute of Medical Education & Research (PGIMER), Chandigarh, India

Rakesh Kumar
School of Chemical Science and Engineering, Lovely Professional University, Phagwara, India

Tashi Lhamo
Technical Training Institute, Khuruthang, Ministry of Education and Skills Development, Bhutan; Department of Mathematics, Lovely Professional University, Phagwara, Punjab, India

Rakesh Malhan
School of Chemical Engineering and Physical Sciences, Lovely Professional University, Phagwara, Punjab, India

Mehak Malhotra
School of Chemical Engineering and Physical Sciences, Lovely Professional University, Phagwara, Punjab, India

Nitin Kumar Mishra
Department of Mathematics, Lovely Professional University, Phagwara, Punjab, India

Mohit Nain,
OM Sterling Global University, India

Renuka Namwad
Department of Mathematics, Lovely Professional University, Phagwara, Punjab, India

Renuka S. Namwad
Department of Mathematics, Lovely Professional University, Phagwara, Punjab, India

Nisha
Department of Mathematics, Lovely Professional University, Phagwara, Punjab, India

Amit Kumar Pathak
College of Economics and Business Administration, University of Technology and Applied Sciences, Ibri, Oman

Hrithik P. M.
Department of Mathematics, School of Chemical Engineering and Physical Sciences, Lovely Professional University, Phagwara, Punjab, India

Ranu
Department of Mathematics, NIILM University, Kaithal, Haryana, India

Sani Haliru Rini
Department of Mathematics, School of Chemical Engineering and Physical Sciences, Lovely Professional University, Phagwara, Punjab, India

Tasneem Shah
Kwantlen Polytechnic University, Surrey, BC, Canada

Sachitanand Singh
Department of Optometry, UIAHS, Chandigarh University, Mohali, Punjab, India
Department of Optometry, CSHS, Chitkara University, Rajpura, Punjab, India

Chukka Sowjanya
Lovely Professional University, Phagwara, Punjab, India

Renu Thakur
Centre for Research Impact and Outcome, Chitkara University, Rajpura, Punjab, India

Abbreviations

ACF	autocorrelation function
AD	Anderson–Darling
ADHD	attention-deficit hyperactivity disorder
AIC	Akaike's information criterion
AIMS	African Institute for Mathematical Sciences
AQI	air quality index
ARIMA	autoregressive integrated moving average
AWMA	African Women in Mathematics Association
BIC	Bayesian information criterion
BMI	body mass index
CNS	cumulative negative sum
CPFR	collaborative planning, forecasting, and replenishment
CPS	cumulative positive sum
CSA	climate-smart agriculture
CUSUM	cumulative sum
DSD	direct store delivery
DTR	decision tree regression
EOQ	economic order quantity
GDPI	gross direct premium income
ICTP	International Centre for Theoretical Physics (ICTP)
IOs	insurance offices
IP	insurance penetration
JIT	just-in-time
KMO	Kaiser–Meyer–Olkin
LCL	lower control limit
MA	moving average
MAE	mean absolute error
MAPE	mean absolute percentage error
MCMC	Markov Chain Monte Carlo
ML	maximum likelihood
MLR	multiple linear regression
MR	moving range
MSE	mean squared error

PACF	partial autocorrelation function
Q–Q	quantile–quantile
RFID	radio-frequency identification
RFR	random forest regression
RMSE	root mean squared error
SDP	state domestic product
SPC	statistical process control
SVM	support vector machine
SVR	support vector regression
UCL	upper control limit
VMI	vendor-managed inventory

Preface

In a world increasingly driven by data and precision, this book, *Integrative Approaches to Quality, Data Analysis, and Interdisciplinary Research,* offers a comprehensive exploration of advanced methodologies and their applications across various domains. This volume aims to bridge the gap between theory and practice, presenting insights that span quality management, risk assessment, environmental analysis, healthcare, and more.

PART I: Data-Driven Analysis in Various Sectors

Part I focuses on the transformative power of data in addressing complex challenges. We begin with an "Analysis of Air Pollution in Delhi Using Machine Learning Techniques," showcasing how advanced algorithms can provide critical insights into environmental health. The chapter on "Modeling Socioeconomic and Regional Factors in the Nonlife Insurance Sector of India through Regression Analysis" highlights the intricate interplay between socioeconomic variables and insurance dynamics. "Quantitative Analysis of Healthcare Costs: Integrating Behavioral, Regional, and Demographic Factors" offers a holistic view of the healthcare landscape, emphasizing the importance of comprehensive data integration.

In the agricultural sector, "A Time-Series Analysis of Lemon Production in Ten Major Cities of India" illustrates the application of statistical techniques to understand and forecast agricultural trends. Finally, "Machine Learning Algorithms for COVID-19 Data Analysis with Python" provides a timely examination of how machine learning can be harnessed to analyze and respond to global health crises.

PART II: Interdisciplinary Studies in Agriculture, Education, and History

Part II underscores the value of cross-disciplinary approaches. "Optimizing Water Management for Sustainable Agriculture: A Multidisciplinary Approach" discusses the integration of various scientific methods to enhance agricultural sustainability. "Factor Analysis for Attention Deficit Hyperactivity Disorder Symptoms Questionnaires (Adult ADHD

Self-Report Scale v1.1) Among HEI Learners" seeks to improve educational support through precise diagnostic tools.

The historical journey from "Ancient Mathematics to Modern Data Science: Africa's Legacy and Future" reveals the profound contributions and future potential of African mathematics. "Exploring Decentralized Inventory Strategies: A Study" examines innovative approaches to inventory management, highlighting the benefits and challenges of decentralization.

PART III: Advanced Techniques in Quality and Risk Management

The final section delves into cutting-edge methodologies in quality and risk management. "Advancing Quality Management: Exploring the Power of CUSUM Control Charts in Process Monitoring and Improvement" demonstrates how these charts can revolutionize quality control processes. "Premium Precision: A Bayesian Approach Using Poisson and Exponential Models in Insurance Risk Assessment" explores advanced statistical methods to enhance the precision of risk assessments.

Finally, "Optimizing Supply Chain Efficiency with Mathematica: Mathematical and Statistical Methods for Finite Planning Horizons" presents sophisticated techniques for optimizing supply chain operations, leveraging the power of Mathematica.

This book serves as a resource for scholars, practitioners, and students, offering a rich tapestry of knowledge and insights across various fields. By integrating diverse perspectives and methodologies, we hope to inspire innovative solutions and foster a deeper understanding of the complex world we navigate. Together, let us embark on this intellectual journey, embracing the power of integrative approaches to advance knowledge and drive meaningful change.

Introduction

The capacity to apply advanced analytical techniques and combine several fields of knowledge is essential for tackling difficult challenges in today's environment of rapid change. There is a growing demand for novel techniques that integrate quality management, data analysis, and interdisciplinary research as sectors and research areas become more interconnected. *Integrative Approaches to Quality, Data Analysis, and Interdisciplinary Research* is a book that attempts to investigate these intersections and provide insights into how these different but related professions might collaborate to promote advancement and innovation.

This book is essentially about embracing a holistic approach to problem-solving and dismantling conventional barriers. Once limited to process control and manufacturing, quality management is today essential to a wide range of industries, including finance, education, and healthcare. The emergence of big data and machine learning has enabled data analysis to provide historically unseen possibilities for pattern recognition, forecasting, and decision optimization in a variety of fields. In the meantime, interdisciplinary study is becoming more and more acknowledged as being crucial to tackling the complex problems of the modern world, whether they involve managing natural resources, comprehending global health crises, or investigating the cultural and historical backgrounds of scientific advancement.

Research and practice can be conducted more entirely because of the integration of various domains. The frameworks and procedures offered by quality management guarantee that procedures are effective, dependable, and always improving. The tools and methods needed to manage big, complicated datasets, derive insightful conclusions, and facilitate data-driven decision-making are brought to bear by data analysis. Interdisciplinary research encourages cooperation between experts from other fields, which stimulates creativity and leads to the development of novel solutions that would not be possible within the boundaries of a single subject.

Readers will come across a wide range of case studies and applications that highlight the effectiveness of these integrative approaches throughout this book. The examples given highlight the practical applications of integrating quality management, data analysis, and multidisciplinary research, from solving urgent environmental challenges to improving public health and company operations. These illustrations not only show the usefulness of this kind of integration but also stress how crucial it is to have an adaptable and flexible attitude when tackling the complexity of today's problems.

This book not only examines these applications but also explores the theoretical foundations of the methods covered. Through a consideration of the guiding principles of quality management, the statistical techniques that propel data analysis, and the cooperative approaches that characterize multidisciplinary research, readers will get a more profound comprehension of the interplay among these components. Anyone hoping to use these ideas in their work—in academia, business, or public policy—needs to have this basic knowledge.

In the end, the book *Integrative Approaches to Quality, Data Analysis, and Interdisciplinary Research* is an appeal to acknowledge the interdependence of knowledge and the importance of cooperation and integration in the advancement of theory and practice. Being able to draw from a wide range of tools and viewpoints is not only useful, but critical in a world where the challenges we confront are becoming more complicated and interconnected. With the help of this book, readers will be able to negotiate this terrain with the knowledge and abilities needed to meaningfully contribute to both their fields and society at large.

PART I
Data-Driven Analysis in Various Sectors

CHAPTER 1

Machine Learning Algorithms for COVID-19 Data Analysis with Python

TASHI LHAMO[1,2*] and GEETA ARORA[2*]

[1]*Technical Training Institute, Khuruthang, Ministry of Education and Skills Development, Bhutan*

[2]*Department of Mathematics, Lovely Professional University, Phagwara, Punjab, India*

*Corresponding author

ABSTRACT

Machine learning algorithms have emerged as a potent tool for COVID-19 data analysis, enabling researchers to identify patterns, predict outcomes, and optimize interventions. The COVID-19 pandemic has led to abundant data from diverse sources, including health organizations, governments, and individuals. This chapter explores the machine learning algorithms for COVID-19 data in Python. An overview of common machine learning algorithms, such as decision trees, random forests, support vector machine, and linear regression, and their applications for COVID-19 data analysis is discussed. Moreover, implementing these algorithms using Python libraries such as scikit-learn is explored. The findings demonstrate that machine learning algorithms can be practical for COVID-19 data analysis, providing insights into the spread of the virus and informing public health interventions.

Integrative Approaches to Quality, Data Analysis, and Interdisciplinary Research.
Amir Ahmad Dar and Waseem Z. Lone (Eds.)

DOI: 10.1201/9781779641014-2

1.1 INTRODUCTION

Machine learning is a field that involves creating models and algorithms capable of learning from data and using that knowledge to make predictions or decisions [1]. These methods involve developing algorithms and mathematical models that are not explicitly programmed but instead learn from data. Machine learning has played a crucial role in forecasting and controlling the spread of COVID-19, making it an indispensable tool in the fight against the pandemic [2]. Similarly, Python has emerged as a highly popular programming language, particularly in data analysis. Its versatility and flexibility have contributed to its widespread adoption within the data science community. The COVID-19 pandemic has led to a significant increase in the demand for data analysis to gain insights into the spread and impact of the virus [3]. With its extensive range of libraries and tools tailored explicitly for data analysis, Python is a powerful and valuable resource for analyzing COVID-19 data. Its versatility and flexibility have been instrumental in meeting the increased demand for data analysis during the COVID-19 pandemic, reassuring us of Python's effectiveness in our data analysis efforts [4].

In January 2020, India reported its first case of COVID-19. Since then, the country has faced a formidable challenge in combating the virus, leading to a significant surge in both cases and fatalities. The peak of COVID-19 cases occurred in September 2020, with a staggering daily count of over 90,000 new cases [5]. This surge placed immense pressure on the healthcare system and prompted urgent measures to control the spread of the virus. However, the situation has gradually improved through concerted efforts and significant public health interventions. As of April 2024, active cases have decreased significantly to 748, indicating a remarkable turnaround in the fight against the pandemic [6].

This chapter delves into the details of machine learning algorithms using Python for COVID-19 data analysis. It uses Python to explore techniques and insights for processing, visualizing, and interpreting COVID-19 data. Popular libraries such as Pandas, Matplotlib, and Seaborn are discussed and demonstrated briefly. Python machine learning algorithms such as decision trees, linear regression, SVM (support vector machine), and random forests can be used to analyze COVID-19 data.

1.2 TYPES OF MACHINE LEARNING ALGORITHMS

Machine learning involves using various techniques to classify datasets. These techniques include supervised, unsupervised, semisupervised, instance-based, and ensemble learning. To understand the COVID-19 data, the study focuses mainly on decision trees, random forests, SVM, and linear regression algorithms.

In machine learning, data is classified as either a classifier or a regressor. The objective of a classification task is to predict the class label of the input data using a classifier data [7]. However, in regression tasks, when the objective is to predict a continuous value, regression or data is employed. Regression problems primarily involve training a learner on the available data and mapping the input to the matching output result to accomplish the prediction goal [8]. Machine learning algorithms for classifier and regressor data are different and require different preprocessing techniques. For classifier data, the data should be labeled, and the labels should be categorical. For regressor data, the data should be continuous, and the labels should be numerical. It is crucial to use the correct machine learning algorithm for the data type to achieve the best results [9].

The machine learning algorithms in this study can be used as classifiers and regressors. However, due to the nature of the data, the regressor algorithms are used to analyze the COVID-19 data. Following are the details, along with a sample flowchart for decision trees, random forests, SVM, and linear regression algorithms:

1.2.1 DECISION TREE

The decision tree is a supervised machine learning algorithm for classification and regression tasks. It is a graphical depiction of every decision-making option based on specific parameters and their results [10]. The algorithm recursively splits the data set into smaller subsets based on the features that best separate the classes or minimize the variance within the class, as shown in Figure 1.1. The decision tree algorithm creates a tree-like model of decisions and their potential outcomes, making it simple to comprehend and apply. It is also flexible and can handle both categorical and numerical data. The decision tree algorithm is an effective and popular tool in machine learning and data analysis, offering insightful analysis and data-driven forecasts [11].

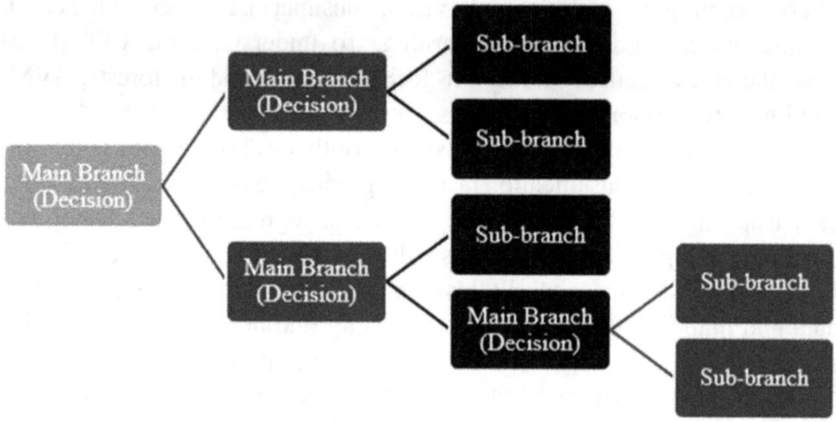

FIGURE 1.1 Decision tree flowchart.

1.2.2 RANDOM FOREST

Random forest is an ensemble learning method combining numerous decision trees [12], as shown in Figure 1.2. It is also a robust machine learning algorithm that can be used as a classifier and a regressor. Random forests can be used in COVID-19 data analysis to categorize patients into groups according to their symptoms and demographics, identify risk factors, and forecast the severity of the condition. Random forest is a versatile and widely used machine learning algorithm that can provide valuable insights into COVID-19 data analysis [13].

1.2.3 SUPPORT VECTOR MACHINE (SVM)

A SVM finds a hyperplane within an *n*-dimensional space that maximally divides the input points into distinct classes [14] as shown in Figure 1.3.

In classification tasks, SVMs classify data points into different categories. The objective is to identify a hyperplane with the most significant feasible margin of separation that divides the data points into distinct categories. The margin separates each class's closest data points and the hyperplane [15]. SVM uses a set of input variables and a regression job to predict a continuous output variable. The objective is to identify a hyperplane with the most negligible error that fits the data points. The SVM technique produces a regressor with strong outlier resistance and strong generalization capabilities by identifying the hyperplane that minimizes the mean squared error (MSE) between the predicted and actual values [16].

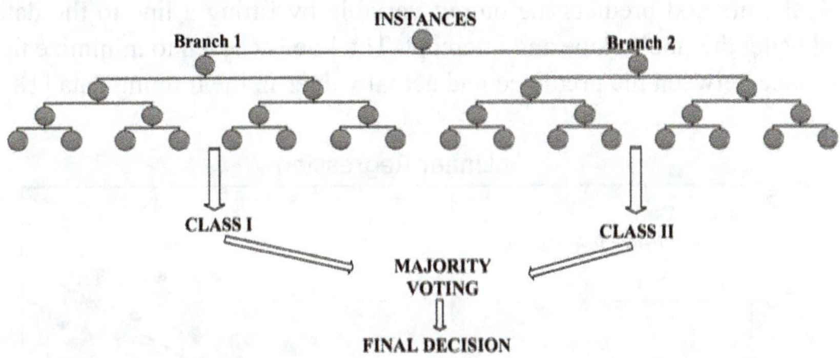

FIGURE 1.2 Flowchart of random forest.

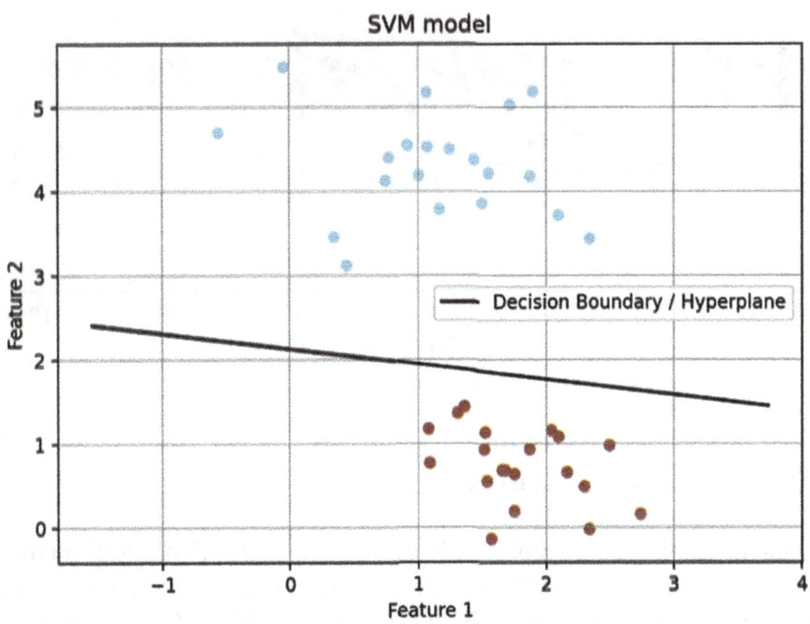

FIGURE 1.3 Sample SVM model showing the hyperplane.

1.2.4 LINEAR REGRESSION

Linear regression is a versatile machine learning algorithm that applies to regression and classification tasks. Linear regression can be used as a binary classifier to predict whether a given data point belongs to one of two possible classes. It forecasts a continuous output variable as a regressor based on one or more input variables [17]. As seen in Figure 1.4, the method predicts the output variable by fitting a line to the data and using the line's slope and intercept. The line is chosen to minimize the distance between the predicted and actual values in the training data [18].

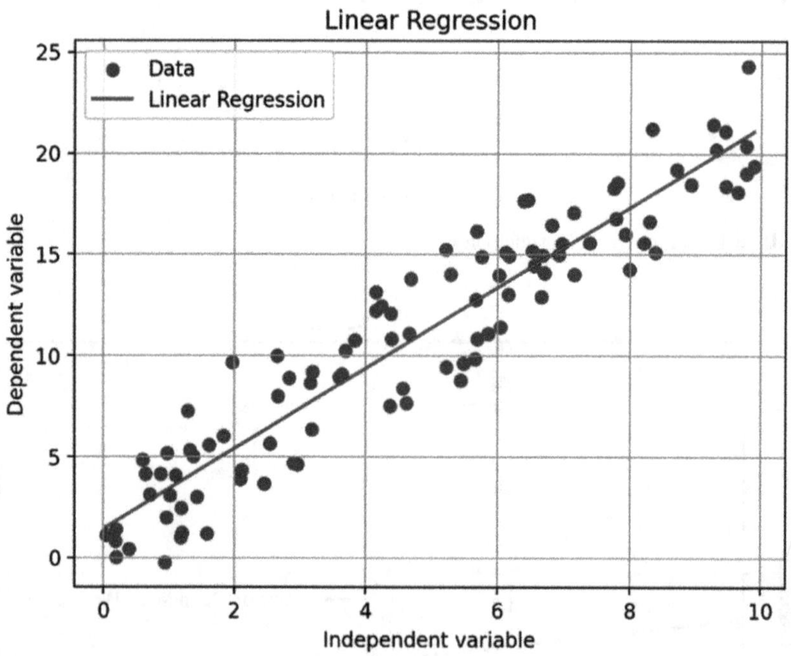

FIGURE 1.4 Sample plot of linear regression.

1.3 EVALUATION METRICS

Evaluation metrics are employed to evaluate the algorithms' performance. These metrics help assess the accuracy of the predictive models and determine their effectiveness in predicting the spread of the COVID-19 virus.

The following are the details of the evaluation metrics [19]:

1. **Mean squared error (MSE):** It calculates the mean of the squared difference between the actual and predicted values.

$$\frac{1}{n}\sum_{i=1}^{n}(y_i - \hat{y}_i)^2$$

2. **Root mean squared error (RMSE):** It is the square root of the MSE.

$$\sqrt{\frac{1}{n}\sum_{i=1}^{n}(y_i - \hat{y}_i)^2}$$

3. **Mean absolute error (MAE):** It evaluates the absolute difference between the expected and actual numbers and finds the mean.

$$\frac{1}{n}\sum_{i=1}^{n}|y_i - \hat{y}_i|$$

where,

n = number of samples in dataset
y_i = actual value for ith sample
$\hat{y}_i$ = predicted value for ith sample

4. ***R*-squared:** It is a statistical metric used to evaluate the accuracy of the regression model, ranging from 0 to 1. Higher values indicate a better fit, where 1 means the model accounts for all the variation in the dependent variable [20]. Conversely, a value of 0 means the model does not fit the data accurately.

R-squared is calculated using the formula as follows:

$$R\text{-}squared = 1 - \left(\frac{SS_{res}}{SS_{tot}}\right)$$

where,

$$SS_{res} = \sum_{i=1}^{n}(y_i - \hat{y}_i)^2$$

$$SS_{tot} = \sum_{i=1}^{n}(y_i - \bar{y}_i)^2$$

- SS_{res} is the sum of squares of residuals (the difference between the dependent variable's actual and predicted values)
- SS_{tot} is the total sum of squares (the difference between the dependent variable's actual values and mean)
- y_i is the observed value for the ith observation
- $\hat{y}_i$ is the predicted value for the ith observation
- $\bar{y}_i$ is the mean of the observed value

1.4 PYTHON LIBRARIES

Various libraries are used in Python to analyze the COVID-19 data, such as Pandas, NumPy, Matplotlib, and scikit-learn. Pandas, NumPy, and Matplotlib are three powerful libraries widely used for data analysis and visualization, whereas scikit-learn is a library used for machine learning in Python [21]. The following are brief descriptions of the libraries:

- **Pandas** is a popular library used for data analysis. It provides data structures such as data frames and series that make it easy to manipulate and analyze data. Pandas can read data from various file formats, such as CSV, Excel, SQL databases, etc [22].
- **NumPy** is a numerical computing library in Python that supports large, multidimensional arrays and matrices. It also provides functionalities for mathematical operations such as linear algebra, Fourier transform, and random number generation [23]. NumPy is a fast and efficient library that makes data analysis more efficient and effective.
- **Matplotlib** is a plotting library in Python that supports creating various types of plots, such as line plots, scatter plots, bar plots, etc. This library provides functionalities to customize the plots, add titles, labels, and legends, and save them in various formats [24]. Matplotlib is an exceptional tool for data visualization, making it easier to communicate insights and conclusions from data.
- The **scikit-learn/sklearn** library is a popular machine learning library in Python. It provides a range of algorithms for machine learning tasks involving classification, regression, and clustering [25]. Scikit-learn also includes a range of utilities for data preprocessing, such as scaling, normalization, and imputation. These tools make preparing data for machine learning tasks easy and ensure that models are trained on high-quality data [26].

1.5 DATA ANALYSIS AND RESULTS

The COVID-19 data for this study range from January 30, 2020 to March 9, 2023, and it is retrieved from Kaggle, a data repository for research purposes. The analysis of the spread of the COVID-19 virus utilizes some of the most advanced tools and techniques available in machine learning. The study involves using Python, a robust programming language, and the scikit-learn library, one of the most commonly used machine learning frameworks. Regression data is used for this study, which enables the creation of predictive models for the spread of the virus.

To start with the data analysis, it is necessary to import the required libraries. Code 1.1 presents the code to import the libraries in Python.

```
import pandas as pd
import numpy as np
import matplotlib.pyplot as plt
import seaborn as sns
from sklearn.model_selection import train_test_split
from sklearn.linear_model import LinearRegression
from sklearn.svm import SVR
from sklearn.tree import DecisionTreeRegressor
from sklearn.ensemble import RandomForestRegressor
from matplotlib import rcParams
from sklearn import metrics
%matplotlib inline
from scipy import stats
from sklearn.metrics import r2_score
```

CODE 1.1 Importing required libraries.

After importing all the required libraries, the dataset should be loaded using the Panda's library as shown in Figure 1.5. Data cleaning can remove features not required for the analysis.

Defining the features (X) and target variables (*y*) to be predicted is essential. After defining the data, using the train_test_split model, the data is split into training and testing data. The model is then called on, and the data is fitted to the model. For example, the data is fitted to the linear regression model with the test_size of 0.3, meaning that 30% of the total data is used as the testing data and the remaining 70% as the training data. The code for fitting the training data to the linear regression is mentioned in Code 1.2, along with the output plot in Figure 1.6.

```
data = pd.read_csv("COVID-19 data.csv")
data.head()
```

[4]:

	day	date	infected	deaths	recovered	tests	vaccines	people_vaccinated	people_fully_vaccinated
0	1	30-01-20	1	0	0	0	0	0	0
1	2	31-01-20	1	0	0	0	0	0	0
2	3	01-02-20	1	0	0	0	0	0	0
3	4	02-02-20	2	0	0	0	0	0	0
4	5	03-02-20	3	0	0	0	0	0	0

FIGURE 1.5 The dataset used for the study.

```
df.drop(columns = ['vaccines','people_vaccinated','people_fully_vaccinated',
'day'], inplace = True)
X = df.drop(columns = 'infected')
y = df['infected']
X_train, X_test, y_train, y_test = train_test_split(X, y, test_size=0.3, ran-
dom_state=0)
lm = LinearRegression()
lm.fit(X_train,y_train)
y_pred_train = lm.predict(X_train)
plt.scatter(y_train,y_pred_train, linewidth = 0.2, s=5.5, c= 'orange', label =
'Original data')
plt.xlabel('Actual infection')
plt.ylabel('Predicted infection')
slope, intercept, rvalue, stderr, intercept_stderr =  stats.linregress(y_train,
y_pred_train)
plt.plot(y_train, slope*y_train+intercept, label = 'Regression line')
```

CODE 1.2 Fitting training data to linear regression.

Verifying the fit of testing data to the linear regression model is essential. If the training and testing data graphs do not match, the model has not performed well. Figure 1.7 presents the output graph from Code 1.3, which shows the code to fit the testing data to the linear regression model.

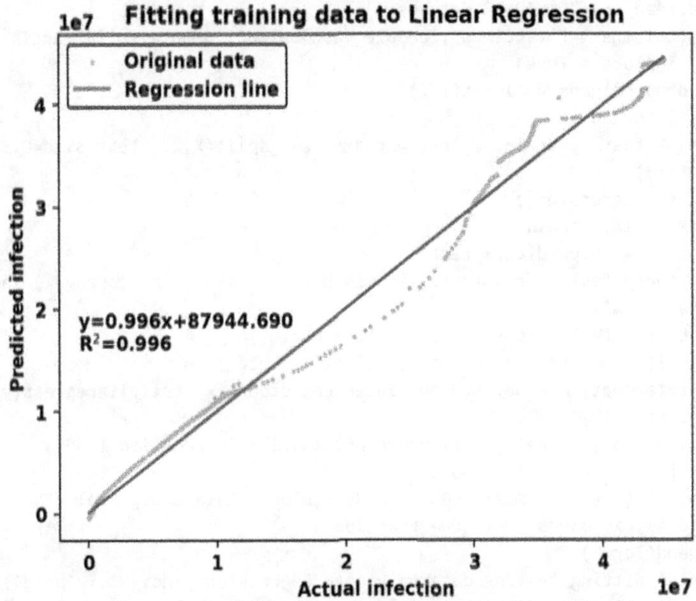

FIGURE 1.6 Graph showing the fitting of training data to linear regression.

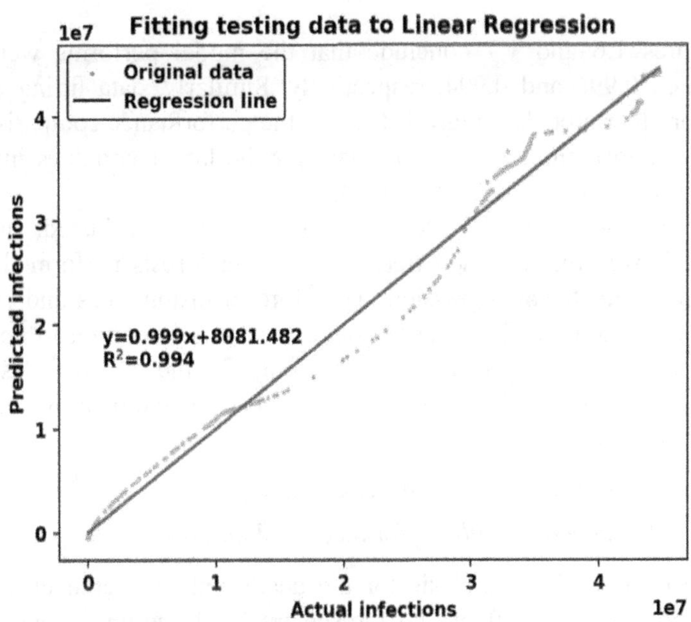

FIGURE 1.7 Graph showing the fitting of testing data to linear regression.

```
df = pd.read_csv("COVID-19 data.csv")
df.drop(columns = ['vaccines','people_vaccinated','people_fully_vaccinated',
'day'], inplace = True)
X = df.drop(columns = 'infected')
y = df['infected']
X_train, X_test, y_train, y_test = train_test_split(X, y, test_size=0.3, ran-
dom_state=0)
lm = LinearRegression()
lm.fit(X_train,y_train)
y_pred_test = lm.predict(X_test)
plt.scatter(y_test,y_pred_test, linewidth = 0.2, s=5.5, c= 'orange', label =
'Original data')
plt.xlabel('Actual infections', weight = 'bold')
plt.ylabel('Predicted infections', weight = 'bold')
slope, intercept, rvalue, stderr, intercept_stderr = stats.linregress(y_test,
y_pred_test)
plt.plot(y_test, slope*y_test+intercept, label = 'Regression line')
rcParams['font.weight'] = 'bold'
plt.annotate("y=%.3fx+%.3f \nR$^2$=%.3f"%(slope, intercept, rvalue**2), xy =
(0.13, 0.4), xycoords = 'figure fraction')
plt.legend(loc=0)
plt.title('Fitting testing data to Linear Regression', weight = 'bold')
plt.savefig('testing data LR.png', dpi = 200, bbox_inches='tight')
```

CODE 1.3 Fitting testing data to linear regression.

Figures 1.6 and 1.7 conclude that the model performs well with *R*-squared 0.996 and 0.994, respectively. Similarly, data fitting can be done for other models. Figure 1.8 shows the performance comparison for the four algorithms by fitting the data for the target variables infected, deaths, and recovered using Code 1.4.

The performance of different algorithms was evaluated, and the results showed that decision trees and random forests performed better than SVM and linear regression. Therefore, decision trees and random forests are recommended over the other two. It is important to note that the comparison shown in Figure 1.8 is only for the infected class. The same code can be used to analyze death and recovered data by replacing the "*y*" value, that is,

$y = df[\text{'}death\text{'}].values$ (for deceased class)

$y = df[\text{'}recovered\text{'}].values$ (for recovered class)

The results of the analysis for the death and recovered classes are presented in Figures 1.9 and 1.10, respectively. Based on the evaluation, it has been observed that the decision tree and random forest perform better in fitting the data than the SVM and linear regression methods. This implies that the decision tree and random forest models are more accurate and reliable in predicting the outcomes for the given dataset.

```
# Load COVID-19 time-series data
data = pd.read_csv("COVID-19.csv")
df = data.dropna()
# Prepare data
X = df['day'].values.reshape(-1, 1)
y = df['infected'].values
# Split data into train and test sets
X_train, X_test, y_train, y_test = train_test_split(X, y, test_size=0.2, random_state=42)
# Plot predictions
plt.figure(figsize=(12, 8))
rcParams['font.weight'] = 'bold'
plt.show()
```

```
# Linear Regression
lr_model = LinearRegression()
lr_model.fit(X_train, y_train)
lr_predictions = lr_model.predict(X_test)
# Linear Regression
plt.subplot(2, 2, 1)
plt.scatter(X_test, y_test, color='blue',
label='Actual')
plt.scatter(X_test, lr_predictions,
color='red', label='Predicted', s = 5.7)
plt.title('Linear Regression', weight =
'bold')
plt.xlabel('Day', weight = 'bold')
plt.ylabel('Infections', weight = 'bold')
plt.legend()
```

```
# Support Vector Machine (SVM)
svm_model = SVR(kernel='rbf')
svm_model.fit(X_train, y_train)
svm_predictions = svm_model.pre-
dict(X_test)
# Support Vector Machine (SVM)
plt.subplot(2, 2, 2)
plt.scatter(X_test, y_test, color='blue',
label='Actual')
plt.scatter(X_test, svm_predictions,
color='red', label='Predicted', s = 5.7)
plt.title('SVM', weight = 'bold')
plt.xlabel('Day', weight = 'bold')
plt.ylabel('Infections', weight = 'bold')
plt.legend()
```

```
# Decision Tree
dt_model = DecisionTreeRegressor(ran-
dom_state=42)
dt_model.fit(X_train, y_train)
dt_predictions = dt_model.predict(X_test)
# Decision Tree
plt.subplot(2, 2, 3)
plt.scatter(X_test, y_test, color='blue',
label='Actual')
plt.scatter(X_test, dt_predictions,
color='red', label='Predicted', s = 5.7)
plt.title('Decision Tree', weight =
'bold')
plt.xlabel('Day', weight = 'bold')
plt.ylabel('Infections', weight = 'bold')
plt.legend()
```

```
# Random Forest
rf_model = RandomForestRegressor(n_estima-
tors=100, random_state=42)
rf_model.fit(X_train, y_train)
rf_predictions = rf_model.predict(X_test)
# Random Forest
plt.subplot(2, 2, 4)
plt.scatter(X_test, y_test, color='blue',
label='Actual')
plt.scatter(X_test, rf_predictions,
color='red', label='Predicted', s = 5.7)
plt.title('Random Forest', weight =
'bold')
plt.xlabel('Day', weight = 'bold')
plt.ylabel('Infections', weight = 'bold')
plt.legend()
```

CODE 1.4 Comparing the performance of the four algorithms.

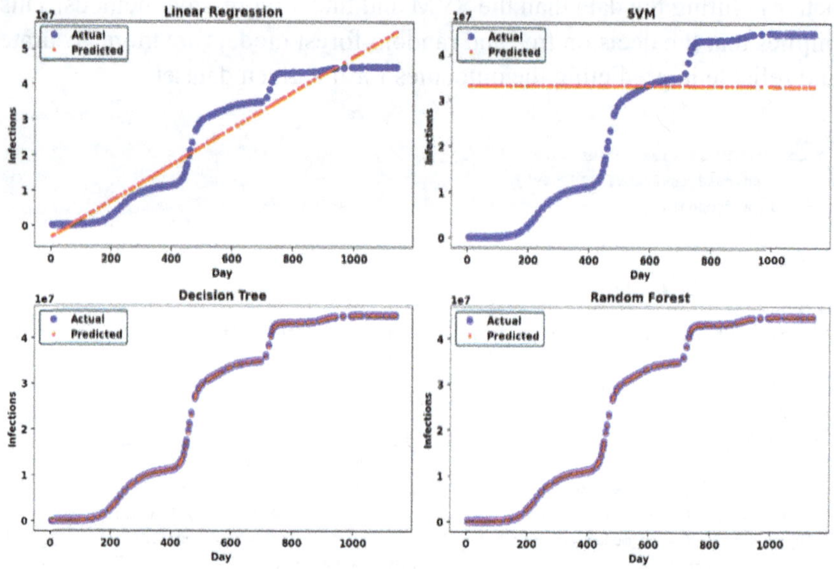

FIGURE 1.8 Comparison of the performance of the algorithms for infected class.

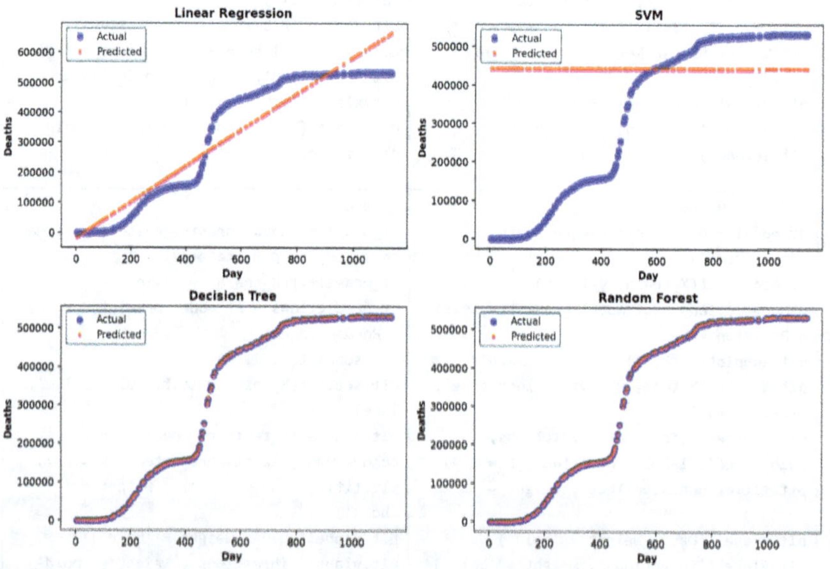

FIGURE 1.9 Comparison of the algorithms for deceased class.

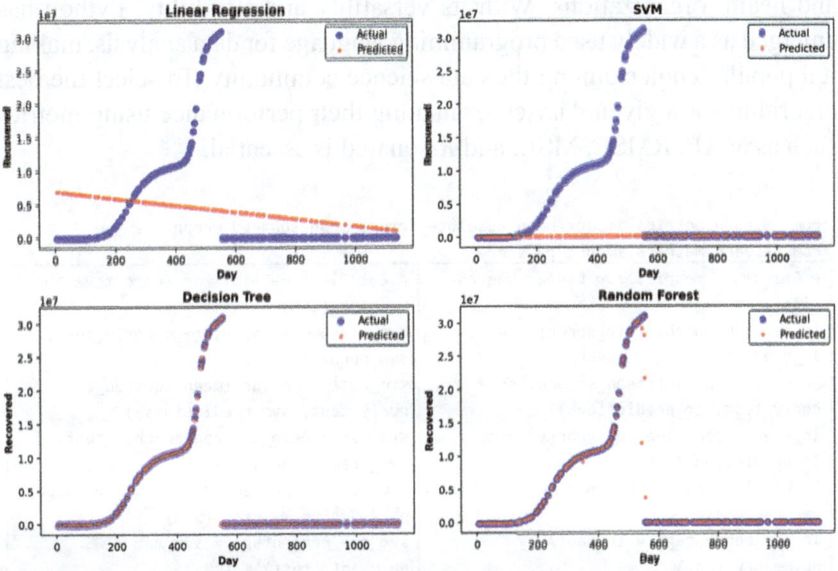

FIGURE 1.10 Comparison of the algorithms for recovered class.

The MSE, MAE, RMSE, and *R*-squared for the four algorithms are compared to see which is best suited for forecasting using Code 1.5, and result is presented in Table 1.1.

Table 1.1 presents the performance metrics of four machine learning algorithms: linear regression, SVM, decision tree, and random forest. The metrics include MAE, RMSE, MSE, and *R*-squared. These metrics are commonly used to evaluate the accuracy of machine learning models.

In general, if the values of MAE, RMSE, and MSE are low, the algorithm performs well. The *R*-squared value measures the accuracy of the model fit, and a higher *R*-squared value means a better fit. Table 1.1 concludes that random forest is the best-performing algorithm, followed by linear regression, decision tree, and SVM.

1.6 CONCLUSION

An unprecedented amount of data has been released by the COVID-19 pandemic from various sources, including individuals, governments, and health organizations. With its versatility and flexibility, Python has emerged as a widely used programming language for data analysis, making it a popular choice among the data science community. To select the best algorithm for a given dataset, evaluating their performance using metrics such as MAE, RMSE, MSE, and *R*-squared is essential.

```
from sklearn.metrics import mean_absolute_error, mean_squared_error
from sklearn.metrics import r2_score
```

```
# Calculate metrics for Linear Regres-
sion
lr_mae = mean_absolute_error(y_test,
lr_predictions)
lr_rmse = np.sqrt(mean_squared_er-
ror(y_test, lr_predictions))
lr_mse = mean_squared_error(y_test,
lr_predictions)
# Calculate percentage metrics for Lin-
ear Regression
lr_mae_percentage = lr_mae /
np.mean(y_test) * 100
lr_rmse_percentage = lr_rmse /
np.mean(y_test) * 100
lr_mse_percentage = lr_mse /
np.mean(y_test) * 100
# Calculate R-squared for Linear Re-
gression
lr_r_squared = r2_score(y_test, lr_pre-
dictions)
```

```
# Calculate metrics for Support Vector
Machine (SVM)
svm_mae = mean_absolute_error(y_test,
svm_predictions)
svm_rmse = np.sqrt(mean_squared_er-
ror(y_test, svm_predictions))
svm_mse = mean_squared_error(y_test,
svm_predictions)
# Calculate percentage metrics for Sup-
port Vector Machine (SVM)
svm_mae_percentage = svm_mae /
np.mean(y_test) * 100
svm_rmse_percentage = svm_rmse /
np.mean(y_test) * 100
svm_mse_percentage = svm_mse /
np.mean(y_test) * 100
# Calculate R-squared for Support Vec-
tor Machine (SVM)
svm_r_squared = r2_score(y_test,
svm_predictions)
```

```
# Calculate metrics for Decision Tree
dt_mae = mean_absolute_error(y_test,
dt_predictions)
dt_rmse = np.sqrt(mean_squared_er-
ror(y_test, dt_predictions))
dt_mse = mean_squared_error(y_test,
dt_predictions)
# Calculate percentage metrics for De-
cision Tree
dt_mae_percentage = dt_mae /
np.mean(y_test) * 100
dt_rmse_percentage = dt_rmse /
np.mean(y_test) * 100
dt_mse_percentage = dt_mse /
np.mean(y_test) * 100
# Calculate R-squared for Decision Tree
dt_r_squared = r2_score(y_test, dt_pre-
dictions)
```

```
# Calculate metrics for Random Forest
rf_mae = mean_absolute_error(y_test,
rf_predictions)
rf_rmse = np.sqrt(mean_squared_er-
ror(y_test, rf_predictions))
rf_mse = mean_squared_error(y_test,
rf_predictions)
# Calculate percentage metrics for Ran-
dom Forest
rf_mae_percentage = rf_mae /
np.mean(y_test) * 100
rf_rmse_percentage = rf_rmse /
np.mean(y_test) * 100
rf_mse_percentage = rf_mse /
np.mean(y_test) * 100
# Calculate R-squared for Random Forest
rf_r_squared = r2_score(y_test, rf_pre-
dictions)
```

CODE 1.5 Evaluation metrics code for the algorithms.

TABLE 1.1 Metrics for Algorithms (in Percentage)

Algorithm	MAE (%)	RMSE (%)	MSE (%)	*R*-squared
Linear regression	17.674191	20.220322	9.707627e + 07	0.923639
Support vector machine	69.366424	83.146241	1.641429e + 09	−0.291170
Decision tree	0.186361	0.393602	3.678329e + 04	0.999971
Random forest	0.095913	0.221826	1.168318e + 04	0.999991

The dataset of COVID-19 is taken from Kaggle (January 30, 2020–March 9, 2023) for analysis using machine learning algorithms. It is also observed from this study that the decision tree and random forest algorithms outperformed SVM and linear regression with minimal MAE, MSE, and RMSE. This study also highlights the importance of continued research in machine learning techniques in analyzing COVID-19 data and provides valuable insights into this topic.

KEYWORDS

- **COVID-19**
- **machine learning algorithms**
- **data analysis**
- **Python**

REFERENCES

1. Alkhatib, R., Sahwan, W., Alkhatieb, A., & Schütt, B. (2023). A brief review of machine learning algorithms in forest fires science. *Applied Sciences, 13*(14), 8275.
2. Mahesh, B. (2020). Machine learning algorithms—a review. *International Journal of Science and Research (IJSR), 9*(1), 381–386.
3. Jalolov, T. S. (2023). Teaching the basics of python programming. *International Multidisciplinary Journal for Research & Development, 10*(11).
4. Sultonov, S. (2023). Importance of python programming language in machine learning. *International Bulletin of Engineering and Technology, 3*(9), 28–30.
5. Kwekha-Rashid, A. S., Abduljabbar, H. N., & Alhayani, B. (2023). Coronavirus disease (COVID-19) cases analysis using machine-learning applications. *Applied Nanoscience, 13*(3), 2013–2025.

6. Ananthalakshmi, V. (2021). The current situation of COVID-19 in India. *Brain, Behavior, & Immunity-Health, 11*, 100200.
7. An, Q., Rahman, S., Zhou, J., & Kang, J. J. (2023). A comprehensive review on machine learning in healthcare industry: Classification, restrictions, opportunities and challenges. *Sensors, 23*(9), 4178.
8. Huang, J. C., Ko, K. M., Shu, M. H., & Hsu, B. M. (2020). Application and comparison of several machine learning algorithms and their integration models in regression problems. *Neural Computing and Applications, 32*(10), 5461–5469.
9. Sonkavde, G., Dharrao, D. S., Bongale, A. M., Deokate, S. T., Doreswamy, D., & Bhat, S. K. (2023). Forecasting stock market prices using machine learning and deep learning models: A systematic review, performance analysis and discussion of implications. *International Journal of Financial Studies, 11*(3), 94.
10. Ahmed, S. R., Ahmed, A. K., & Jwmaa, S. J. (2023, June). Analyzing the employee turnover by using decision tree algorithm. In: *2023 5th International Congress on Human-Computer Interaction, Optimization and Robotic Applications (HORA)* (pp. 1–4). IEEE.
11. Costa, V. G., & Pedreira, C. E. (2023). Recent advances in decision trees: An updated survey. *Artificial Intelligence Review, 56*(5), 4765–4800.
12. Hu, J., & Szymczak, S. (2023). A review on longitudinal data analysis with random forest. *Briefings in Bioinformatics, 24*(2), bbad002.
13. Anggrawan, A., Mayadi, C. S., Triwijoyo, B. K., & Rismayati, R. (2023). Comparative analysis of machine learning in predicting the treatment status of COVID-19 patients. *Journal of Advances in Information Technology, 14*(1), 56–65.
14. Roy, A., & Chakraborty, S. (2023). Support vector machine in structural reliability analysis: A review. *Reliability Engineering & System Safety, 233*, 109126.
15. Muawanah, S., Muzayanah, U., Pandin, M. G., Alam, M. D., & Trisnaningtyas, J. P. (2023). Stress and coping strategies of Madrasah's teachers on applying distance learning during COVID-19 pandemic in Indonesia. *Qubahan Academic Journal, 3*(4), 206–218.
16. El Hamdaoui, H., Boujraf, S., Chaoui, N. E. H., Alami, B., & Maaroufi, M. (2021). Improving heart disease prediction using random forest and adaboost algorithms. *iJOE, 17*(11), 61.
17. Amphan, S., & Songmuang, P. (2023, March). Data imputation with genetic algorithm and multiple linear regression for improving performance of prediction model. In: *2023 IEEE International Conference on Cybernetics and Innovations (ICCI)* (pp. 1–5). IEEE.
18. Keer, M., Lohiya, H., & Chouhan, S. (2023). Linear Regression Comprehensive in Machine Learning: A survey. *International Research Journal of Modernization in Engineering Technology and Science, 5*(3), 1691–1697.
19. Chicco, D., Warrens, M. J., & Jurman, G. (2021). The coefficient of determination R-squared is more informative than SMAPE, MAE, MAPE, MSE and RMSE in regression analysis evaluation. *PeerJ Computer Science, 7*, e623.
20. Ozili, P. K. (2023). The acceptable R-square in empirical modelling for social science research. In: *Social Research Methodology and Publishing Results: A Guide to Non-native English Speakers* (pp. 134–143). IGI Global.

21. Rajamani, S. K., & Iyer, R. S. (2023). Machine learning-based mobile applications using python and scikit-learn. In: *Designing and Developing Innovative Mobile Applications* (pp. 282–306). IGI Global.
22. Bhardwaj, P., Choudhury, C., & Batra, P. (2023, November). Automating data analysis with python: a comparative study of popular libraries and their application. In: *2023 3rd International Conference on Technological Advancements in Computational Sciences (ICTACS)* (pp. 1243–1248). IEEE.
23. Vadlamani, A., Kalicheti, R., & Chimalakonda, S. (2021, May). APIScanner-towards automated detection of deprecated APIs in python libraries. In: *2021 IEEE/ACM 43rd International Conference on Software Engineering: Companion Proceedings (ICSE-Companion)* (pp. 5–8). IEEE.
24. Lavanya, A., Gaurav, L., Sindhuja, S., Seam, H., Joydeep, M., Uppalapati, V., Ali, W., & SD, V. S. (2023). Assessing the performance of python data visualization libraries: A review. *International Journal of Computer Engineering in Research Trends, 10*(1), 29–39.
25. Mahdi, R. O., & Hacham, W. S. (2024). Applying scikit-learn of machine learning to predict consumed energy in Al-Khwarizmi college of engineering, Baghdad, Iraq. *Al-Khwarizmi Engineering Journal, 20*(1), 76–88.
26. Kavuncuoglu, E. (2024). Exploring the performance of PySpark and Scikit-Learn libraries in developing fall detection systems. *Niğde Ömer Halisdemir Üniversitesi Mühendislik Bilimleri Dergisi, 13*(2), 582–592.

CHAPTER 2

Analysis of Air Pollution in Delhi Using Machine Learning Techniques

HRITHIK P. M.[1] and MOHIT NAIN[2*]

[1]*Department of Mathematics, School of Chemical Engineering and Physical Sciences, Lovely Professional University, Phagwara, Punjab, India*

[2]*OM Sterling Global University, Hisar, Haryana, India*

*Corresponding author

ABSTRACT

The study uses Central Pollution Control Board data and focuses on important pollutants from Delhi monitoring sites, including $PM_{2.5}$, PM_{10}, NO_2, SO_2, CO, and O_3. The predictive accuracy of several machine learning regression models, such as random forest regression (RFR), decision tree regression (DTR), support vector regression (SVR), and multiple linear regression (MLR), was investigated. To find patterns, trends, and correlations in the dataset, the study starts with exploratory data analysis. To extract pertinent characteristics from the pollutant concentration data, feature engineering techniques are utilized. The findings show that the SVR model performed better in predicting AQI with greater accuracy than MLR, DTR, and RFR. The investigation shows how AQI prediction accuracy could be improved by applying machine learning techniques. The results show promise for revolutionizing the monitoring and management of air quality in urban areas, with a particular focus on Delhi. The region's public health and air quality may eventually be improved by the integration of various data sources and cutting-edge machine learning algorithms, which can result in more precise forecasts and proactive actions. The study

Integrative Approaches to Quality, Data Analysis, and Interdisciplinary Research.
Amir Ahmad Dar and Waseem Z. Lone (Eds.)

DOI: 10.1201/9781779641014-3

emphasizes how crucial it is to choose the most precise forecasting model to support the creation of efficient air pollution management plans.

2.1 INTRODUCTION

In this modern era, many metropolitan cities inside and outside India are at their peak in pollution. Among the various types of pollution, people are mostly affected by air pollution. According to estimates from the World Health Organization, indoor and outdoor air pollution kills close to seven million people globally each year.

Delhi has the highest level of pollution among Indian cities [1]. It is necessary to calculate the air quality of Delhi to take precautions. The government uses the Air Quality Index (AQI) to inform the public about the state of the air [3]. Pollutant concentration increases lead to a decline in air quality. For the average person, the level of pollution is represented by the AQI. The AQI focuses on the possible health consequences that breathing in polluted air can have hours or days later [8, 12]. The AQI measurement requires an air monitor and the air pollutant concentration over a predefined averaging period. The data are divided into ranges, and each range is assigned a color code, descriptor, and standardized public health advisory [11]. By using cutting-edge statistical methods to analyze and forecast AQI values, such as multiple linear regression (MLR), decision tree regression (DTR), random forest regression (RFR), and support vector regression (SVR) [8, 12, 13], this study hopes to further the current conversation.

There is serious concern about air pollution [9] due to the presence of microscopic particles in the atmosphere called PM2.5 and PM10, which have diameters of 2.5 μm or less and 10 μm or less, respectively. The combustion of fossil fuels, burning biomass, industrial emissions, vehicle emissions (particularly from heavy vehicles), agricultural practices, domestic heating and cooking, and meteorological conditions are some of the sources of these particles [7]. Nitric oxide and nitrogen dioxide make up the majority of nitrogen oxides (NOx), which further exacerbate environmental problems. The use of vehicles, industrial processes, and agricultural practices all produce NOx emissions, which have an effect on the quality of the air in urban and industrial areas. These pollutants have the ability to combine with other substances to produce ground-level ozone and particulate matter, which can aggravate respiratory disorders and environmental issues like soil and water acidification and biodiversity loss. Another major air pollutant that comes from sources like car emissions, burning waste, heating homes, and volcanic activity is sulfur dioxide (SO_2). Acid rain is one of SO_2's negative effects, as it can damage vegetation, soil, and aquatic ecosystems. Furthermore, SO_2 is a respiratory irritant that can be harmful to one's health, particularly for those who already have a medical condition like asthma. One of the main causes of air pollution is carbon monoxide (CO), which is produced by burning fossil fuels, smoking cigarettes, and natural processes like volcanic eruptions. In conclusion, there are serious health and environmental risks associated with the release of different pollutants into the atmosphere, such as PM, NO_x, SO_2, and CO, which also affect ecosystems and air quality [14].

In the present chapter, we have analyzed the data provided by the Central Pollution Board and categorized it. Various machine learning techniques [10], along with various regression models, are examined. All this analysis is carried out using different packages of R Programming. We hope to find the best method for precise and trustworthy AQI predictions by clarifying the subtleties of each model. The results of this study can educate public health officials, urban planners, and environmental policy-makers, encouraging a proactive and data-driven approach to air quality management.

2.2 MATERIALS AND METHODS

2.2.1 LOCATION OF THE STUDY

Delhi is a city in northern India shown in Figure 2.1, which is bounded to the east and three sides by the state of Haryana. The latitudinal and longitudinal coverage is approximately 28°4′–28°9′N and 76°8′–77°3′E. We chose Anand Vihar in the eastern part of Delhi, Patparganj, and Jahangir Puri to study AQI. In this study, the data provided by the Central Pollution Board are needed for the AQI analysis. It was raw data. We use the ETL data extraction process to make it relevant to our analysis.

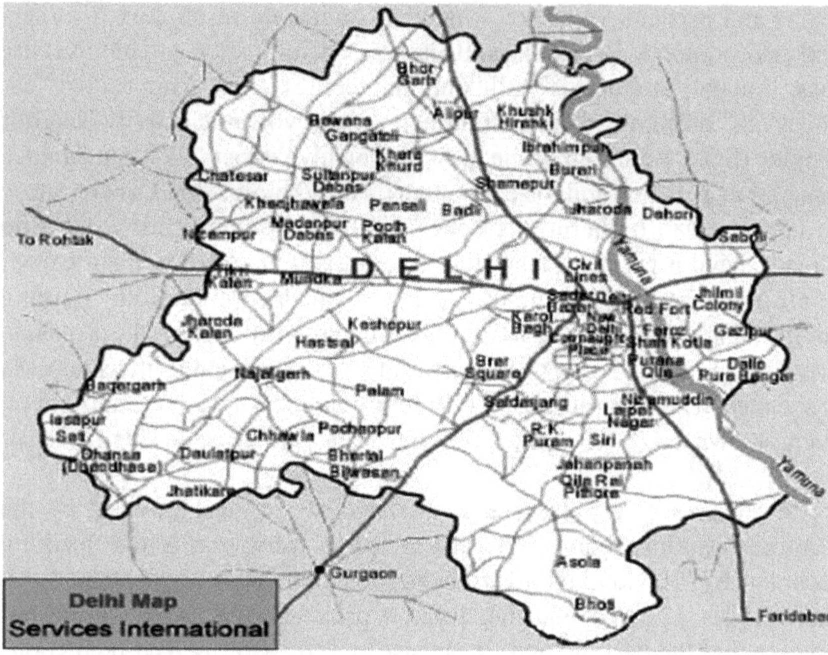

FIGURE 2.1 Location of study.

2.2.2 MACHINE LEARNING METHODS

2.2.2.1 MULTIPLE LINEAR REGRESSION

A statistical technique called MLR, or multiple regression, combines some [4] explanatory variables to predict a response variable's outcome. One explanatory variable is used in multiple regression, which is a variation of linear regression (ordinary least squares).

$$Y = b_0 + b_1 * X_1 + b_2 * X_2 + , \ldots, + b_n * X_n + \varepsilon$$

where,

Y is the dependent variable

$X_1, X_2, \ldots, X_n$ are independent variables

b_0 is the y-intercept

$b_1, b_2, \ldots, b_n$ are the regression coefficients

ε is the residual or random error

The assumptions of MLR [6] include a linear relationship between the variables, normally distributed errors, and constant variance of the errors (homoscedasticity). The validity of the results may be impacted by violations of these presumptions. The performance of an MLR model can be commonly assessed using adjusted *R*-squared, significance tests for individual coefficients, and *R*-squared, or the percentage of variance explained by the model. Many disciplines, including economics, finance, biology, and social sciences, use MLR extensively to forecast and comprehend the relationships between variables.

2.2.2.2 SUPPORT VECTOR REGRESSION

Strong machine learning algorithms such as SVR are used for tasks such as regression, outlier detection, and linear or nonlinear classification. Text classification, image classification, handwriting identification, spam detection, face detection, gene expression analysis, and anomaly detection are just a few of the many applications for SVMs. Because SVMs can handle high-dimensional data and nonlinear relationships, they are versatile and effective in various applications. SVR's basic concept [13] is comparable to support vector classification for classification tasks, but it has been modified to make it more regression-friendly. SVR looks for a hyperplane that best captures the relationship between input features and the target variable in a continuous space, as opposed to attempting to identify a hyperplane that best divides classes. SVM algorithms work extremely well when attempting to identify the largest separating hyperplane between the various classes in the target feature.

2.2.2.3 DECISION TREE REGRESSION

A decision tree is a type of tree data structure in which each node can have any number of branches. An internal node is a node with outgoing edges. "Leaf" refers to other nodes. One or more internal nodes divide the instance used for regression or classification into groups based on a particular function. During the training phase, the values of the input variable(s) take a specific function into account. An algorithm that creates a decision tree from given instances is the decision tree's stimulant. By minimizing the fitness function, the implemented algorithm seeks to identify the ideal decision tree [5, 12]. Given that the dataset used in this study lacks classes, each independent variable is used to fit a regression model to the target variable. Each independent variable has multiple split points in the dataset. The implemented algorithm determines the error between the actual and predicted values with respect to the predefined fitness function at each split point. After comparing the split point errors for each variable, the split point is determined by examining the variable that produces the lowest fitness function value. Recursively, this process continues.

2.2.2.4 *RANDOM FOREST REGRESSION*

With the use of several decision trees and a method known as bootstrap aggregation (or bagging), random forest is an ensemble technique that can handle both regression and classification tasks. The fundamental idea here is to use a combination of decision trees instead of depending only on one to determine the result [2]. Many decision trees serve as foundational learning models for random forest. We create sample datasets for each model by randomly selecting rows and features from the dataset. This section is known as bootstrap. We must approach the RFR technique like any other machine learning technique. As an ensemble learning technique, random forest integrates the predictions of various models to enhance overall robustness and performance. In the random forest, every tree is a decision tree. Decision trees recursively split the data based on features to produce a tree-like structure of decisions that leads to a final prediction. Random forest adds a random element to the process of creating trees. Only a random subset of features is considered at each split, and each tree is trained on a random subset of the training data (bootstrapped samples). The model becomes more robust and less prone to overfitting because of this randomization.

2.3 RESULTS AND DISCUSSION

Table A.1 shows the data provided by the CPCB used to study the trend of AQI in Delhi. Air quality indices are modeled and predicted using a variety of machine learning algorithms, such as SVR, RFR, and DTR. The accuracy and reliability of the models were assessed using a variety of performance metrics, including R-squared, mean absolute error, and root mean square error (RMSE). Figures 2.2, 2.3, 2.4, and 2.5 represent the trend of the predicted and actual values of MLR, SVR, DTR, and RFR, respectively. The respective R^2, MSE, and RMSE values are tabulated in Tables 2.1, 2.2, 2.3, and 2.4, respectively.

The results obtained using the MLR model are presented in Table 2.1 and show that the AQI station in Anand Vihar had an accuracy of 72.07%, the station in Patparganj had an accuracy of 80.06%, and the station in Jahangir Puri had an accuracy of 88.65%.

TABLE 2.1 Values Calculated Using the MLR

Location	R^2	MSE	RMSE
Anand Vihar	0.7207	2620.96	51.19
Patparganj	0.8006	1985.60	44.56
Jahangir Puri	0.8865	1280.46	35.78

The MLR machine learning regression model's predicted values versus actual values are visually represented in Figure 2.2's graphs. The real versus predicted graphs for the stations in Anand Vihar, Patparganj, and Jahangir Puri are displayed in Figures 2(a), (b), and (c), respectively.

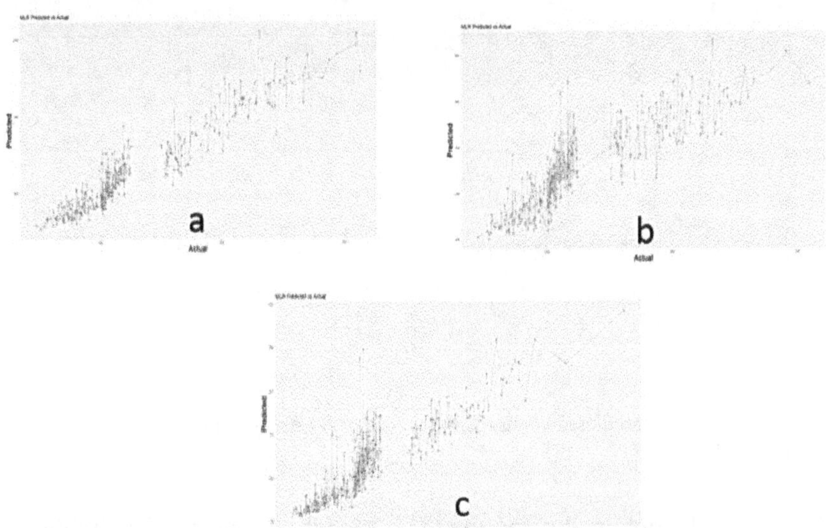

FIGURE 2.2 MLR predicted versus actual values of (a) Anand Vihar, (b) Patparganj, and (c) Jahangir Puri.

The results obtained using the SVR regression model are displayed in Table 2.2 and show that the AQI station in Anand Vihar had an accuracy of 79.24%, the station in Patparganj had an accuracy of 89.64%, and the station in Jahangir Puri had an accuracy of 92.45%. The graphs in Figure 2.3 show the actual values versus the predicted values obtained using the SVR machine learning regression model. The real versus predicted graphs for the stations in Anand Vihar, Patparganj, and Jahangir Puri are displayed in Figures 2.3(a), (b), and (c), respectively.

TABLE 2.2 Values Calculated Using the SVR

Location	R^2	MSE	RMSE
Anand Vihar	0.7923	2118.93	46.03
Patparganj	0.8964	929.74	30.49
Jahangir Puri	0.9245	904.03	30.06

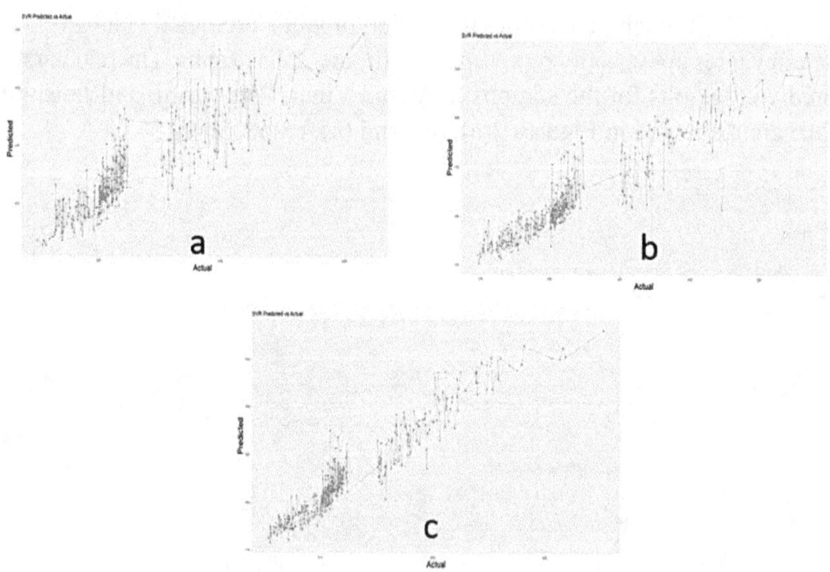

FIGURE 2.3 SVR predicted versus actual values of (a) Anand Vihar, (b) Patparganj, and (c) Jahangir Puri.

The results obtained using the DTR model are displayed in Table 2.3 and show that the AQI station in Anand Vihar had an accuracy of 64.87%, the station in Patparganj had an accuracy of 83.40%, and the station in Jahangir Puri had an accuracy of 82.39%.

The graphs in Figure 2.4 show the actual values versus the predicted values obtained using the SVR machine learning regression model. The actual versus predicted graphs for the stations in Anand Vihar, Patparganj, and Jahangir Puri are displayed in Figures 2.4(a), (b), and (c), respectively.

TABLE 2.3 Values Calculated Using the DTR

Location	R^2	MSE	RMSE
Anand Vihar	0.6487	3368.08	58.03
Patparganj	0.8340	1374.02	37.06
Jahangir Puri	0.8239	2143.60	46.29

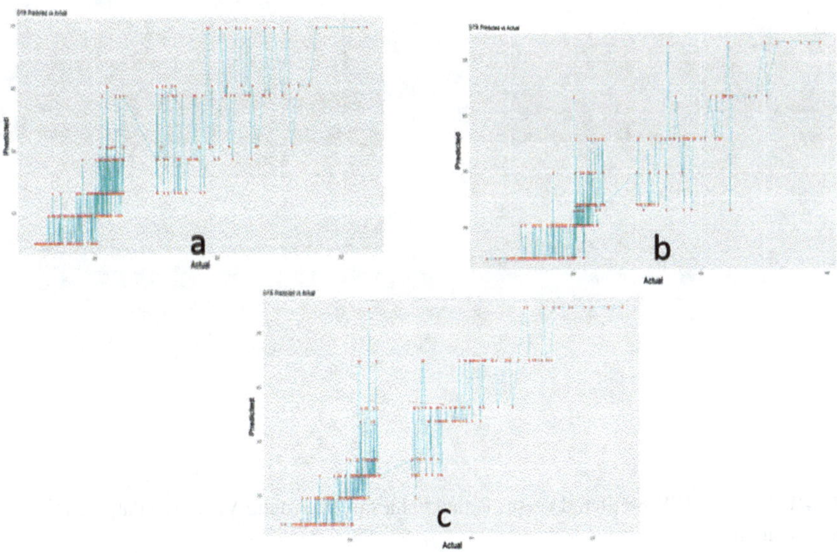

FIGURE 2.4 DTR predicted versus actual values of (a) Anand Vihar, (b) Patparganj, and (c) Jahangir Puri.

The results obtained using the RFR model are displayed in Table 2.4 and show that the AQI station in Anand Vihar had an accuracy of 70.66%, the station in Patparganj had an accuracy of 84.74%, and the station in Jahangir Puri had an accuracy of 90.89%.

The graphs in Figure 2.5 show the actual values versus the predicted values obtained using the SVR machine learning regression model. The actual versus predicted graphs for the stations in Anand Vihar, Patparganj, and Jahangir Puri are displayed in Figures 2.5(a), (b), and (c), respectively.

TABLE 2.4 Values Calculated Using the RFR

Location	R^2	MSE	RMSE
Anand Vihar	0.7066	2647.09	51.44
Patparganj	0.8474	1297.91	36.02
Jahangir Puri	0.9089	1233.60	35.12

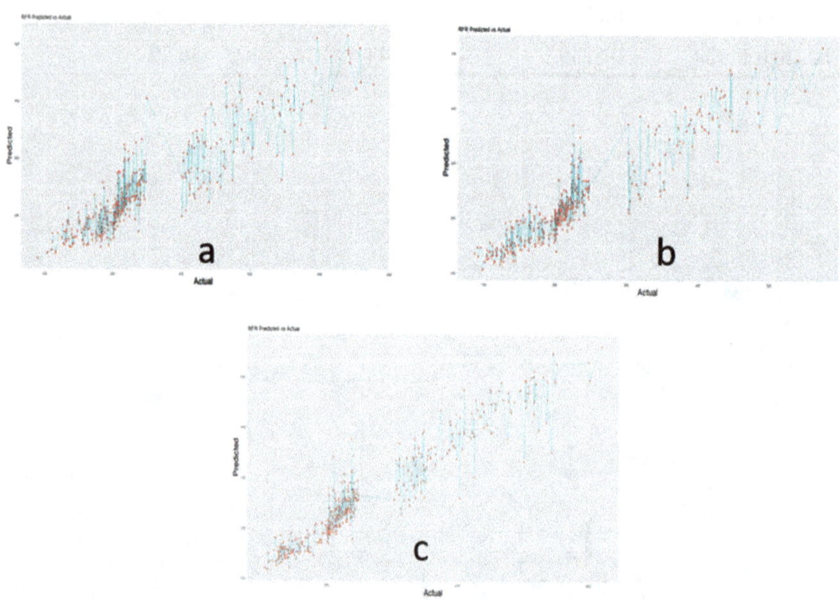

FIGURE 2.5 RFR predicted versus actual values of (a) Anand Vihar, (b) Patparganj, and (c) Jahangir Puri.

In comparison to the other three models—MLR, DTR, and RFR—the machine learning regression model, SVR algorithm, has an accuracy of 79.23% in Anand Vihar, 89.64% in Patparganj, and 92.45% in Jahangir-puri, while DTR has the lowest accuracy, scoring 64.87%, 83.40%, and 82.34% in Anand Vihar, Patparganj, and Jahangir Puri, respectively. In this case, the accuracy of the regression models, that is, RFR and MLR, is nearly equal.

Based on all the calculations, SVR is the top machine learning regression model for AQI prediction.

Comparing individual stations across states when comparing Delhi's various states also aids in predicting Delhi's overall pollution levels, for the government to implement specific pollution control measures. We notice through analysis that the precise machine learning model is the same across stations. So that the Delhi government can, on the whole, implement various policies, specific techniques, and preventive measures to lower pollution in Delhi.

2.4 FUTURE STUDIES

2.4.1 INTEGRATION OF ADDITIONAL DATA SOURCES

To further improve the precision and resilience of AQI forecasts, future studies can include data from other sources, such as satellite imaging, traffic patterns, industrial activity, and meteorological data. An understanding of Delhi's pollution dynamics that is more thorough can be achieved by integrating data from many sources.

2.4.2 ADVANCED MACHINE LEARNING ALGORITHMS

The prediction performance could be further enhanced by investigating more sophisticated machine learning algorithms and approaches, such as deep learning, neural networks, and ensemble methods. The effectiveness of these sophisticated models in air quality forecasting may be better understood by contrasting them with more conventional regression models.

2.4.3 LONGITUDINAL ANALYSIS

Lengthy-term trends and patterns in air pollution could be identified by performing a longitudinal investigation over a lengthy period. This would facilitate comprehension of how seasonal variations, socioeconomic factors, and policy changes affect air quality.

2.4.4 REAL-TIME MONITORING AND PREDICTION

Using machine learning algorithms and Internet of Things (IoT) devices, real-time monitoring and prediction systems might be developed to give the public and policymakers immediate alerts and actionable insights. Establishing an AQI monitoring network in real-time throughout Delhi might greatly improve the city's capacity to handle pollution outbursts.

2.5 CONCLUSION

The analysis's findings shed light on the connections between air pollutants, weather, and other contextual variables, which helps in the creation of air quality prediction models. The results aid in the development of policies and programs aimed at reducing air pollution and enhancing the quality of the environment in cities such as Delhi. From the analysis using different regression methods, we can conclude that SVR is the most suitable and best method for the analysis of AQI of Anand Vihar, Patparganj, and Jahangirpuri, the cities of different parts of Delhi. Using various kernel functions (such as linear, polynomial, or radial basis function kernels), SVR can model nonlinear relationships between variables. It can identify intricate patterns in the data because of its adaptability. With regard to outliers, SVR is less susceptible to certain other regression models. The utilization of machine learning models has demonstrated efficacy in forecasting and tracking the levels of air quality in Delhi. These models are able to provide real-time predictions by utilizing historical data, which helps authorities take proactive steps to reduce pollution. By making it easier to analyze the temporal and spatial patterns of air pollution, machine learning contributes to a better understanding of the ways in which pollution levels fluctuate over time and space. With this knowledge, authorities can effectively allocate resources and implement location-specific interventions. The precision and detail of pollution data are improved by combining machine learning with IoT devices, like air quality sensors. A comprehensive network for controlling and monitoring Delhi's air quality is created by this networked system. In conclusion, a strong framework for decision-making, policy creation, and community involvement is provided by the use of machine learning techniques in the analysis of Delhi's air pollution.

These realizations are crucial for creating a multifaceted strategy to address the various issues raised by air pollution in a dynamic urban setting.

KEYWORDS

- **Air Quality Index**
- **pollution**
- **chemicals**
- **regression**
- **machine learning**

REFERENCES

1. Dutta, A., & Jinsart, W. (2022). Air pollution in Delhi, India: It's status and association with respiratory diseases. *PLoS One, 17*(9), e0274444.
2. Hanif, W. H., & Gunawan, F. E. (2022). Random forest regression to predict catalyst deactivation in industrial catalytic process. *TEM Journal, 11*(1), 104–110.
3. Horn, S. A., & Dasgupta, P. K. (2023). The Air Quality Index (AQI) in historical and analytical perspective a tutorial review. *Talanta, 267*, 125260.
4. Kumar, R., Kumar, P., & Kumar, Y. (2020). Time series data prediction using IoT and machine learning technique. *Procedia Computer Science, 167*, 373–381.
5. Pekel, E. (2020). Estimation of soil moisture using decision tree regression. *Theoretical and Applied Climatology, 139*(3), 1111–1119.
6. Rath, S., Tripathy, A., & Tripathy, A. R. (2020). Prediction of new active cases of coronavirus disease (COVID-19) pandemic using multiple linear regression model. *Diabetes & Metabolic Syndrome: Clinical Research & Reviews, 14*(5), 1467–1474.
7. Ravishankara, A. R., David, L. M., Pierce, J. R., & Venkataraman, C. (2020). Outdoor air pollution in India is not only an urban problem. *Proceedings of the National Academy of Sciences, 117*(46), 28640–28644.
8. Sharma, N., Taneja, S., Sagar, V., & Bhatt, A. (2018). Forecasting air pollution load in Delhi using data analysis tools. *Procedia Computer Science, 132*, 1077–1085.
9. Sharma, R., Kumar, R., Sharma, D. K., Son, L. H., Priyadarshini, I., Pham, B. T., Bui, D. T., & Rai, S. (2019). Inferring air pollution from air quality index by different geographical areas: Case study in India. *Air Quality, Atmosphere & Health, 12*, 1347–1357.

10. Udristioiu, M. T., Mghouchi, Y. E., & Yildizhan, H. (2023). Prediction, modelling, and forecasting of PM and AQI using hybrid machine learning. *Journal of Cleaner Production, 421*, 138496.
11. Wu, C. Y., Wu, C. Y., Li, M. C., Ho, H. J., & Ao, C. K. (2024). Association of Air Quality Index (AQI) with incidence of atopic dermatitis in Taiwan: A nationwide population-based cohort Study. *Journal of the American Academy of Dermatology, 90*(6), 1218–1225.
12. Zhang, C., Kotz, A., Kelly, K., & Rippelmeyer, L. (2021). Development of heavy-duty vehicle representative driving cycles via decision tree regression. *Transportation Research Part D: Transport and Environment, 95*, 102843.
13. Zhang, F., & O'Donnell, L. J. (2020). Support vector regression. In: *Machine Learning* (pp. 123–140). Academic Press.
14. Zhang, J., Tao, Y., Wang, Y., Ji, X., Wu, Y., Zhang, F., & Wang, Z. (2024). Independent and interaction effects of prenatal exposure to high AQI and extreme Humidex on the risk of preterm birth: A large sample population study in northern China. *Reproductive Toxicology, 124*, 108544.

APPENDIX A

TABLE A.1 Dataset from CPCB About Anand Vihar

From Date	To Date	PM2.5	PM10	NO	NO_2	CO	SO_2	AQI	Outcome
01-02-2018 00:00	02-02-2018 00:00	193.92	440.44	108.37	339.27	4.08	13.78	343.02	Hazardous
02-02-2018 00:00	03-02-2018 00:00	128.64	331.54	84.83	230.52	2.23	16.49	237.76	Very Unhealthy
03-02-2018 00:00	04-02-2018 00:00	104.89	256.5	80.84	203.93	4.11	17.58	225.50	Very Unhealthy
04-02-2018 00:00	05-02-2018 00:00	135.79	276.49	89.4	245.11	6.36	15	241.45	Very Unhealthy
05-02-2018 00:00	06-02-2018 00:00	178.25	415.84	117.69	305.67	2.17	14.23	327.50	Hazardous
06-02-2018 00:00	07-02-2018 00:00	129.92	311.36	90.27	168.16	1.81	18.07	238.42	Very Unhealthy
07-02-2018 00:00	08-02-2018 00:00	135.2	290.25	96.65	166.88	1.93	13.38	241.15	Very Unhealthy
08-02-2018 00:00	09-02-2018 00:00	228.65	411.25	118.67	112.2	3.33	17.17	377.44	Hazardous
09-02-2018 00:00	10-02-2018 00:00	225.2	491.05	109.98	159.01	2.74	12.49	374.02	Hazardous
10-02-2018 00:00	11-02-2018 00:00	303.98	411.52	116.04	108.5	3.95	24.79	452.99	Hazardous
11-02-2018 00:00	12-02-2018 00:00	165.12	358.31	76.43	109.03	1.81	17.32	314.48	Hazardous
12-02-2018 00:00	13-02-2018 00:00	61.63	149.46	39.53	55.55	2.77	7.13	203.16	Very Unhealthy
13-02-2018 00:00	14-02-2018 00:00	118.92	237.48	68.28	134.17	2.1	18.84	232.74	Very Unhealthy
14-02-2018 00:00	15-02-2018 00:00	69.25	218.5	72.11	111.48	1.58	19.28	207.09	Very Unhealthy
15-02-2018 00:00	16-02-2018 00:00	91.25	217.77	77.61	140.14	1.6	18.64	218.45	Very Unhealthy
16-02-2018 00:00	17-02-2018 00:00	123.83	291.97	100.58	183.31	1.76	13.03	235.28	Very Unhealthy
17-02-2018 00:00	18-02-2018 00:00	135.17	347.79	91.38	162.47	2.82	16.86	241.13	Very Unhealthy

TABLE A.1 *(Continued)*

From Date	To Date	PM2.5	PM10	NO	NO_2	CO	SO_2	AQI	Outcome
18-02-2018 00:00	19-02-2018 00:00	161.5	342.91	96.31	147.13	2.97	17.13	310.90	Hazardous
19-02-2018 00:00	20-02-2018 00:00	261.25	386.2	127.63	113.43	3.44	21.48	410.65	Hazardous
20-02-2018 00:00	21-02-2018 00:00	231.17	516.43	117.3	132.04	3.45	19.25	379.94	Hazardous
21-02-2018 00:00	22-02-2018 00:00	252.88	381.79	104.77	130.7	3	21.82	402.35	Hazardous
22-02-2018 00:00	23-02-2018 00:00	215.91	443.33	98.88	156.37	2.82	17.73	364.82	Hazardous
23-02-2018 00:00	24-02-2018 00:00	238.29	543.08	93.89	169.03	2.61	19.24	386.99	Hazardous
24-02-2018 00:00	25-02-2018 00:00	183.22	414.13	65.19	97.3	2.41	15.15	332.42	Hazardous
25-02-2018 00:00	26-02-2018 00:00	125	312.38	66.65	107.71	1.71	22.85	235.88	Very Unhealthy

CHAPTER 3

Modeling Socioeconomic and Regional Factors in the Nonlife Insurance Sector of India through Regression Analysis

AKSHAT JAIN[1*], RAKESH MALHAN[1], and IMRAN AZAD[2]

[1]*School of Chemical Engineering and Physical Sciences, Lovely Professional University, Phagwara, Punjab, India*

[2]*University of Technology and Applied Science, Oman*

*Corresponding author

ABSTRACT

In India's dynamic life insurance market, shaped by social and economic forces, this study undertakes an investigative and exploratory analysis covering the years 2019–2023. Using a systematic approach that includes data analysis, regional comparison, correlation analysis, policy impact evaluation, and regression analysis, the research examines the factors influencing the sector's growth and resilience. Geographical differences reveal regions with high insurance penetration alongside areas with significant coverage gaps. Correlation analysis highlights interactions between population density, literacy rates, and insurance uptake, offering insights into key socioeconomic drivers. Policy impact assessment demonstrates the industry's ability to adapt to regulatory changes and economic fluctuations, with a steady increase in premium income (PI) throughout the study period. Further analysis links population dynamics, economic prosperity, and educational attainment to patterns of insurance consumption. Regression results uncover a complex network of relationships that shape the sector's development, providing valuable inputs for scholars,

Integrative Approaches to Quality, Data Analysis, and Interdisciplinary Research.
Amir Ahmad Dar and Waseem Z. Lone (Eds.)

DOI: 10.1201/9781779641014-4

policymakers, and industry stakeholders. The findings depict a resilient and evolving industry with significant potential for future expansion. This study not only identifies the challenges and opportunities ahead but also underscores the critical role of insurance in fostering financial stability and economic security in India's changing environment.

3.1 INTRODUCTION

India's life insurance industry is a monument to the nation's social progress and economic endurance. Several variables, including rising disposable incomes, shifting consumer preferences, and legislative changes meant to improve consumer safety and market efficiency, have contributed to the industry's notable expansion in recent years. In this context of change, players in the business as well as policymakers and scholars must comprehend the intricacies of the intricate interactions between economic, demographic, and regulatory factors to comprehend the dynamics of the Indian life insurance market [1, 2].

The General Insurance Council's 2022–2023 Indian Life Insurance Industry Year Book is a useful source of information about the sector's performance and future directions. This study explores the dynamics of the Indian life insurance market from 2019 to 2023 by utilizing the plethora of data offered by this all-inclusive resource. Through the examination of significant indicators like the number of insurance offices (IOs), gross direct premium income (GDPI), population size, literacy rates, and state domestic product (SDP), this study attempts to identify the fundamental factors that influence the expansion and effectiveness of the industry in various parts of the nation [3].

Opportunities and problems abound in the Indian life insurance market, which is indicative of the nation's varied socioeconomic makeup and regulatory framework. On the one hand, the industry has enormous development potential because of favorable demographic trends and growing awareness of risk management and financial planning. However, there are several obstacles to market expansion and inclusivity, including unequal regional development, low insurance coverage rates, and changing consumer behaviors [4–6].

This study uses a multidimensional approach that includes regression analysis, policy effect assessment, correlation analysis, and geographical comparison to give a thorough understanding of the dynamics of the

Indian life insurance sector. The study intends to shed light on regional differences and their consequences for industry development through a comparative examination of key performance metrics across states and union territories, including insurance penetration (IP), premium income (PI) growth rate, and SDP growth rate [7, 8].

In addition, the study aims to identify the socioeconomic variables influencing the adoption of life insurance products across various population segments by analyzing the correlations between demographic variables like population size, literacy rates, and IP per capita. To evaluate the influence of economic events and regulatory changes on the industry's growth trajectory, a policy impact analysis is also carried out. This provides insights into the sector's resilience and adaptation to external shocks [9, 10].

A review of pertinent studies and publications on subjects including insurance market dynamics, regional economic development, and policy effect analysis is conducted to place this research within the context of the body of current literature. The introduction's listed references offer a starting point for comprehending the intricacies of the Indian life insurance market and the several elements affecting its expansion and efficacy.

In conclusion, the goal of this research is to further our knowledge of the dynamics of the Indian life insurance market and how it interacts with larger demographic and economic trends. Through the application of rigorous analytical tools and thorough data analysis, the research aims to influence industry strategies, encourage sustainable growth and development in the Indian life insurance sector, and inform the government.

3.2 LITERATURE REVIEW

The crucial role that the Indian life insurance market plays in promoting financial inclusion and economic growth has attracted the attention of both scholars and practitioners. Numerous studies have looked at several facets of the sector, including consumer behavior, industry performance, and regulatory changes, as well as market trends.

The causes propelling the development and expansion of the Indian life insurance industry are an important field of study. While underlining the significance of technology innovation in changing business processes and improving customer experience, stressed the relevance of legislative changes and technical advancements in determining the industry's trajectory.

This research emphasized how dynamic the insurance business is and how insurers must adjust to shifting consumer preferences and market conditions [11, 12].

Additionally, researchers have examined the connection between demographic variables and IP in India. Socioeconomic determinants like income levels, education, and urbanization have a significant impact on people's inclination to buy life insurance products. Likewise, demographic variables like age, gender, and occupation are significant predictors of insurance demand, emphasizing the necessity for insurers to customize their offerings and distribution networks to satisfy the varied needs of various population segments. Additionally, studies have looked at how regulatory changes have affected the Indian life insurance market. In their 2020 analysis, Rajput and Choudhury emphasized the significance of regulatory stability and clarity in promoting investor confidence and industry growth. They also examined the consequences of policy changes on market development and consumer welfare. A long-term study of regulatory actions and market results showed the important influence of policy frameworks on industry dynamics and competitiveness [13–15].

The research on the effects of socioeconomic factors and geographical differences on the dynamics of the insurance market in India is still lacking, despite these contributions. The necessity for greater regional assessments that account for regional differences in economic growth, literacy rates, and population density was emphasized. The need to comprehend regional variations in customer conduct and market inclinations to craft focused marketing approaches and routes of distribution [16, 17].

Research on the life insurance sector in India offers insightful information on a range of topics, including customer behavior, legislative changes, and market dynamics. To provide a more thorough picture of industrial growth and development in India, further research is necessary that incorporates demographic and regional views into the study.

The literature on the complex interactions between socioeconomic determinants, regional dynamics, and industry performance is noticeably lacking, even with the wealth of studies on the Indian life insurance sector. Several previous studies have looked at market trends, consumer behavior, regulatory changes, and other aspects of the industry; however, very few have conducted a thorough analysis that incorporates demographic and regional differences into the analysis of industry growth and development. In this study, the focus is low on regional differences in IP and market dynamics among Indian states and union territories. Previous research frequently offers evaluations at an aggregate level that ignore the variability within the Indian market, missing out on the unique opportunities and constraints that each area faces. To close this knowledge gap, this study compares important performance indicators at the state and union territory levels, providing insights into the regional influences influencing the development of the life insurance market [18, 19].

This study attempts to shed light on the connections between IP and demographic factors by correlation analysis and regression modeling, which will advance knowledge of the socioeconomic factors influencing industry performance. This study provides an in-depth investigation of regional dynamics, demographic factors, and policy consequences, thereby addressing numerous significant research gaps in the literature on the Indian life insurance business. By filling in these gaps, the research hopes to provide academia, business professionals, and policymakers with insightful information that would, in turn, enable evidence-based decision-making and promote the sector's sustainable growth and development [20].

3.3 METHODOLOGY

The present study's methodology is to analyze the dynamics of the nonlife insurance sector in India, with a specific focus on the years 2019–2023. The Indian Life Insurance Industry Year Book 2022–23, which is released yearly by the General Insurance Council, provided the primary data used in this study. The link to the data is given in the references. Particularly, information on the number of offices in each state, the GDPI, the population, the rate of literacy, and the SDP was carefully collected. These factors are taken into consideration and are described as follows:

- **Statewise Number of Offices:** This variable shows where life insurance businesses are located and how many of them are active in each state.
- **GDPI:** GDPI shows the entire amount of premiums that life insurance firms have received, net of reinsurance and ceding commissions. It functions as a gauge of the industry's total size and financial success.
- **Population:** Information on the population is essential for placing the penetration and reach of life insurance products across state lines and demographic categories.

- **Literacy Rates:** A measure of a state's educational attainment, literacy rates can affect customer behavior, product comprehension, and awareness of insurance.
- **SDP:** Over a given period, SDP shows the entire value of products and services generated in a state. It offers information about the state of the economy and the size of the prospective market for life insurance products.

These factors were selected because they are important for evaluating the effectiveness and influence of the life insurance industry in various Indian states. The R programming language was used to do statistical analysis after data preprocessing.

A regional comparison was carried out to evaluate the performance of the states and union territories in several important metrics after the data from the Indian Life Insurance Industry Yearbook were gathered and organized. These measures comprised PI growth rates and SDP growth rates, as well as IP, which was calculated as the number of IOs per capita. Regarding the insurance market penetration and economic growth dynamics of various states and union territories, this comparison analysis sheds important light on the relative advantages and disadvantages of each. Overall, the comprehension of the differences in the development of the insurance industry and the economic performance of various geographical regions within India was greatly aided by this regional comparison.

A correlation study was carried out after the regional comparison to investigate the connections between different demographic characteristics and the insurance industry's performance. The study specifically looked at relationships between IP, population sizes, and literacy rates. The number of IOs per capita, or IP, was computed by dividing the total number of IOs in 2022–2023 by the population data from 2011. This measure sheds light on how widely available insurance services are for each region's population. The study was to clarify how demographic variables, such as population figures and literacy rates, impact the functioning of the insurance industry by examining connections between IP and them. The patterns and trends found through this analysis provided insight into the socioeconomic factors influencing the growth of the insurance business in India's various regions.

In summary, the correlation analysis proved to be a useful instrument in comprehending the intricate relationship between demographic variables and the performance of the insurance industry. This has led to a more profound understanding of the elements that influence market penetration and accessibility within the insurance landscape of India.

A policy impact study was carried out after the correlation analysis to see how policy modifications or economic events will affect the insurance industry. For this analysis, the number of IOs and PI were tracked across time, with particular attention paid to times when there were notable policy changes or volatility in the economy. To identify patterns and trends suggestive of the effects of policy changes or economic events on the insurance industry, the study monitored variations in PI and the number of IOs. This study offered insightful information about how economic policies, regulatory changes, and external shocks affected the expansion and stability of the insurance industry. The policy impact analysis has facilitated informed decision-making and policy formulation in the area of insurance regulation and governance by providing a comprehensive understanding of the dynamic interactions between policy frameworks, economic conditions, and the performance of the insurance sector.

Regression analysis was done after policy impact analysis to investigate the connections between IP and important socioeconomic variables, such as number of IO, SDP, literacy rates, and population numbers. Using the previously described socio-economic factors as independent variables and IP as the dependent variable, an ordinary least squares regression model was built.

The model equation looks like this:

$$\text{PI} = \beta_0 + \beta_1(\text{IO}) + \beta_2(\text{SDP}) + \beta_3(\text{Literacy}) + \beta_4(\text{Population}) + \varepsilon \quad (3.1)$$

where β_0 is intercept term, and β_1, β_2, β_3, and β_4 are the coefficients associated with the independent variables (IO, SDP, literacy, population), respectively, and ε is the error term.

The purpose of the regression analysis was to determine how much the number of IOs, state GDP, literacy rates, and population data in various states and union territories could account for variances in IP. The regression analysis provided insights into the direction and magnitude of the independent factors' respective impacts on IP by estimating the coefficients of the independent variables. Furthermore, statistical analyses were performed to appraise the overall goodness-of-fit of the regression model and determine the significance of these associations.

3.4 RESULT AND ANALYSIS

3.4.1 REGIONAL COMPARISON

The study evaluated the performance of Indian states and union territories in terms of IP, PI growth rate, and SDP growth rate using a comparative analysis. The purpose of this comparison was to pinpoint areas that were functioning well and investigate any possible relationships between the dynamics of the insurance industry and economic variables. The outcome of this is shown below.

1. The investigation showed that there is a significant regional variance in the penetration of insurance. With roughly 0.00005689 IOs per capita, Chandigarh was found to have the highest IP rate. In contrast, Bihar had the lowest rate of IP, with a per-capita IO count of just 0.000002341.
2. With a remarkable growth rate of 116.3%, Sikkim showed the greatest PI growth rate. As a result of the reduction in premium revenue within the region, Lakshadweep suffered a negative growth rate of −81.82%.
3. With an impressive growth rate of 43.68%, Assam was the best performer in terms of SDP growth rate. The SDP growth rate in Chandigarh, on the other hand, decreased and was negative, at −9.067%.

The average IP, PI growth rate, and SDP growth rate by region were displayed using bar plots as shown in Figures 3.1–3.3 as a visual aid to the quantitative analysis. These graphics offer a clear representation of the trends and geographical differences found for the chosen variables.

Overall, the results highlight the diverse landscape of the Indian insurance market and its intersection with economic development indicators at the regional level. The results highlight the significance of regional context in influencing the dynamics of the insurance market and point to possible directions for future research and policy initiatives to support equal development and financial resilience in India's various regions.

3.4.2 CORRELATION ANALYSIS

A correlation analysis was carried out to investigate the relationships between important demographic variables and performance metrics for the insurance industry. The population, IP per capita, and literacy rate were the specific variables that were examined. The ratio of the number of IOs in 2022–2023 to the population in 2011 was used to compute the IP per capita.

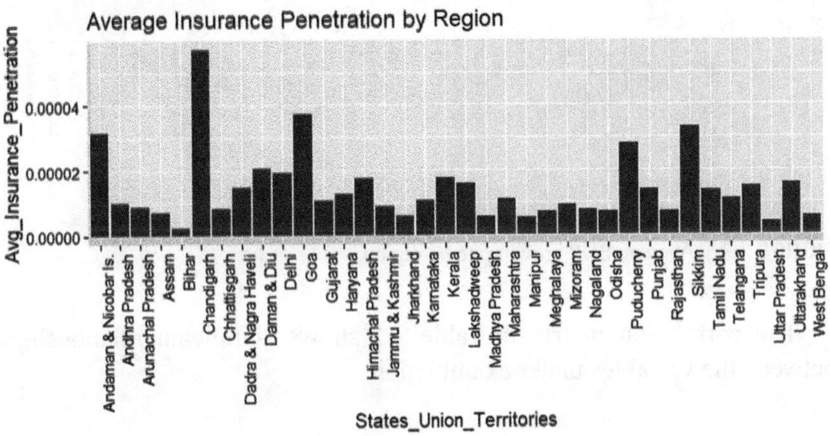

FIGURE 3.1 Average insurance penetration by region.

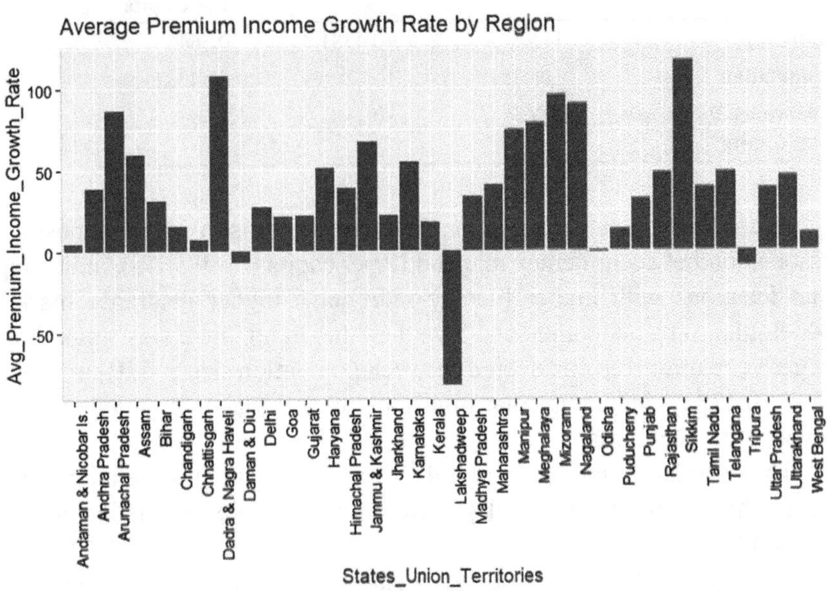

FIGURE 3.2 Average premium income growth rate by region.

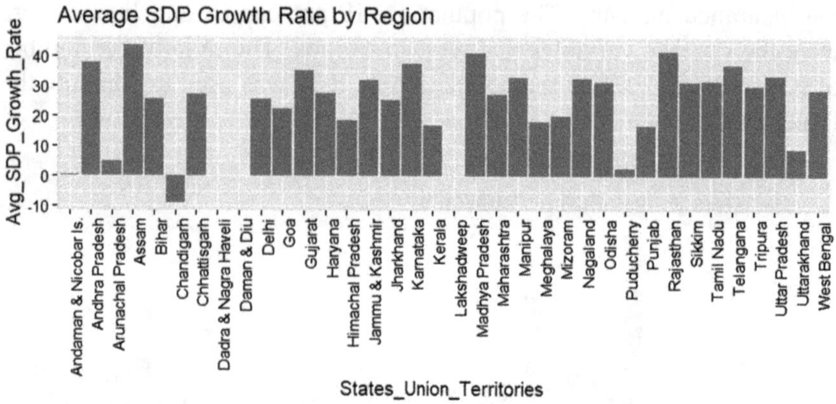

FIGURE 3.3 Average SDP growth rate by region.

The correlation matrix in Table 3.1 shows significant relationships between the variables under examination.

TABLE 3.1 Correlation Matrix

	Literacy	Population	Insurance Penetration Per Capita
Literacy	1	−0.4381	0.5645
Population	−0.4381	1	−0.4383
Insurance Penetration Per Capita	0.5645	−0.4383	1

According to the correlation matrix, there is a modest positive association between literacy rate and IP per capita ($r = 0.5645$), indicating that locations with higher literacy rates have higher insurance market penetration on a per capita level. On the other hand, there was a moderate negative relationship discovered between population size and IP per capita ($r = -0.4383$), indicating that highly populated places may have lower levels of IP per capita.

The correlation plot (Figure 3.4) visually depicts these relationships, further highlighting the interplay between literacy rate, population, and IP per capita.

The plot highlighted the observed patterns of correlation, emphasizing the role of demographic considerations in driving the dynamics of the insurance business across different geographical regions. Overall, the correlation analysis offered insightful information about the relationship between demographic traits and the performance of the insurance sector, highlighting the importance of population density and literacy rates in affecting the uptake of insurance services across different population segments.

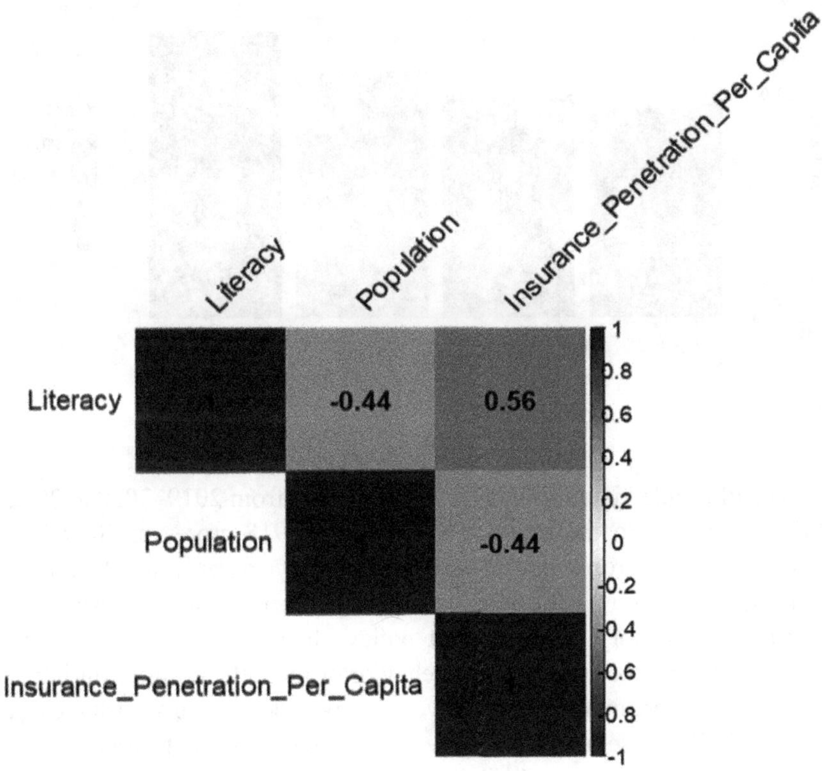

FIGURE 3.4 Correlation plot.

3.4.3 IMPACT ANALYSIS OF POLICIES

With a focus on analyzing changes in PI and the number of IOs across the years under examination, the policy impact analysis examined the effects of policy changes or economic events on the Indian insurance sector. PI trends are displayed in Table 3.2 and Figure 3.5 over time.

TABLE 3.2 Premium Income Trends

Year	Premium Income
2019–2020	188,918
2020–2021	198,715
2021–2022	220,701
2022–2023	256,894

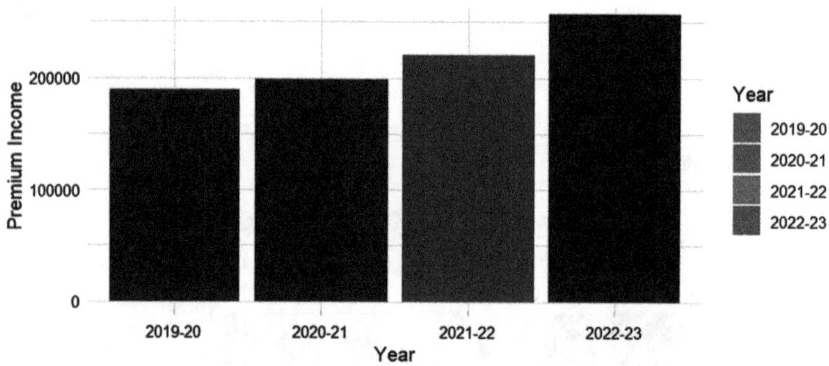

FIGURE 3.5 Premium income over time.

The PI trended increasing over the four years from 2019–2020 to 2022–2023, according to the report. From INR 188,918 crores in 2019–2020 to INR 256,894 crores in 2022–2023—a steady increase in PI indicates a strong expansion in the money made by the insurance industry. This increasing trajectory indicates that policy changes or economic stimuli that may have affected consumer behavior or market dynamics during the study period were met with a positive response. Plots serve as visual aids to further clarify these trends and give a clear picture of the PI trajectory for the study. IO numbers are displayed in Table 3.3 and Figure 3.6 over time.

Over the same period, there was a slight decrease in the number of IOs, which was in contrast to the trend found in PI. In 2019–20, there were 11,375 IOs nationwide; in 2022–2023, there were 9928. Even while this drop can seem alarming at first, it is important to consider market dynamics and structural changes within the insurance business when interpreting this pattern. Plots serve as visual aids to further clarify these trends and give a clear picture of the growth trajectory of the number of IOs during the study.

TABLE 3.3 Number of Insurance Office

Year	Insurance Office Numbers
2019–2020	11,375
2020–2021	11,248
2021–2022	10,786
2022–2023	9928

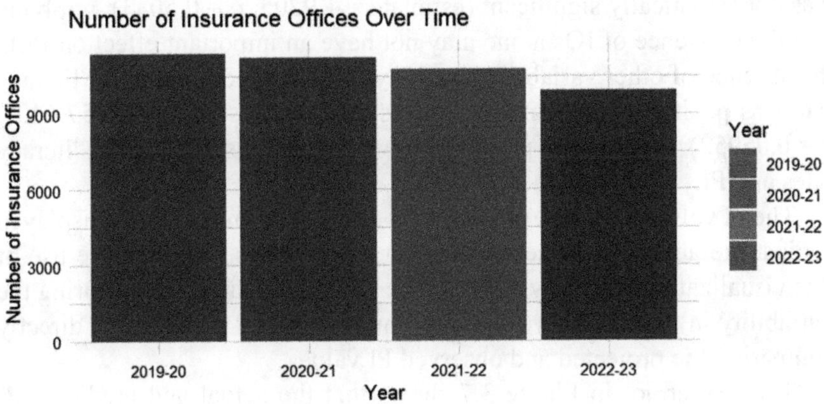

FIGURE 3.6 Number of insurance offices over time.

3.4.4 *REGRESSION ANALYSIS*

Regression analysis was used to investigate the link between PI and a variety of important variables, such as the population, SDP, number of IO, and literacy rate. Table 3.4 displays the regression model's results.

TABLE 3.4 Regression Result

	Estimate	St. Error	*t*-value	*p*-value
Intercept	−80,910.367	3597.137	−2.25	0.02621*
IO	1.9205	2.8612	0.67	0.50330
SDP	0.0132	0.0013	10.26	0.0000000002***
Literacy	8557.6401	4500.8785	1.90	0.05952
Population	−0.00005	0.00001	−3.96	0.00012***

SDP showed a significant coefficient in the model (estimate = 0.0132, $p < 0.0001$), suggesting a positive correlation between SDP and PI.

This implies that PI in the life insurance industry tends to be higher in areas with higher economic activity. Furthermore, a significant negative population coefficient (estimate = −0.00005, $p = 0.00012$) was found in the regression model, indicating a possible correlation between lower PI and higher population densities. The significance of taking demographic variables like population size into account when examining PI in the insurance industry is shown by this finding. The coefficient for the number of IO was not statistically significant (estimate = 1.9205, $p = 0.5033$), implying that the existence of IOs alone may not have an important effect on PI in the absence of other variables. Similarly, while the coefficient for literacy rate was positive, it was marginally insignificant (estimate = 8557.6401, $p = 0.05952$), indicating a possible but weak relationship between literacy rates and PI.

The PI values that were predicted by the regression model are displayed against the actual PI values in the plot that follows. Through the use of this visualization, one may evaluate the model's accuracy in capturing the variability in premium revenue based on the chosen variables by directly comparing the projected and observed PI values.

The scatterplot in Figure 3.7 shows that the actual and predicted PI values are closely aligned, suggesting that the regression model does a good job of capturing the variation in premium revenue depending on the factors it includes. The points form a tight cluster around the diagonal line, indicating that the model's predictions and the observed PI levels are fairly close to each other.

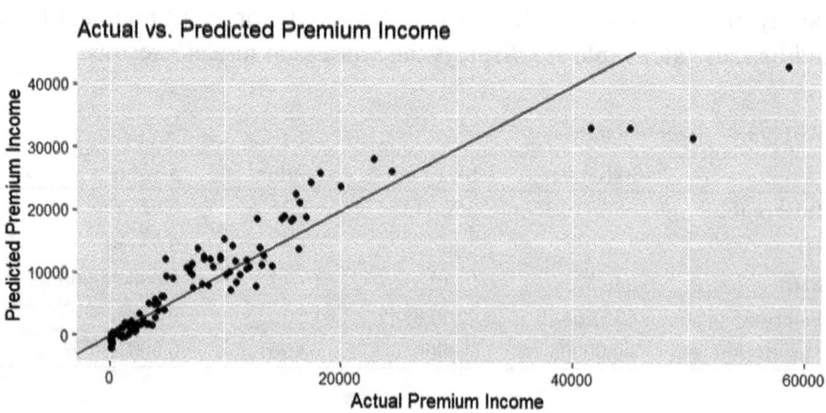

FIGURE 3.7 Actual vs. predicted premium income.

Overall, the regression model had an excellent fit, with an adjusted *R*-squared value of 0.867, indicating that it explains about 86.7% of the variation in premium revenue based on the factors considered. This high explanatory power indicates that the selected variables, taken together, provide useful insights into the determinants of PI in the Indian life insurance business.

3.5 FINDING AND DISCUSSION

The study investigated the dynamics of the life insurance business in India from 2019 to 2023, using a comprehensive methodology that included data analysis, regional comparison, correlation analysis, policy impact assessment, and regression analysis. The findings shed light on various crucial areas of the Indian insurance environment, providing useful information for policymakers, industry stakeholders, and scholars. The findings of the regional comparison indicated notable differences in the rates of IP, PI growth, and SDP growth among the Indian states and union territories. The success of insurance distribution channels in the area is demonstrated by Chandigarh's rise to the top of the IP rankings. Bihar, on the other hand, showed the lowest IP, suggesting possible difficulties in increasing insurance coverage in underdeveloped regions. While Lakshadweep's growth rate is negative, raising worries about both market saturation and economic issues, Sikkim's impressive PI growth rate highlights the promise in specific places. The necessity for focused initiatives and specialized tactics to support inclusive insurance expansion across a range of geographic contexts is highlighted by these regional discrepancies.

The correlation study revealed significant relationships between IP and demographic factors. Studies show that literacy rates and IP per capita are positively correlated, indicating that education is a critical factor in raising insurance knowledge and uptake. On the other hand, a negative relationship between population size and IP per capita suggests that providing insurance services to densely populated areas may be difficult. To increase insurance coverage in densely populated areas and promote resilience and financial inclusion, these findings highlight the significance of tackling literacy gaps and developing focused outreach programs. The analysis of policy impact showed the insurance industry's adaptability to shifts in both economic conditions and policy. It is clear from the PI trend that the industry has been able to adjust to changing consumer preferences and regulatory environments throughout the study period. This drop in IOs, however, is noteworthy and suggests that it may be difficult to continue being accessible and present in the market. To maintain sector growth and protect consumers, policymakers need to give top priority to projects that strengthen distribution networks and expedite regulatory procedures.

The factors influencing PI in the Indian life insurance market were clarified by the regression analysis. The SDP was found to be a significant predictor of PI, suggesting that the demand and consumption of insurance are positively impacted by economic development. On the other hand, there was a negative correlation found between PI and population density, indicating that places with high population density would have trouble reaching the ideal level of IP. The existence of IOs and literacy rates suggested possible relationships between PI and policyholders, but their relevance was only slight, highlighting the complex web of variables affecting insurance uptake and consumption patterns.

To unlock the full potential of the Indian insurance market and support sustainable socioeconomic development, future research efforts should concentrate on investigating novel distribution channels, utilizing digital technologies, and improving risk management practices. The study's findings provide insightful information about the dynamics of the Indian life insurance sector and its intersection with demographic, economic, and policy variables. Addressing regional disparities, enhancing financial literacy, and fostering a supportive policy environment are imperative to promote inclusive insurance growth and financial resilience across India.

3.6 LIMITATIONS AND FUTURE SCOPE

Even with such a careful methodology, there are still some limits to the study. The use of information from the General Insurance Council's Indian Life Insurance Industry Yearbook 2022–2023 is one noteworthy feature. This dataset may still be susceptible to limitations common to any industry study, such as potential data gaps, reporting biases, or methodological restrictions, even while it provides insightful information about the dynamics of the life insurance market in India. Furthermore, the temporal scope of the analysis, which is limited to the years 2019–2023, can miss longer-term trends or cyclical patterns that could have an impact on the insurance market's dynamics. Furthermore, the study mostly used quantitative methods, which may cause it to ignore qualitative factors like customer preferences, business practices, or legal issues that may provide more complex answers to the research questions. Lastly, although the study takes into account economic and demographic characteristics, it does not take into account other external effects or contextual elements like technological advancements, regulatory changes, or sociocultural trends that could affect the dynamics of the insurance industry.

Future studies on the Indian insurance market may employ a variety of approaches to expand on present findings, overcome these limitations and these shortcomings, and improve our understanding of the industry. The integration of qualitative techniques such as case studies and interviews would provide deeper insights into the experiences of stakeholders and the complexities of the sector. To improve prediction accuracy, longitudinal studies with longer periods would be able to identify subtle trends and cyclical patterns. A fine-grained examination conducted at the subregional or demographic levels may reveal specific differences in the adoption of insurance and the habits of consumers. Prospective insights and prediction powers could be obtained by applying cutting-edge data sources and analytical methods like machine learning and geographic analysis. To promote inclusive insurance growth and financial resilience, comparative studies between nations or regions would provide useful benchmarks and ease cross-country learning. Using these methods would help us better understand the insurance market in India and provide evidence for evidence-based policies that promote financial security and sustainable socioeconomic growth.

3.7 CONCLUSION

The life insurance industry in India is adaptable and full of opportunities in a world where uncertainty is the norm and financial stability is crucial. This study offers valuable insights into the complex insurance environment of India using a thorough investigation that involved years of data collection, regional comparison, correlation analysis, policy impact assessment, and regression scrutiny. From economic success to educational attainment, from policy winds to demographic currents, the research essentially presents a clear picture of a sector impacted by multiple causes. A patchwork of regional differences is exposed, with parts begging for coverage coexisting with areas with great penetration. However, a strand of hope does seem to be emerging despite this complexity; this hope is driven by the possibility of focused interventions, well-informed policy, and technological innovation. The results highlight the need for diversity and call on relevant parties to close the inequalities in economic empowerment, accessibility, and literacy. They put pressure on politicians to develop complex plans that speak to the particular requirements of various communities and work toward a time when every Indian has access to insurance protection. Rather than calling this exploration of possibilities to an end, we want to leave you with a call to action, asking you to imagine a time when everyone has access to insurance and financial stability transcends all boundaries. It is a story of resiliency, empowerment, and opportunity that is waiting to be told by those brave enough to pick up the pen, wrapped up in the colorful tapestry that is India's insurance industry.

KEYWORDS

- **insurance**
- **gross direct premium income**
- **state domestic population**
- **literacy**

REFERENCES

1. Sinha, T. (2005). The Indian insurance industry: Challenges and prospects. *SSRN Electronic Journal*. https://doi.org/10.2139/ssrn.792166.
2. Ghosh, A. (2013). Life insurance in India: The relationship between reforms and growth in business. *Geneva Papers on Risk and Insurance—Issues and Practice, 38*, 88–112.
3. Jaiswal, A., Agarwal, N., Kumar, R., Singh, N., & Maan, H. (2024). Assessing the strategic transformation of the Indian insurance sector evolution amidst COVID-19. *Revolutionizing Customer-Centric Banking Through ICT*, 239–257.
4. Ray, S., Thakur, V., & Bandyopadhyay, K. (2020). India's insurance sector: Challenges and opportunities. Indian Council for Research on International Economic Relations (ICRIER) Working Paper 394, Indian Council for Research on International Economic Relations (ICRIER), New Delhi, India.
5. Birau, R., Kayarthakdka, V., Rai, S., Puttanna, R., & Ninulescu, P. (2023). Influence of demographic and household factors on surrender of life insurance policies in India.

6. Fernando, K. D. U. D., Tharanga, T. M. N., Dewasiri, N. J., Sood, K., Grima, S., & Thalassinos, E. (2023). Insurance penetration and institutional spillover on economic growth: A dynamic spatial econometric approach on the Asian and Europe region. *Journal of Risk and Financial Management, 16*(8), 365.
7. Trivellas, P., Malindretos, G., & Reklitis, P. (2020). Implications of green logistics management on sustainable business and supply chain performance: Evidence from a survey in the Greek agri-food sector. *Sustainability, 12*(24), 10515.
8. Senthil, M. K. (2024). Insurance penetration and density in India. *International Journal of Early Childhood Special Education, 14*(03), 2022.
9. Chakraborty, K., Dutta, A. & Sengupta, P. (2012). Efficiency and productivity of Indian life insurance industry. *Asia-Pacific Journal of Risk and Insurance*, *7*(1). doi: https://10.1515/2153-3792.1164
10. Dash, G., & Im, J. (2018). Determinants of life insurance demand: Evidence from India. *Asia Pacific Journal of Advanced Business and Social Studies, 4*(2), 86–99.
11. Suresh, K. S., & Kamalakannan, T. (2023). Digital image steganography in the spatial domain using block-chain technology to provide double-layered protection to confidential data without transferring the stego-object. *International Journal of Intelligent Systems and Applications in Engineering, 11*(2s), 61–68.
12. Jandaghi, G., & Moradpour, Z. (2015). Segmentation of life insurance customers based on their profile using fuzzy clustering. *International Letters of Social and Humanistic Sciences, 61*, 17–24.
13. Rathod, K. (2023). Recent trends of Green Finance in India. *Vidhyayana—An International Multidisciplinary Peer-Reviewed E-Journal-ISSN 2454-8596, 8*(5), 11.
14. Paramasivan, C., & Naidu, C. K. (2014). A study on the role of Bancassurance in the Indian life insurance business. *SELP Journal of Social Science, 5*(20).
15. Sehgal, R. (2017). A comparative study of customer satisfaction and level of loyalty between public insurance sector and private insurance sector. *Asian Journal of Management, 8*(4), 1271–1279.
16. Babu, S. (2015). Financial inclusion: Challenges and opportunities in India. *International Journal of Research in Commerce & Management, 6*(3).
17. Tomar, J. S. (2020). Employee engagement in India: Organizational effectiveness, people, and performance in IT companies. In: Misra, S., & Adewumi, A. (Eds.), *Handbook of Research on the Role of Human Factors in IT Project Management* (pp. 420–451). IGI Global.
18. Pandey, D., Khurana, P., & Misra, A. (2021, December). Towards understanding the psychological effects of the COVID-19 pandemic on the indian population. In: *2021 20th IEEE International Conference on Machine Learning and Applications (ICMLA)* (pp. 1449–1454). IEEE.
19. van den Eynde, E. The need for a tailored approach within integrated childhood obesity care.
20. Rohilla, R. L. Comparative performance of distribution channels of public and private life insurers in India. *International Journal of Current Science Research and Review*, *6*(3), 1968–1992.

CHAPTER 4

Quantitative Analysis of Healthcare Costs: Integrating Behavioral, Regional, and Demographic Factors

MEHAK MALHOTRA[1*], RAKESH MALHAN[1], and ATAUR RAHMAN FAROOQI[2]

[1]*School of Chemical Engineering and Physical Sciences, Lovely Professional University, Phagwara, Punjab, India*

[2]*CEBA, University of Technology and Applied Science, Nizwa, Oman*

*Corresponding author

ABSTRACT

Understanding the factors influencing healthcare costs is critical for global policymaking and resource allocation, enabling strategies that ensure equitable access and optimize service delivery. This study analyzes healthcare cost dynamics using a large dataset containing key health variables, applying rigorous statistical methods and R-based visualization techniques. It examines the interplay of behavioral, demographic, and regional factors to identify cost determinants. Findings highlight smoking status as a major predictor, with smokers incurring substantially higher costs. Age and body mass index (BMI) also significantly impact expenses, underscoring the need to address the healthcare requirements of the elderly and obese populations. While notable regional cost differences exist, gender shows minimal influence. These results emphasize the importance of targeted interventions, such as smoking cessation programs and specialized care for high-risk demographic groups, to reduce costs and improve health outcomes. By revealing the complex relationships among behavioral,

Integrative Approaches to Quality, Data Analysis, and Interdisciplinary Research.
Amir Ahmad Dar and Waseem Z. Lone (Eds.)

DOI: 10.1201/9781779641014-5

demographic, and geographic variables, the study provides actionable insights for policymakers, healthcare providers, and researchers. Addressing lifestyle-related risks and regional disparities is a crucial step toward more efficient, equitable, and accessible healthcare systems. The research offers a comprehensive foundation for evidence-based policy design to enhance affordability and ensure better health for diverse populations.

4.1 INTRODUCTION

The distribution of resources and the formulation of global policies are significantly influenced by healthcare costs, which are crucial for both guaranteeing fair access to healthcare services and streamlining their provision. Due to the intricacy of healthcare cost dynamics, a thorough grasp of the several elements affecting these prices is necessary. Through the utilization of R programming language to perform rigorous statistical analyses and visualization techniques on large datasets containing important health variables, researchers can clarify the complex interplay between behavioral, demographic, and regional factors influencing healthcare costs [1, 2].

This study emphasizes the value of using a multimodal approach to healthcare cost management, taking into account how behavioral, demographic, and geographic factors are interrelated. Policymakers may create focused interventions targeted at lowering costs and enhancing health outcomes for a variety of groups by recognizing these drivers [3–6].

One of the study's important conclusions is that smoking status has a considerable effect on healthcare expenditures, with smokers having to pay a notably higher price. Age and body mass index (BMI) also show up as significant predictors, highlighting the significance of attending to the healthcare requirements of the elderly and obese people [7–10].

Although there are clear geographical differences in healthcare expenditures, gender does not seem to have much of an impact on these differences. As a result, those who live in some areas pay less for healthcare than those who live in others [11–14].

This study establishes the groundwork for the development of evidence-based policies that are strategically targeted at improving the affordability and accessibility of healthcare services by providing deep insights into the dynamics of healthcare prices. Addressing smoking behaviors and meeting the healthcare needs of the elderly and people with high BMIs are critical first steps in accomplishing this aim [15–18].

To optimize resource allocation and enhance healthcare affordability and accessibility, researchers, policymakers, and healthcare providers may benefit greatly from the thorough examination of the factors impacting healthcare prices provided by this study.

4.2 LITERATURE REVIEW

Globally, there is a great deal of worry about healthcare prices, and academics, politicians, and healthcare providers are working to better understand the many variables that affect these costs. Behavioral, demographic, and geographical characteristics are among the major predictors of healthcare costs that are shown by a thorough assessment of the research.

Many studies have been conducted on the relationship between behavioral factors—like smoking habits—and healthcare expenditures. Studies have continuously shown a clear correlation between being a smoker and higher healthcare costs. Due to a higher frequency of smoking-related disorders like heart disease, lung cancer, and respiratory ailments, smokers often have higher medical expenses [19, 20].

Age is yet another important factor that affects healthcare expenses. Population aging has effect on healthcare spending, with a focus on the heightened healthcare requirements of the elderly. People are more likely to acquire chronic health disorders as they become older and need continuous medical care, which drives up the cost of healthcare [21].

Healthcare expenses are significantly predicted by BMI. A comprehensive analysis shows a favorable relationship between healthcare spending and obesity. Obese people are frequently more likely to acquire diseases, including diabetes, hypertension, and joint issues, which can be expensive to cure and require medical procedures [22].

Although behavioral and demographic variables are significant contributors to healthcare costs, it is also important to pay attention to regional inequalities. A geographical study shows significant regional differences in healthcare spending. Healthcare prices are influenced by several factors, including socioeconomic position, healthcare infrastructure, and population density. Residents in different locations may have cheaper or higher healthcare expenditures [23].

Numerous studies have looked into the gaps in healthcare expenditures across genders. A comparative investigation revealed few differences in healthcare spending by gender. There is a need for more research in this area since men and women may have different healthcare expenses due to gender-specific healthcare demands and utilization patterns [24, 25].

The literature study highlights the complexity of healthcare cost dynamics overall. Healthcare costs are greatly impacted by behavioral variables, such as obesity and smoking, which emphasizes the need for health promotion and preventative measures. Age is another important demographic aspect; as the population ages, healthcare expenditures increase. Furthermore, specific interventions are required to alleviate inequities in access to healthcare services due to regional variations in healthcare expenditure.

Even while our understanding of the factors that influence healthcare costs has advanced significantly, there are still areas of uncertainty that need more investigation. For instance, more research is needed to fully understand how behavioral, demographic, and geographical characteristics interact and how this affects the cost of healthcare. Furthermore, careful evaluation of the efficacy of treatments targeted at lowering healthcare expenditures and enhancing health outcomes is required through longitudinal research and randomized controlled trials.

The literature evaluation offers insightful information about the variables affecting healthcare costs and establishes the foundation for resource allocation and policy decisions based on facts. Policymakers and healthcare professionals may create focused interventions to improve the accessibility and cost of healthcare services by addressing behavioral, demographic, and geographical factors. This will eventually improve health outcomes for a variety of groups.

4.3 METHODOLOGY

The dataset used in this study was obtained from Kaggle, a well-known platform that offers datasets in a variety of fields. This dataset includes important health data for 1338 patients, including demographics like age, gender, and BMI, as well as critical health variables like residency area and smoking status. It also offers thorough records of the expenses that were billed to each insurance company for the specific year. The foundation of the research into different facets of healthcare utilization, cost distribution, and potentially significant factors therein is provided by this dataset. The primary analytical tool used in the study for data processing, statistical analysis, and visualization was the R programming language. R is an open-source programming language that is widely used and well known for its powerful statistical features, and a large library of packages designed specifically for data analysis.

To give a comprehensive overview of the dataset, descriptive statistics were computed. Basic statistics like mean, median, mode, range, and standard deviation were calculated for numerical variables like age, BMI, and charges. The central tendency, variability, and distribution of these variables within the dataset are all revealed by these metrics. A variety of data visualization methods were used to obtain more insights from the dataset. To see the distributions of numerical variables like age, BMI, and charges, histograms were created. These histograms help visualize each variable's frequency distribution, which makes it easier to comprehend its variability and central tendencies. The distribution of categorical factors, such as sex, smoking status, and region, was shown using bar charts. These charts make it easier to compare and identify trends by providing a clear picture of the proportions or frequencies of each category within the dataset.

Correlation analysis was done to further look into the correlations between the variables in the dataset. The purpose of this analysis was to use correlation matrices or scatter plots to find any meaningful correlations between numerical variables. For numerical factors like age, BMI, and medical costs, a correlation matrix was calculated to measure the direction and strength of linear correlations. A graphical depiction of any possible correlations was also provided by scatter plots, which were used to visually examine these interactions. Investigations were also conducted into the effects of particular variables on medical costs, including age, BMI, and smoking status. In order to provide insight into the relative influence of each component on healthcare expenditures, the correlation coefficients between these factors and medical expenses were evaluated.

A linear regression model was created after the exploratory data analysis to look into the relationship between the response variable (charges) and the predictor variables (age, gender, BMI, smoking status, and region). The lm() function in R was used to fit the model, known as model1, with charges serving as the dependent variable and the other variables serving as independent predictors. The mathematical expression of the linear regression model is as follows:

$$\begin{aligned}\text{Charges} &= \beta_0 + \beta_1(\text{Age}) + \beta_2(\text{Sex}) + \beta_3(\text{BMI}) \\ &\quad + \beta_4 + (\text{Smoker}) + \beta_5 + (\text{Regoin}) + \varepsilon \end{aligned} \tag{4.1}$$

where β_0 is the intercept and $\beta_1, \beta_2, \beta_3, \beta_4$, and β_5 are the coefficients associated with age, sex, BMI, smoker, and region, respectively, and ε is the error term.

The null and alternative hypotheses for this case: According to the null hypothesis, there is no significant linear relationship between any of the predictor variables and the costs that are billed to insurance companies. Then, the alternative theory would be that at least one of the coefficients is not zero, meaning that there is a meaningful correlation between the charges and at least one predictor variable. A scatter plot was used to display the regression results, contrasting the actual charges with the charges that the linear regression model predicted.

Following the preliminary regression analysis, more models were built to investigate the effects of eliminating particular variables from the regression formula. Three distinct linear regression models were developed: one that only took into account the variable "sex," one that excluded the variable "smoker," and a third model that eliminated the variable "region." To determine the proportion of charge variance that the predictor variables account for, the coefficient of determination (R-squared) was calculated for each model. After removing each variable from the model, the R-squared values produced from these models are used to quantify the contribution of each variable to the explanation of the variability in charges.

4.4 RESULT AND ANALYSIS

4.4.1 DESCRIPTIVE STATISTICS

By giving information about the distributions and central tendencies of important variables, descriptive statistics help to provide a basic knowledge of the dataset being studied. They also provide both the numerical and categorical variables' descriptive statistics in this section. To provide an overview of the main variables in our dataset, descriptive statistics were performed. Basic data for numerical variables, including age, BMI, and costs, are summarized in Table 4.1.

Table 4.1 indicates that the patients' mean age was 39.21 years, with a 39-year median age and an 18-year mode. With a median BMI of 30.4 and a mode of 32.3, the average BMI was 30.66. With respect to fees, the average was $13,270.42, while the median was $9,382.03 and the mode was $1,639.56. The range for charges was $62,648.55, the range for age was 46 years, and the range for BMI was 37.17. Age, BMI, and charges had standard deviations of 14.05, 6.10, and $12,110.01, respectively. Moreover, the distribution of categorical characteristics such as region, sex, and smoker status was studied. The frequency counts for each category are shown in the result. Binary variables were indicated by the two separate categories for both sex and smoking status. However, region featured four unique categories that each represented a different geographic location."

TABLE 4.1 Descriptive Statistics

	Age	BMI	Charges
Mean	39.2070254110613	30.6633968609865	13,270.4222651413
Median	39	30.4	9382.033
Mode	18	32.3	1639.5631
Range	46	37.17	62,648.55411
SD	14.0499603792162	6.09818691167901	12,110.011236694

A variety of data visualization methods were used to obtain more insights from the dataset. To see the distributions of numerical data like age, BMI, and charges, histograms were created, as seen in Figure 4.1.

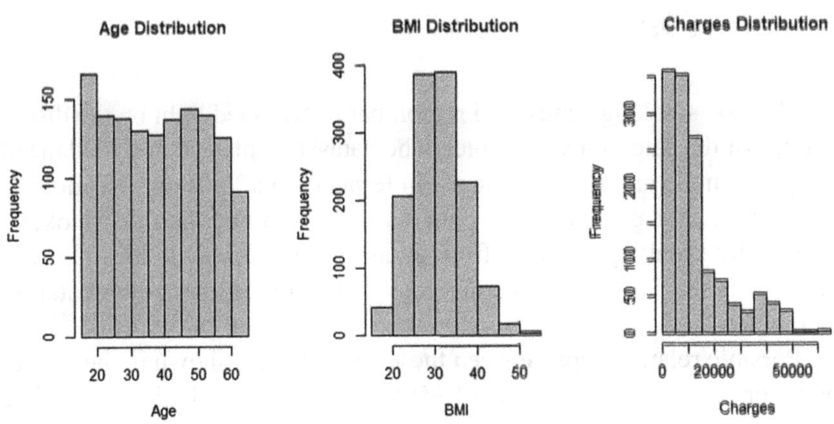

FIGURE 4.1 Distributions of numerical data.

The age, BMI, and charge distributions within the dataset are shown in the histograms. The histogram's depiction of age distribution shows a fairly uniform distribution of ages among the patients, with a peak located around the middle age range. The majority of patients fall into the normal to overweight BMI categories, as indicated by the slight right-skewness in the BMI distribution. A considerable fraction of patients had reduced medical costs, whereas a smaller subset had significantly higher charges, as seen by the charges histogram, which shows a highly right-skewed distribution.

The distribution of categorical variables, such as sex, smoking status, and region, is shown using bar charts in Figure 4.2.

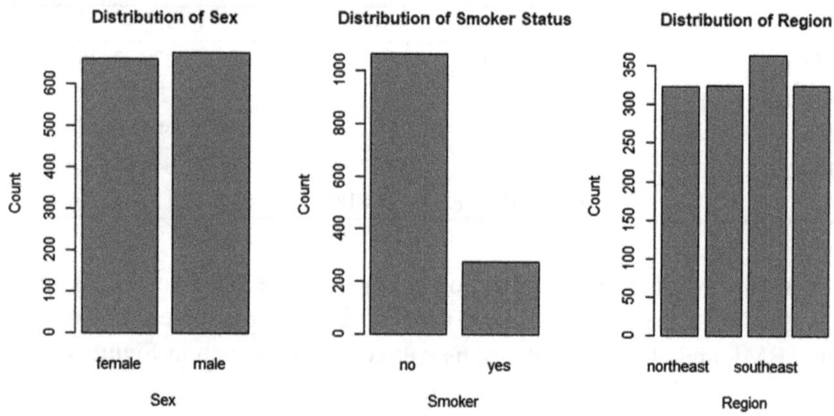

FIGURE 4.2 Distributions of categorical data.

The sex, smoking status, and region bar charts shed light on the distributions of the categorical variables. The dataset displays a fairly balanced sample of male and female patients in terms of sex. In terms of smoking status, a greater percentage of patients do not smoke than do smokers. Regionally speaking, patients from a variety of geographic locations are included in the dataset, with certain regions having a higher representation than others.

Possible relationships between these variables are shown in the scatter plots for age versus charges and BMI versus charges, which differentiate color according to smoker status. Smoking status may have an impact on healthcare use patterns, as evidenced by the age versus charges plot, which shows that nonsmokers have a wider range of medical expenses across various age groups than do smokers. A possible correlation between smoking status and healthcare costs is also indicated by the BMI versus charges plot, which shows that nonsmokers have distinct medical expenses across different BMI levels, while smokers tend to cluster toward greater charges.

4.4.2 CORRELATION ANALYSIS

For comprehending the relationships between the variables in a dataset, correlation analysis is an indispensable tool. An investigation of correlations between numerical factors, including age, BMI, and medical costs, was done in this study. To find any possible influence of smoking habits on healthcare costs, the relationship between medical charges and smoking status was also examined. The correlation matrix is shown in Table 4.2.

TABLE 4.2 Correlation Matrix

	Age	BMI	Charges
Age	1.0000000	0.1092719	0.2990082
BMI	0.1092719	1.0000000	0.1983410
Charges	0.2990082	0.1983410	1.0000000

An examination of the correlation between variables provided interesting new information. A positive connection ($r = 0.299$) between age and medical costs was found in the correlation matrix, indicating that medical costs often grow with age. In the same way, a lesser but still positive correlation ($r = 0.198$) was found between medical costs and BMI, suggesting a minor relationship between the two. To further investigate possible correlations between variables, scatter plots were made. To be more precise, scatter plots were created that show age versus charges and BMI versus charges. Figure 4.3 illustrates how the colors were differentiated according to whether or not the smoker was present.

Possible relationships between these variables are shown in the scatter plots for age versus charges and BMI versus charges, which differentiate color according to smoker status. Smoking status may have an impact on healthcare use patterns, as evidenced by the age versus charges plot, which shows that nonsmokers have a wider range of medical expenses across various age groups than do smokers. A possible correlation between smoking status and healthcare costs is also indicated by the BMI versus charges plot, which shows that nonsmokers have distinct medical expenses across different BMI levels while smokers tend to cluster toward greater charges.

Furthermore, with a correlation coefficient of 0.787, the relationship between smoking status and medical costs was noticeably strong.

This suggests a substantial positive relationship between healthcare costs and smoking behaviors. Figure 4.4 shows the box plot that was created to graphically depict this association between smoking status (smoker versus nonsmoker) and medical costs.

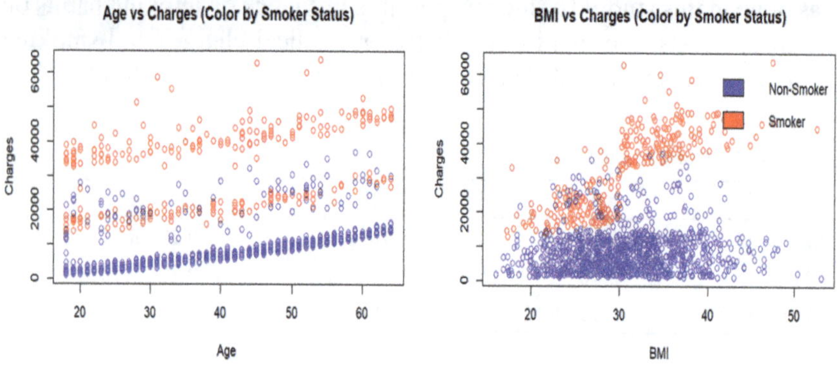

FIGURE 4.3 Correlation plot.

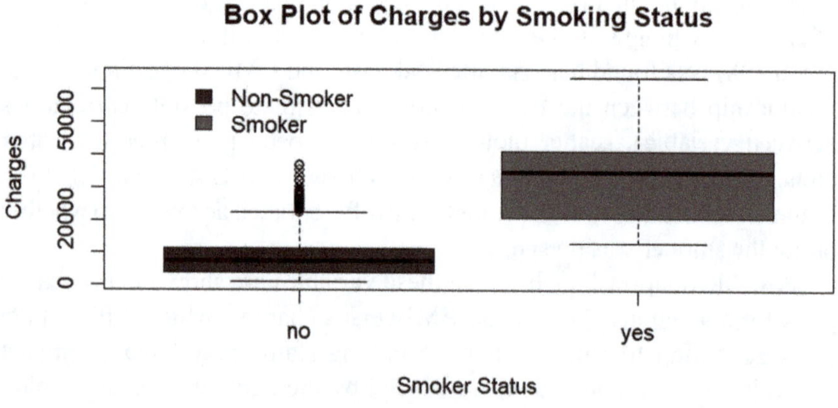

FIGURE 4.4 Plot of charges by smoking status.

The box plot highlights the possible effects of smoking on healthcare utilization and costs by showing greater median charges for smokers compared to nonsmokers. These results, taken together, highlight how crucial it is to take lifestyle and demographic variables, including age and smoking status, into account when examining healthcare costs and usage. In order to reduce healthcare expenditures and enhance public health outcomes, policymakers and healthcare professionals can better devise focused interventions and strategies by studying these relationships.

4.4.3 REGRESSION ANALYSIS

Understanding the relationship between different predictors and healthcare costs was made possible by the results of the linear regression analysis. The result of the regression analysis is shown in Table 4.3.

TABLE 4.3 Regression Result

	Estimate	St. Error	*t*-value	*p*-value
Intercept	−11,833.41	1214.17	−9.75	2e−16
Age	253.81	14.79	17.16	2e−16***
Sex(Male)	−128.42	415.47	−0.31	0.75732
BMI	348.28	35.61	9.78	2e−16***
Children	519.88	176.79	2.94	0.00336**
Smoker(Yes)	24,339.40	513.56	47.39	2e−16***
Region(Northwest)	−207.85	597.89	−0.348	0.72818
Region(Southeast)	−1671.78	596.30	−2.804	0.00516
Region(Southwest)	−1042.73	595.11	−1.752	0.08008

According to the results, age and charges had a positive correlation, with an estimated $253.81 increase for every year of life. Likewise, BMI demonstrated a noteworthy influence, indicating an approximate increase of $348.28 for every unit increase. In addition, those classified as smokers paid significantly more than those classified as nonsmokers—an estimated $24,000 more than the former. This stark contrast highlights the significant impact that smoking status has on healthcare expenditures. Furthermore, the presence of children was found to positively contribute to charges, indicating higher costs for those who have dependents. More analysis of categorical variables—like region and sex—uncovered more subtle information. Regional differences stood out as significant factors even though the coefficient for sex was not statistically significant, suggesting a minimal impact on charges between genders. In particular, residents in the southeast region incurred substantially less in fees than residents in other regions—an estimated $1671.78 less. On the other hand, living in the northwest and southwest had relatively small and insignificant effects.

The R-squared value was used to evaluate the overall fit of the model and showed that the predictors in the model could account for roughly 74.3% of the variance in charges. This significant percentage highlights how well the model captures the variation in healthcare costs depending on the chosen predictors.

By comparing the actual charges with the predicted charges derived from the linear regression model, a scatter plot was used to visualize the regression results, shown in Figure 4.5.

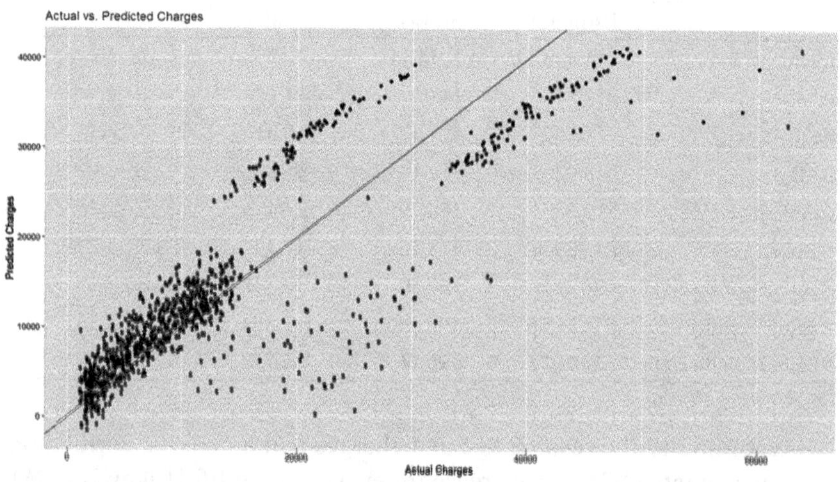

FIGURE 4.5 Actual vs. predicted charges.

The actual charges are indicated by the *x*-axis, while the predicted charges are represented by the *y*-axis. Each data point is an observation. To further denote perfect prediction alignment, a reference line was added. The performance and accuracy of the model can be evaluated with the help of this visualization, which provides an intuitive comparison between the observed charges and those predicted by the regression model.

To evaluate each categorical predictor's contribution to explaining the variance in charges, the analysis entailed methodically eliminating them from the regression model. The percentage of the response variable's variance that the predictors account for was indicated by the coefficient of determination (R-squared), which was used as a measure of model fit.

When the sex category was eliminated from the model, the R-squared value was found to be 0.74295. Since adding sex does not significantly increase the model's ability to explain charges, it appears that sex is not a significant predictor of charges. Conversely, the R-squared value significantly dropped to 0.1202076 when the smoker category was eliminated. As its exclusion resulted in a significant reduction in the model's predictive ability, this suggests that smoking status plays a significant role in explaining the variance in charges. Similarly, the R-squared value did not change when the region category was eliminated, suggesting that the region does not appreciably increase the explanatory power of the model.

These results highlight the significance of smoking status as a predictor of healthcare costs, albeit they also raise the possibility that sex and geography may not be as significant factors as they seem.

4.5 DISCUSSION AND FINDINGS

Important information about the variables affecting healthcare costs in a sample population can be gleaned from the study analysis sections' findings. The substantial effect that smoking status has on medical expenses is one of the main conclusions. The results of the regression analysis showed that those who were classified as smokers paid significantly more than those who were not, with an estimated $24,000 difference. This striking disparity emphasizes how crucial it is to address smoking habits in strategies for controlling healthcare costs. It implies the possibility of significant cost savings for the healthcare system from interventions meant to lower the prevalence of smoking. Furthermore, the examination revealed significant correlations between specific health-related and demographic factors and medical expenses. Age and BMI showed positive relationships with costs, suggesting that older people and those with higher BMIs typically spend more on healthcare. This result is consistent with previous research on the topic, which emphasizes the hazards and increased healthcare requirements linked to aging and a larger body mass. These findings highlight how crucial it is to take demographics into account when allocating healthcare resources and developing policy.

Regression analysis also showed notable regional differences in healthcare costs, even though it failed to find a statistically significant difference in charges between genders. It was discovered that charges for residents in the southeast region are significantly lower than those in other regions—roughly $1,671.78 in difference. This regional variation indicates the existence of regional variations in healthcare pricing structures or utilization patterns, underscoring the complexity of healthcare cost dynamics. To guarantee equitable access to healthcare services and optimize resource allocation across various geographic areas, it is imperative to comprehend and address these regional disparities. A deeper understanding of the factors influencing healthcare costs is provided by the interaction effects among predictor variables. The relationship between smoking status and variables like age and BMI can be dynamic, based on an individual's smoking habits, according to visualizations showing the interactions between these variables and charges. This result emphasizes how crucial it is to take into account potential interactions between variables when analyzing healthcare costs and how specific interventions are required to take these intricate relationships into account.

The study's conclusions have a big impact on healthcare practice and policy overall. Policymakers can create focused interventions targeted at lowering healthcare costs while improving health outcomes by identifying variables like smoking status, age, BMI, and region that are linked to variations in healthcare costs. The knowledge gained from this study also emphasizes how critical it is to take a multifaceted approach to healthcare cost management that takes into account how behavioral, regional, and demographic factors interact. Healthcare systems can aim to achieve more equitable and efficient healthcare delivery through targeted interventions and evidence-based policymaking.

4.6 LIMITATIONS

Although this study offers insightful information, it should be noted that it has certain limitations. First of all, the dataset used in this study was sourced from Kaggle, which could introduce biases or limitations related to the process of gathering and curating the dataset. Although Kaggle datasets are frequently extensive and extensively utilized, it is possible that they do not accurately reflect the diversity of healthcare systems or populations across the globe, which could restrict the findings' ability to be applied broadly. It is not possible to completely rule out the possibility of unmeasured or unknown uncertainties, which could have an impact on the validity of the results, even though thorough statistical analyses were carried out to investigate associations between variables.

Furthermore, by concentrating on a small number of predictor variables, the study may have ignored other variables like multiple medical conditions, socioeconomic status, or patterns of healthcare utilization that may have an impact on healthcare costs. The omission of these variables could lead to a partial comprehension of the factors that influence healthcare costs. However, even though interactions between predictor variables were investigated, more complex analyses may be necessary to fully capture the interplay between various factors due to the complexity of healthcare cost dynamics. In short, this study provides insightful information about the variables affecting healthcare costs; however, its conclusions should be interpreted in light of these limitations, and future investigations should focus on resolving these issues to deepen our comprehension of the dynamics affecting healthcare costs.

4.7 FUTURE SCOPE

The foundation for several lines of future research in healthcare cost analysis is laid by this study. First, broadening the range of variables taken into account—for example, by incorporating comorbidities, socio-economic variables, and healthcare utilization patterns—might yield a more thorough understanding of the dynamics of healthcare costs. Furthermore, longitudinal studies that monitor variations in healthcare costs over time and among various populations may shed light on patterns and factors that influence cost variance. Additionally, evaluating the efficacy of focused interventions meant to cut healthcare costs—especially in expensive domains like smoking cessation programs—may help guide evidence-based policy choices. Lastly, the use of cutting-edge analytical methods like machine learning algorithms may improve the capacity for predictive modeling and reveal intricate connections between predictor factors and healthcare expenses, opening the door to more exacting cost-controlling tactics.

4.8 CONCLUSION

The study offers insightful information about the variables affecting healthcare costs in a sample population, with a focus on behavioral and demographic factors in particular. The substantial influence of smoking status on healthcare costs is one of the main conclusions of this study. It was discovered that smokers pay significantly more than nonsmokers, which emphasizes the necessity of focused interventions meant to lower the prevalence of smoking to save healthcare costs. Furthermore, age and BMI showed positive relationships with healthcare costs, meaning that older people and people with higher BMI typically spend more. This emphasizes how crucial it is to address the healthcare requirements of the elderly and obese to reduce financial burdens. Although there was no significant correlation found between gender and healthcare costs, there were clear regional differences, with residents in the southeast region paying significantly less than residents in other regions. To guarantee equitable access to healthcare services and optimize resource allocation across various geographic areas, it is imperative to comprehend and address these regional variations in healthcare costs. The results of the study have significant ramifications for healthcare practice and policy. Through the process of identifying the variables that contribute to variations in healthcare costs, policymakers can create focused interventions that lower healthcare costs while enhancing health outcomes. The research's conclusions also highlight the significance of using a multifaceted strategy for healthcare cost management that takes into account the interactions between behavioral, regional, and demographic variables. In summary, the research advances our knowledge of the dynamics of healthcare costs and lays the groundwork for future studies focused on creating evidence-based plans for efficient healthcare delivery. Legislators and healthcare professionals can endeavor to create more effective and equitable healthcare systems by tackling the factors that have been found to influence healthcare costs.

KEYWORDS

- **healthcare costs**
- **smoking status**
- **body mass index**
- **regional**
- **regression**
- **expenses**

REFERENCES

1. Gallet, C. A., & Doucouliagos, H. (2017). The impact of healthcare spending on health outcomes: A meta-regression analysis. *Social Science & Medicine*, *179*, 9–17.
2. Sisko, A. M., Keehan, S. P., Poisal, J. A., Cuckler, G. A., Smith, S. D., Madison, A. J., Rennie, K. E., & Hardesty, J. C. (2019). National health expenditure projections, 2018–2027: Economic and demographic trends drive spending and enrollment growth. *Health Affairs*, *38*(3), 491–501.
3. Rosenthal, T. (2012). Geographic variation in health care. *Annual Review of Medicine*, *63*, 493–509.
4. Salvi, M., Loh, H. W., Seoni, S., Barua, P. D., García, S., Molinari, F., & Acharya, U. R. (2023). Multi-modality approaches for medical support systems: A systematic review of the last decade. *Information Fusion*, *103*, 102134.
5. Wrathall, J., & Belnap, T. (2017). Reducing health care costs through patient targeting: Risk adjustment modeling to predict patients remaining high cost. *eGEMs*, *5*(2), 4.
6. Mays, G. P., & Scutchfield, F. D. (2010). Improving public health system performance through multiorganizational partnerships. *Preventing Chronic Disease*, *7*(6), A116.
7. Rezaei, S., Sari, A. A., Arab, M., Majdzadeh, R., & Poorasl, A. M. (2016). Economic burden of smoking: A systematic review of direct and indirect costs. *Medical Journal of the Islamic Republic of Iran*, *30*, 397.
8. Warner, D. O., Borah, B. J., Moriarty, J., Schroeder, D. R., Shi, Y., & Shah, N. D. (2014). Smoking status and health care costs in the perioperative period: A population-based study. *JAMA Surgery*, *149*(3), 259–266.
9. De Meijer, C., Wouterse, B., Polder, J., & Koopmanschap, M. (2013). The effect of population aging on health expenditure growth: A critical review. *European Journal of Ageing*, *10*, 353–361.
10. Kent, S., Fusco, F., Gray, A., Jebb, S. A., Cairns, B. J., & Mihaylova, B. (2017). Body mass index and healthcare costs: A systematic literature review of individual participant data studies. *Obesity Reviews*, *18*(8), 869–879.
11. Owens, G. (2008). Gender differences in health care expenditures, resource utilization, and quality of care. *Journal of Managed Care Pharmacy*, *14*(3), 2–6.
12. Saikia, N., Moradhvaj, & Bora, J. K. (2016). Gender difference in health-care expenditure: Evidence from India human development survey. *PLoS One*, *11*(7), e0158332.
13. Mina, A., & Seyyed Meysam, M. (2014). Regional disparities in the distribution of health care facilities: Building evidence for evidence-based policy making. *Iranian Journal of Public Health*, *43*(7), 1020–1021.
14. Zhang, Y., Baik, S. H., Fendrick, A. M., & Baicker, K. (2012). Comparing local and regional variation in health care spending. *New England Journal of Medicine*, *367*(18), 1724–1731.
15. Brownson, R. C., Fielding, J. E., & Maylahn, C. M. (2009). Evidence-based public health: A fundamental concept for public health practice. *Annual Review of Public Health*, *30*, 175–201.
16. Bright, T., Felix, L., Kuper, H., & Polack, S. (2017). A systematic review of strategies to increase access to health services among children in low and middle income countries. *BMC Health Services Research*, *17*, 1–19.

17. Secker-Walker, R., Gnich, W., Platt, S., Lancaster, T., & Cochrane Tobacco Addiction Group. (1996). Community interventions for reducing smoking among adults. *Cochrane Database of Systematic Reviews, 2010*(1).
18. Jones, C. H., & Dolsten, M. (2024). Healthcare on the brink: Navigating the challenges of an aging society in the United States. *npj Aging, 10*(1), 22.
19. Castillo-Riquelme, M., Bardach, A., Palacios, A., & Pichón-Riviere, A. (2020). Health burden and economic costs of smoking in Chile: The potential impact of increasing cigarettes prices. *PLoS One, 15*(8), e0237967.
20. Barendregt, J. J., Bonneux, L., & van der Maas, P. J. (1997). The health care costs of smoking. *New England Journal of Medicine, 337*(15), 1052–1057.
21. Cristea, M., Noja, G. G., Stefea, P., & Sala, A. L. (2020). The impact of population aging and public health support on EU labor markets. *International Journal of Environmental Research and Public Health, 17*(4), 1439.
22. Lam, B. C. C., Lim, A. Y. L., Chan, S. L., Yum, M. P. S., Koh, N. S. Y., & Finkelstein, E. A. (2023). The impact of obesity: A narrative review. *Singapore Medical Journal, 64*(3), 163–171.
23. Percoco, M. (2021). Spatial health inequality and regional disparities historical evidence from Malaria in Italy. *Region, 8*(1), 53–73.
24. Bertakis, K. D., Azari, R., Helms, L. J., Callahan, E. J., & Robbins, J. A. (2000). Gender differences in the utilization of health care services. *Journal of Family Practice, 49*(2), 147–152.
25. Godoy-Bermúdez, A., Rojo-Gallego-Burin, A., Delgado-Márquez, L., Martín-Martín, J. J., Sánchez-Martínez, M. T., & López del Amo-González, M. P. (2023). Variation in perceived health across gender, working status, educational level, and regional health care expenditure in Spain (2014–2017). *PLos One, 18*(7), e0269613.

CHAPTER 5

A Time-Series Analysis of Lemon Production in Ten Major Cities in India

ANIL KUMAR[1], MOHIT NAIN[2*], and AMIT KUMAR PATHAK[3]

[1]*Department of Mathematics, Lovely Professional University, Phagwara, Punjab, India*

[2]*OM Sterling Global University, Hisar, Haryana, India*

[3]*College of Economics and Business Administration, University of Technology and Applied Sciences, Ibri, Oman*

ABSTRACT

The study is based on the agricultural sector in India to make well-informed decisions, and accurate forecasting of lemon production, and to help farmers make decisions regarding lemon production. This study uses autoregressive integrated moving average (ARIMA) models to forecast future lemon production. Monthly data for 10 major cities of India is collected from the National Horticulture Board. autocorrelation and partial autocorrelation functions are used for selecting the parameters of ARIMA models. Each city ARIMA model is implemented using the R programming language. The two cities which are Delhi [(3,0,0) (0,1,1)] and Jaipur [(1,0,2) (0,1,1)], are the best models among all the cities.

5.1 INTRODUCTION

India's agricultural sector includes a large amount of lemon cultivation, which has a major effect on domestic as well as global trade. Lemon is

Integrative Approaches to Quality, Data Analysis, and Interdisciplinary Research.
Amir Ahmad Dar and Waseem Z. Lone (Eds.)

DOI: 10.1201/9781779641014-6

well-known for its numerous health advantages and for being extremely rich in vitamin C. Lemons are used for soaps, various recipes, and pickles, too. Agriculture is dynamic and subject to various external factors, including consumer preferences, market trends, and variations in climate. Accurate forecasting is necessary to effectively manage the challenges involved in the lemon production process. The main objective of the study is to utilize ARIMA (autoregressive integrated moving average) models and time series to increase the accuracy of lemon production forecasting.

ARIMA approach is a widely used technique for forecasting time series based on previous data patterns [1, 2]. Using ARIMA models to predict sugarcane production in the major states for 2025 [3]. Lemon production is dependent on variations in weather, economic conditions, and methods of farming. For the analysis of time series data, ARIMA models are implemented in this research.

A brief look at the data shows that forecasting accuracy varies from state to state. For example, certain cities like Ahmedabad, Bengaluru, Chandigarh, Hyderabad, and Kolkata have nonseasonal data; on the other hand, Chennai, Mumbai, Pune, Delhi, and Jaipur have nested seasonality patterns.

Ray and Bhattacharyya [1] discovered that ARIMA (1,1,1) was more suitable for pulse production. There is an essential instrument for predicting the market price is the price prediction, and it is essential for developing policies that ensure stable output and fair prices. When Savadatti [4] used the ARIMA model for projections, found growth in productivity and pulse production.

The ARIMA model has been utilized for forecasting in numerous different research; for instance, it has been used to forecast sugarcane production. ARIMA models are used in Tamil Nadu for forecasting sugarcane yield [5, 6] as well as the area, productivity, and production of a variety of crops.

5.2 MATERIALS AND METHODS

For this study, data was extracted from the National Horticulture Board. The data is presented in a monthly format spanning from January 2002 to December 2022. The analysis is for the 10 states in India with significant lemon production, namely Chandigarh, Pune, Kolkata, Mumbai, Hyderabad, Chennai, Bengaluru, Ahmedabad, Delhi, and Jaipur. The statistical application R was utilized for the ARIMA model building.

5.2.1 ARIMA MODELS

ARIMA models were initially introduced by Jenkins and Box in 1976; hence, in the literature, it can also be referred to as the Box-Jenkins method [7]. Moving average (MA) and autoregressive (AR) models are parts of the ARIMA model. The ARIMA model is used in nonstationary series even these are the models appropriate for the series stationary.

The simplest way to make a time series stationary is the differencing technique. In this case, the difference operation involves subtracting a certain time period value from the time series final value and an ARIMA (p,q) model in a nonstationary time series can be converted into an ARIMA (p,d,q) model by calculating the d-order difference in order to make the series stationary.

In ARIMA (p,d,q) models, three parameters represent different aspects of the time series data. The order of the AR model is represented by parameter "p," the MA model is represented by "q," and "d" is the number of times that the data needs to be differenced to achieve stationarity [3, 8] and seasonal ARIMA is represented by the notation (p,d,q) (P, D, Q) [X], in this notation "P" represents seasonal autoregressive, "D" represents seasonal differencing order, "Q" represents seasonal moving average and "'X" represent the seasonal period.

The ARIMA model equation is as follows:

$$Yt = \varphi 1Yt - 1 + \varphi 2Yt - 2 + \cdots + \varphi pYt - p + \alpha 1 - \theta 1\alpha t - 1 - \alpha 2 - \theta 2$$
$$\alpha t - 2 - \cdots - \alpha q - \theta q\alpha t - q$$

In this case, φ_p stands for the AR operator's parameter values, αq for the error coefficient, θq for the MA operator's parameter values, and Yt for the data with the difference (d) from the original data [9].

The procedure for fitting time-series data to an ARIMA model is as follows [10]:

Step 1: Plot the data, check for additional observations, and adjust the data if necessary to normalize the variance.

Step 2: To identify the values of p and q, analyze the autocorrelation function (ACF) and the partial ACF (PACF). Following this, select the most effective ARIMA model by using Akaike's information criterion (AIC).

Step 3: To analyze the residuals from the best model, plot the ACF and PACF. Adjust the model if the graphical plot ACF and PACF do not seem to be white noise.

Step 4: If the residuals seem like white noise, compute the forecasts. The Bayesian information criterion (BIC), mean absolute error (MAE), mean absolute percentage error (MAPE), mean squared error (MSE), root mean square error (RMSE), and AIC are the statistical metrics used to assess the forecasting performance for model selection. For a time series, the residuals provide the foundation for the goodness-of-fit technique. Consequently, the forecast accuracy measure should be verified using several metrics. The most effective forecasting model is the one with the lowest error criteria value.

$$\text{MSE} = \frac{1}{n}\sum_{i=1}^{n} e_t^2,$$

$$\text{RMSE} = \sqrt{\frac{1}{\eta}\sum_{i=1}^{n} e_t^2},$$

$$\text{MAE} = \frac{1}{n}\sum_{i=1}^{n} |e_t|,$$

$$\text{MAPE} = \frac{100\%}{\eta}\sum_{t=1}^{n}\left|\frac{e_t}{y_t}\right|,$$

where e_t error term, y_t is the observation, and $\tilde{y}_t$ is the forecast, $e_t = y_t - \tilde{y}_t$.

$$\text{AIC} = -2LL + 2k$$

$$\text{BIC} = k^{*}\ln(n) - 2l$$

In this case, n stands for sample sizes, L for the model's likelihood function, and k for the number of estimated parameters in the model.

Mostly the ARIMA models, which are most effective, were identified using R's "auto. Arima ()" function. As a result, performed the other steps. Also, tested different models that would be suitable based on ACF and PACF graphs using R's Arima () function.

5.3 RESULTS AND DISCUSSION

Table 5.1 presents descriptivse information for the entire lemon production in Ahmedabad, Bengaluru, Chandigarh, Hyderabad, Kolkata, Chennai, Mumbai, Pune, Delhi, and Jaipur from 2002 to 2022. Between 2002 and

2022, the total lemon production in 10 cities ranged from a minimum of 380 to a maximum of 87,537. Thus, it can be concluded that since 2002, the total amount of lemon production has huge increment. Hyderabad has the greatest average lemon production (18,456), and Chandigarh has the lowest (3061). Based on an analysis of the standard deviations of lemon production, Hyderabad has the largest standard deviation at 3021.72.

TABLE 5.1 Descriptive Statistical Information for Lemon Production

Region	Minimum	Maximum	Skewness	Kurtosis	Standard Deviation
Ahmedabad	8	4483	5.35	42.58	429.0674
Bangalore	9	5037	1.65	3.06	901.29
Chandigarh	53	3061	4.57	35.89	278.20
Chennai	40	4870	2.47	14.03	567.30
Hyderabad	14	18,456	2.48	7.52	3021.72
Kolkata	36	8380	2.77	14.93	1019.42
Mumbai	22	17,249	4.82	30.76	1790.60
Pune	12	5750	1.73	2.75	1119.66
Delhi	162	15,613	1.07	0.79	2702.472
Jaipur	24	4638	1.43	1.69	902.13

The ACF and PACF graphs of the series' first differences are shown in Figure 5.1. The accurate models were used to forecast the production between 2023 and 2024 for the top 10 cities based on the models in Table 5.2. Based on Table 5.2 and Figure 5.1, the data for Bengaluru, Hyderabad, Kolkata, Chennai, Mumbai, and Pune became stationary at their first differences, while the data for Ahmedabad, Chandigarh, Delhi, and Jaipur were already stationary. From Table 5.2, Ahmedabad, Bengaluru, Chandigarh, Hyderabad, and Kolkata have nonseasonality ARIMA models, but Chennai, Mumbai, Pune, Delhi, and Jaipur have seasonality. The goodness of fit for ARIMA models was evaluated using various types of parameters, including MAE, MAPE, and so on.

A time series is the main tool for forecasting models used to forecast future values based on current information [3]. The purpose of the research was to predict the production of lemons in various major Indian cities for the years 2023 and 2024 using ARIMA models. Point forecasts and 95% prediction intervals were generated for 10 cities as listed in Table 5.2. The lower and upper bounds of the prediction intervals are represented by Lo95

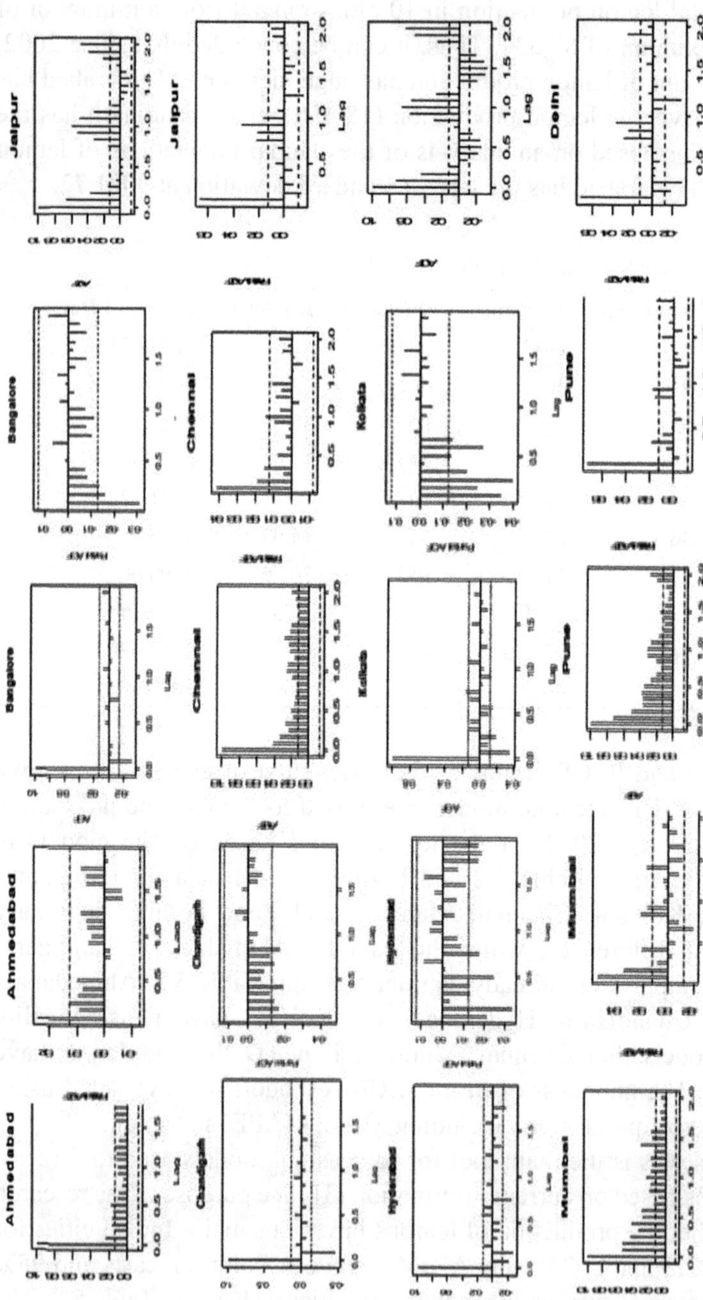

FIGURE 5.1 Partial autocorrelation function and autocorrelation function (ACF) graphs of lemon production using ARIMA models in the 10 major Indian cities.

TABLE 5.2 The Model Selection on Overall Lemon Production

Cities	ARIMA Model	MAE	MSE	RMSE	MAPE
Ahmedabad	(1,0,2)	222.9175	171,319.1	413.9071	52.38647
Bangalore	(1,1,2)	342.1727	303,150.6	550.5911	136.3344
Chandigarh	(2,0,1)	118.7692	47,267.03	217.4098	37.78623
Chennai	(1,1,1) (2,0,0) [12]	274.1385	240,823.3	490.7375	44.54372
Hyderabad	(0,1,2)	1121.75	4203,192	2050.169	220.0874
Kolkata	(0,1,2)	494.9815	679,431.3	824.2762	32.9849
Mumbai	(0,1,1) (0,0,1) [12]	632.0769	1,980,875	1407.436	82.95482
Pune	(1,1,1) (0,0,2) [12]	472.3204	544,273.9	737.7492	26.05213
Delhi	(3,0,0) (0,1,1) [12]	938.5351	1,869,091	1367.147	35.82569
Jaipur	(1,0,2) (0,1,1) [12]	373.1597	336,093.3	579.7356	37.70586

Note: RMSE is for root mean squared error; MAE stands for mean absolute error; MAPE stands for mean absolute percentage error; and ARIMA stands for autoregressive integrated moving average.

and Hi95 for a significance level $\alpha = 0.05$. Based on the tables and forecasted graphs, lemon production in Bangalore and Pune is continuously rising, while on the other hand, in Ahmadabad, Chennai, Chandigarh, Hyderabad, Kolkata, and Mumbai, there is not much change. The ARIMA models for Delhi and Jaipur are the best out of all the cities, Figure 5.2.

Based on the forecast, lemon production is expected to increase in Bangalore and Pune over the next two years. The production of lemons is predicted to reach 1013 in Bangalore and 2612 in Pune by 2024. However, the trend in lemon production in Delhi and Jaipur is highly fluctuating, as shown in Figure 5.2. The production trend is similar in Ahmadabad, Chennai, Hyderabad, Kolkata, and Mumbai, also justified by Figure 5.2.

5.4 CONCLUSION

India is one of the world's top producers of lemons with an estimated yearly production of approximately 3 million tons. Here, the results of this research indicate that India is going to have the highest anticipated value in the upcoming years. Delhi and Jaipur have the best models with seasonality. There is no noticeable variation in the output of lemon production in Ahmadabad, Chennai, Chandigarh, Hyderabad, Kolkata, and Mumbai, but there is an increasing trend in Bangalore and Pune. Maintaining this trend depends mainly on investment in the agriculture sector, price assistance initiatives, better farming techniques, study professionals, and various other variables that will impact results over time. This type of research assists in long-term strategic planning for a specific crop, as well as policy implementation.

KEYWORDS

- **lemon production**
- **autoregressive integrated moving average models**
- **time series analysis**
- **forecasting**
- **prediction**
- **modeling**

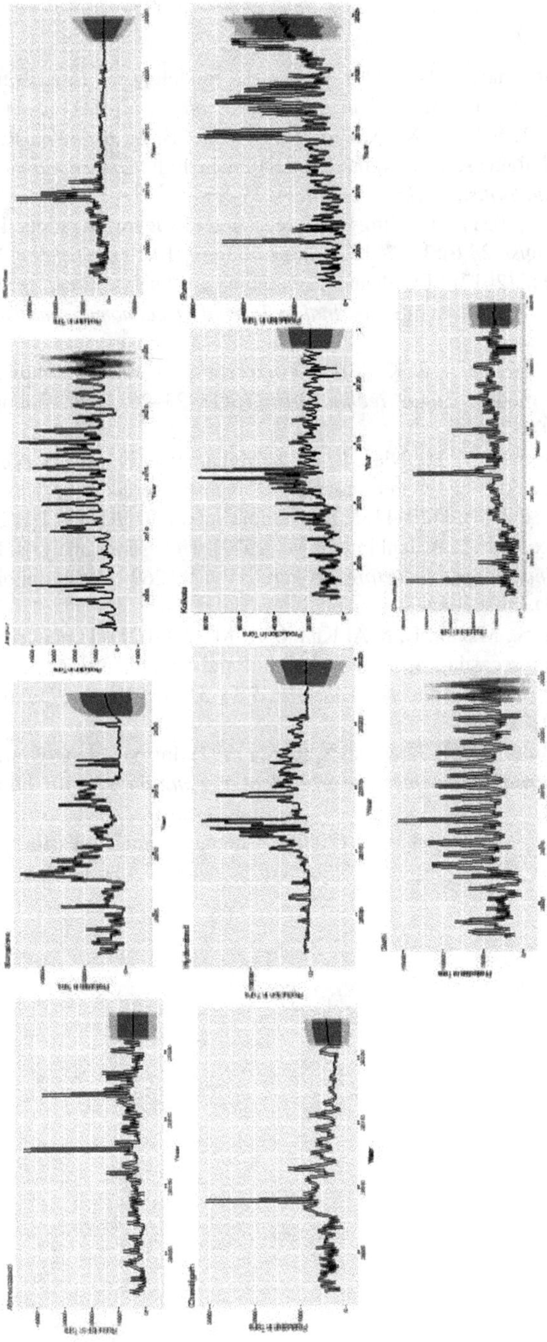

FIGURE 5.2 Autoregressive integrated moving average models were used to provide point forecasts at 95% prediction intervals for lemon production in the 10 major Indian cities (2023–2024).

REFERENCES

1. Ray, S., & Bhattacharyya, B. (2020). Time series modeling and forecasting on pulses production behavior of India. *Indian Journal of Ecology*, *47*(4), 1140–1149.
2. Vishwajith, K. P., Sahu, P. K., Mishra, P., Dhekale, B. S., & Singh, R. B. (2018). Modelling and forecasting of arhar production in India. *International Journal of Agricultural and Statistical Sciences*, *14*(1), 73–86.
3. Mishra, P. et al., (2021). Modeling and forecasting of sugarcane production in India. *Sugar Technologist*, *23*(6), 1317–1324, https://doi.org/10.1007/s12355-021-01004-3.
4. Savadatti, P. M. (2017). Trend and forecasting analysis of area, production and productivity of total pulses in India. *Indian Journal of Economics and Development*, *5*(12).
5. Suresh, K. K., & Priya, S. R. K. (2011). Forecasting sugarcane yield of Tamil Nadu using ARIMA models. *Sugar Technologist*, *13*(1), 23–26, https://doi.org/10.1007/s12355-011-0071-7.
6. Yaziz, S. R., Ahmad, M. H., Nian, L. C., & Muhammad, N. (2011). A comparative study on Box-Jenkins and Garch models in forecasting crude oil prices. *Journal of Applied Sciences*, *11*(7), 1129–1135, https://doi.org/10.3923/jas.2011.1129.1135.
7. Geurts, M., Box, G. E. P., & Jenkins, G. M. (1977). Time series analysis: Forecasting and control. *Journal of Marketing Research*, *14*(2), 269, https://doi.org/10.2307/3150485.
8. Ray, S., Das, S. S., Mishra, P., & Al Khatib, A. M. G. (2021). Time series SARIMA modelling and forecasting of monthly rainfall and temperature in the South Asian countries. *Earth Systems and Environment*, *5*(3), 531–546, https://doi.org/10.1007/s41748-021-00205-w.
9. Seymour, L., Brockwell, P. J., & Davis, R. A. (1997). Introduction to time series and forecasting. *Journal of the American Statistical Association*, *92*(440), https://doi.org/10.2307/2965440.
10. Hyndman, R. J., & Khandakar, Y. (2008). Automatic time series forecasting: The forecast package for R. *Journal of Statistical Software*, *27*(3), 1–22, https://doi.org/10.18637/jss.v027.i03.

PART II

Interdisciplinary Studies in Agriculture, Education, and History

CHAPTER 6

Optimizing Water Management for Sustainable Agriculture: A Multidisciplinary Approach

PREETY KALRA[1*], NISHA[1*], NAVDEEP KAUR[1*], and TASNEEM SHAH[2*]

[1]*Department of Mathematics, Lovely Professional University, Phagwara, Punjab, India*

[2]*Kwantlen Polytechnic University, Surrey, BC, Canada*

*Corresponding authors

ABSTRACT

This chapter adopts a multidisciplinary approach to examine the intersection of sustainable agriculture and water management, aiming to enhance efficiency and environmental stewardship. Understanding patterns in water-related variables is essential for sustaining agricultural productivity. Using statistical methods in R, the chapter first analyzes the distribution of key datasets to uncover variability and trends. It then applies nonparametric tests—robust statistical tools suitable when data distribution assumptions may not hold—to ensure reliable results and allow deeper exploration of correlations without rigid constraints. This analytical framework supports the development of water management strategies that balance environmental objectives with agricultural needs. By integrating statistical rigor with data-driven insights, the chapter provides practical recommendations for policymakers and practitioners. Its interdisciplinary, language-agnostic methodology fosters collaboration across diverse stakeholders, bridging disciplinary gaps. Ultimately, the chapter underscores the value of evidence-based decision-making

Integrative Approaches to Quality, Data Analysis, and Interdisciplinary Research.
Amir Ahmad Dar and Waseem Z. Lone (Eds.)

DOI: 10.1201/9781779641014-8

to promote sustainable and resilient water use in agriculture, aligning productivity goals with long-term environmental health.

6.1 INTRODUCTION

Sustainable agriculture is centered on water management, which is a vital intersection of food security, economic growth, and environmental care. The demand for effective and efficient water management strategies has never been greater due to the growing global population, the effects of climate change, and the growing competition for water supplies. This chapter examines the interdisciplinary method of improving agricultural water management by utilizing knowledge from a range of disciplines, such as hydrology, agronomy, engineering, economics, and policy. Sustainable agriculture is a critical response to global issues, including resource scarcity, climate change, and population expansion. It guarantees both environmental preservation and food security. As one of the most important aspects of agricultural sustainability, water management stands out. By maximizing water use in agriculture, this interdisciplinary strategy aims to promote efficiency and resilience in the face of changing environmental conditions [1, 2].

Sustainable agriculture's fundamental goal is to satisfy current demands without endangering the capacity of future generations to satisfy their own. One of the most important and limited resources in accomplishing this objective is water. Effective water management techniques protect the environment, guarantee water supply for future generations, and increase agricultural output and farmer livelihoods. A limited and essential resource, water is essential to agricultural environments. The strain on water supplies is increasing along with the need for food. Crop production and the availability of water for future generations are both at risk due to unrestrained water consumption and climatic unpredictability [3, 4]

The complex connections that exist in agricultural systems between water, soil, crops, and socioeconomic issues are acknowledged by a multidisciplinary approach. By results of this chapter, one can create comprehensive methods to deal with the problems of water shortage, water pollution, and water-related conflicts in agriculture by combining information from several fields. This strategy highlights how crucial it is for scientists, decision-makers, farmers, and other stakeholders to work together to develop context-specific solutions that strike a balance between conflicting demands for water supplies. This multidisciplinary method incorporates knowledge from agronomy, hydrology, climatology, and engineering, among other scientific fields. A comprehensive knowledge of the complex interaction between water and agriculture may be achieved by merging the experience from these several sectors. For example, hydrological model-informed precision irrigation technology may be used to optimize water distribution, minimizing waste and guaranteeing crops receive the right quantity of water for maximum growth [5, 6].

The basis for comprehending the flow, distribution, and quality of water in agricultural landscapes is provided by hydrology. Hydrologists can find possibilities for rainwater collecting, groundwater recharge, and erosion management to improve water availability and decrease runoff by examining rainfall patterns, soil properties, and hydrological processes. Crop selection and breeding techniques are equally essential in the field of agronomy. Water-use efficiency is facilitated by cultivating drought-resistant crops and advancing agroecological, concepts, which support sustainable agricultural practices. Furthermore, climate-smart farming methods take into account local climatic trends, allowing farmers to modify their water management plans in response to shifting environmental circumstances [7, 8].

The goal of agronomy is to maximize agricultural yield with the least amount of water and environmental effects possible. Agronomists work to increase water production and resistance to climatic unpredictability through advancements in crop breeding, irrigation technology, and agronomic practices. Farmers may better utilize resources and conserve water by customizing water applications to the unique requirements of their crops via the use of techniques like deficit irrigation and precision agriculture. Moreover, the effective use of sustainable water management techniques in agriculture depends on policy interventions. Governments and international organizations have the power to design policies that encourage sustainable agricultural practices, support research and development in the sector, and provide incentives for the use of water-efficient technology. The success of these projects depends on the cooperation of stakeholders, including farmers, researchers, legislators, and nongovernmental organizations [9]. The design and implementation of water infrastructure and management systems heavily rely on engineering. Engineers provide workable solutions to improve water efficiency and resilience in agriculture, ranging from irrigation networks and drainage systems to water storage facilities and water-saving technology. Engineers may build multifunctional landscapes that offer many advantages, such as habitat restoration, climate adaptation, and water retention, by combining engineering concepts with ecological design ideas, such as bioengineering and landscape restoration. Numerous triumphant case studies highlight the efficacy of a multidisciplinary strategy in agricultural water management. For example, drought-tolerant maize cultivars have been produced by the Water Efficient Maize for Africa project, a partnership between research institutions and agricultural organizations, improving resistance to water shortage in sub-Saharan Africa. These kinds of projects demonstrate the beneficial results that may be attained by multidisciplinary collaboration and well-informed decision-making [10, 11].

The incentives, trade-offs, and decision-making procedures that affect agricultural water management techniques can be better understood through the lens of economics. Economists may guide the creation of financial instruments, regulatory frameworks, and incentive systems that support the sustainable use and distribution of water by doing cost-benefit analysis, market valuation, and policy review. Farmers can be encouraged to adopt water-saving techniques and invest in water-efficient technology via the use of strategies like crop insurance, water price, and payment for ecosystem services. The institutional and regulatory framework for agricultural water management is significantly shaped by policy. Policymakers may establish a supportive climate for sustainable water usage, distribution, and governance by enacting laws, enforcing rules, and offering incentives. Stakeholder engagement tools, participatory decision-making procedures, and integrated approaches to water resource management can help varied stakeholders collaborate and reach a consensus, which will promote group action toward sustainable agriculture [3, 12].

In summary, a multidisciplinary strategy that incorporates information, skills, and viewpoints from hydrology, agronomy, engineering, economics, and politics is needed to optimize water management for sustainable agriculture. One can create creative solutions that improve agricultural systems' resilience, productivity, and water efficiency while preserving water resources for future generations by using the synergies across several disciplines. In conclusion, a multidisciplinary strategy incorporating knowledge from agronomy, hydrology, climatology, and engineering is necessary to optimize water management for sustainable agriculture. Climate-smart agriculture (CSA) techniques, crop breeding for resilience, and the development and application of precision irrigation technology are all included in this strategy. Collaboration between academics, policymakers, and farmers is necessary to create a framework that encourages wise water management and ensures agriculture's long-term survival in the face of global problems. By implementing this all-encompassing plan, we may foster a future in which agricultural methods are environmentally conscious and enhance both ecological sustainability and food security [13].

6.2 LITERATURE REVIEW

Agricultural water management is a complex topic that involves many different fields of study and viewpoints. The difficulties and possibilities of optimizing water consumption for sustainable agriculture practices have been thoroughly studied by academics. The main conclusions and ideas from research in the fields of hydrology, agronomy, engineering, economics, and policy are summarized in this survey of the literature [4, 13].

The significance of comprehending water availability and distribution in agricultural settings is emphasized by hydrological research. To effectively manage water resources for rainfed agriculture, a paradigm change is required, emphasizing methods like rainwater gathering and erosion management. To evaluate water consumption and production, Molden and erosion provide the idea of water accounting, which offers a framework for examining water resources in agricultural systems [8, 14].

The goal of agronomic research is to maximize crop yield using the least amount of water. Go over crop breeding, irrigation technology, and agronomic techniques as ways to increase agricultural water production. Sustainable intensification in agriculture entails raising output while reducing negative effects on the environment, particularly water use [5–12]. When it comes to planning and executing water infrastructure for agriculture, engineering is essential. Their analysis of the irrigation efficiency conundrum emphasizes the trade-offs between possible environmental effects and water savings. An international inventory of groundwater consumption for irrigation is presented by highlighting the significance of sustainable water management techniques in agricultural engineering [2].

Research on economics and policy can shed light on the regulatory structures and incentives that influence agricultural water management choices. The water–energy–food nexus is covered, which also emphasizes the necessity for coordinated strategies to handle conflicting demands on water resources. In their examination of the connections between water, food security, and climate change, emphasize the significance of legislative initiatives that support sustainable water usage in agriculture [9].

Integrated methods of agricultural water management place a strong emphasis on the collaboration of many stakeholders and disciplines. The notion of the "water footprint," which measures the amount of water used in agricultural goods, offers a comprehensive approach to water management. To improve resistance to climate change, suggest green water management techniques, highlighting the significance of green water in maintaining agricultural output [7].

To sum up, research on water management optimization for sustainable agriculture emphasizes the value of a multidisciplinary approach. Researchers and practitioners may create novel approaches to deal with the intricate problems of water shortage, climate change, and food security in agricultural systems by combining knowledge from hydrology, agronomy, engineering, economics, and politics [15].

6.3 METHODOLOGY

The data for this work has been taken from Kaggle (https://www.kaggle.com/datasets/prateekkkumar/crop-water-requirement). Data can be normally distributed, or it can follow a non-normal distribution. If it is normally distributed, we can perform a parametric test, whereas for non-normality, nonparametric tests are performed. In statistical hypothesis testing, the p-value, also known as the probability value, is a metric used to assess the importance of research or experimental findings. The p-value is less than 0.05, indicating that there are statistically significant changes in water use across specific temperature ranges. However, the Kruskal–Wallis test alone does not reveal these discrepancies. Post-hoc pairwise comparisons are required to determine whether temperature ranges have significantly different water use rates. Nonparametric tests, such as the Kruskal–Wallis, frequently use the Dunn test for these comparisons. The "Dunn test" is a statistical technique used to identify which particular groups differ from one another in post-hoc analysis after an analysis of variance. Following an omnibus test, post-hoc tests are carried out. When a significant difference is found between groups according to the omnibus test, Kruskal–Wallis is used to compare all possible pairs of group means. When comparing each treatment group to the control group and having a control group, the Dunn test is especially helpful. After gathering, the data was carefully preprocessed to make sure it was suitable for analysis. To prevent outliers, inconsistencies, or missing values from skewing the findings, the dataset has to be cleaned. Furthermore, tests for normality were performed to evaluate the data's distribution. To determine if the dataset was normal, two main techniques were used: quantile-quantile (Q–Q) plot analysis and the Anderson–Darling (AD) test. The AD test's lower *p*-value (less than 0.005) indicated a considerable departure from a normal distribution and offered strong evidence against the null hypothesis of normalcy. A Q–Q plot was used to visually evaluate normalcy in combination with the AD test. The quantiles of the dataset are shown in this visual comparison with the quantiles of a hypothetical normal distribution. The Q–Q plot and the AD test both agreed to point to large departures from a normal distribution. The collective findings of these analyzes highlight the dataset's non-normal characteristics, which call for the use of suitable nonparametric tests in further statistical analysis. After the non-normal distribution of the dataset was evaluated, additional research was carried out to clarify the effects of temperature, weather, geographical differences, and soil types on the amount of water required in agricultural settings. Graphical representations were used to look at how weather and temperature affected the amount of water required. An analysis of regional differences in water requirements was conducted using a visual depiction. An additional visual representation was employed to investigate the influence of soil type on water requirements. An understanding of how temperature, weather, geographical differences, and soil types affect water use was obtained, which will be helpful in strategic agricultural planning and effective water management. Water use patterns during temperature changes were examined using the Kruskal–Wallis test because of the data's non-normal distribution. The Kruskal–Wallis test does not require a normal distribution, in contrast to parametric tests. Rather, it demands that the groups have comparable forms, the data points be independent, and the data be assessed on an ordinal or continuous scale. The test is robust against departures from normalcy because of these presumptions. The null and alternative hypotheses for the Kruskal–Wallis's test must be developed. The alternative hypothesis (H1) proposes a substantial difference, whereas the null hypothesis (H0) points out that there is no difference in the group medians. A *p*-value is produced by the test and is used to decide whether to reject the null hypothesis. The null hypothesis is rejected, and it is shown that there are significant differences in the group medians if the *p*-value is less than the selected significance level, which is often set at 0.05. A *p*-value over the significance threshold, on the other hand, indicates that there is not enough data to reject the null hypothesis. Post-hoc tests such as Dunn's test technique can be used to identify particular group differences when Kruskal–Wallis test finds significant differences. Accurate reporting of the Kruskal–Wallis test findings is required, together with the test statistic, degrees of freedom, and corresponding value. Contextualizing the results and talking about their practical ramifications are also crucial. When dealing with data that is not normally distributed, researchers might benefit greatly from the use of the Kruskal–Wallis test. Through recognition of the constraints of parametric tests and the use of suitable nonparametric substitutes, investigators may guarantee strong and dependable statistical studies, so augmenting the validity of their discoveries [16–18].

6.3.1 NORMALITY

It is clear from the Q–Q plot and the AD test that the dataset considerably deviates from a normal distribution (Figure 6.1). A total of 30.978 was the result of the AD statistic, which measures the variation between the actual data and the predicted values under the assumption of normalcy. Furthermore, the data is not normally distributed, as indicated by the computed *p*-value of less than 0.005, which provides strong evidence against the null hypothesis of normalcy.

6.4 EXAMINING THE FACTORS AFFECTING THE WATER REQUIREMENT

6.4.1 EFFECT OF TEMPERATURE AND WEATHER CONDITIONS ON WATER REQUIREMENT

Each bar in the figure represents a certain temperature range, and the related water need is shown through different heights. Different heights inside the bars represent different types of weather. This graphic representation makes it easier to compare temperature ranges and the water requirements associated with them, providing a clear picture of how various weather conditions affect water consumption (Figure 6.2).

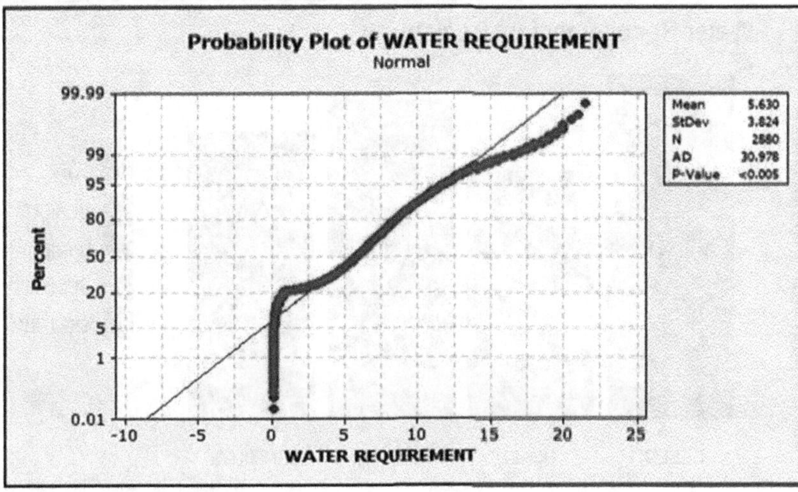

FIGURE 6.1 Q–Q plot.

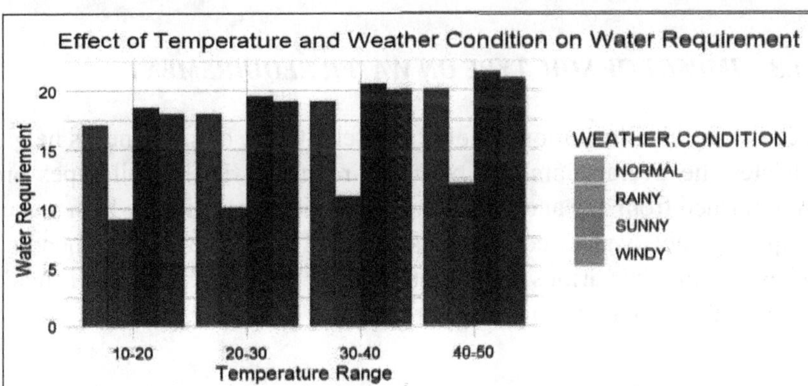

FIGURE 6.2 Effect of temperature.

6.4.2 REGIONAL VARIATION IN WATER REQUIREMENT

Each bar in the visual representation represents a particular location, and its height corresponds to the average amount of water required in that area. Because the bars are color-coded, comparing different regions is easy. This research is crucial for understanding how different locations require different amounts of water, which helps with strategic agricultural planning and efficient water management (Figure 6.3).

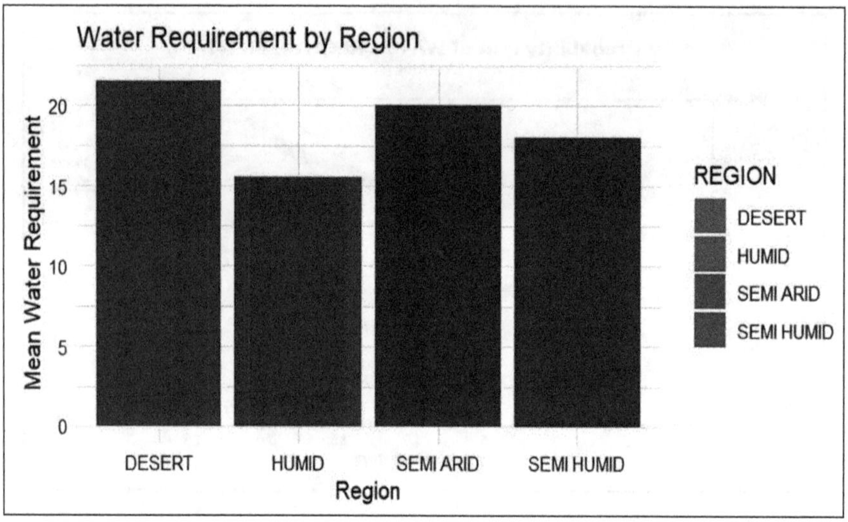

FIGURE 6.3 Water requirement by region.

6.4.3 IMPACT OF SOIL TYPE ON WATER REQUIREMENT

Each bar in this illustration denotes a different type of soil, and its height indicates the average amount of water required. These soil types are distinguished from one another by the use of different colors, which makes comparing their water requirements easier. The task of comprehending and evaluating the various water requirements of each type of soil is made easier by this visual approach (Figure 6.4).

6.4.5 ANALYZING WATER USAGE PATTERNS IN DIFFERENT TEMPERATURE SITUATIONS

Due to the non-normal distribution of the data, the Kruskal–Wallis test was used to analyze water use trends across changing temperatures. The Kruskal–Wallis test revealed substantial differences in water use across temperature settings ($\chi^2 = 235.2$, df = 3, $p < 2.2e{-}16$). This suggests that temperature fluctuations affect water consumption habits. As a result, the temperature has a significant impact on water consumption behaviors. The p-value is less than 0.05, indicating that there are statistically significant changes in water use across specific temperature ranges. However, the

Kruskal–Wallis test alone does not reveal these discrepancies. Post-hoc pairwise comparisons are required to determine whether temperature ranges have significantly different water use rates. Nonparametric tests, such as the Kruskal–Wallis, frequently use the Dunn test for these comparisons.

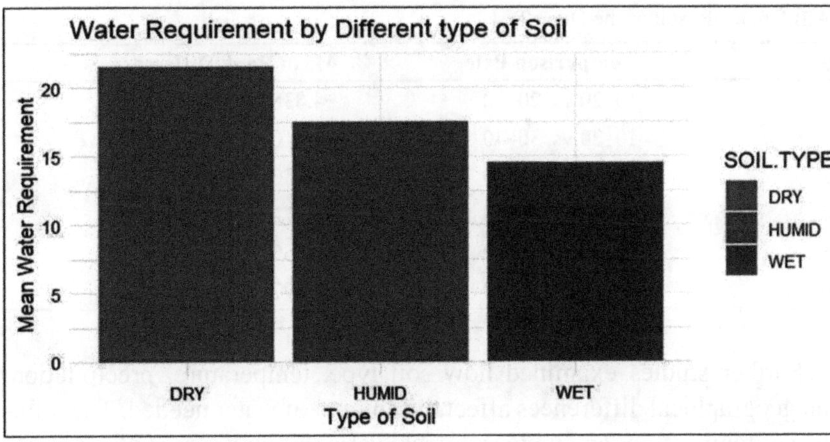

FIGURE 6.4 Water requirement for different soil.

There are notable variations in the amount of water required in each temperature range, according to an examination of water use across temperature ranges. More specifically, crops produced in temperature ranges higher than 10–20° and 20–30° show a much greater water requirement than crops grown in temperature ranges lower than 30–40° and 40–50° (as shown in Table 6.1). Significantly higher mean rankings of water use indicate that crops in the warmer temperature bands consistently need more water when compared pairwise across temperature ranges. These results highlight how crucial it is to take temperature fluctuations into account for efficient water management plans.

6.5 DISCUSSION OF RESULTS

This study's thorough research clarifies the complex variables affecting water requirements in agricultural settings. Significant departures from a normal distribution were found in the first normality evaluation using the Q–Q plot analysis and the AD test, underscoring the need for using alternative statistical techniques appropriate for non-normal data. This result is consistent with other studies that highlighted the non-normal distribution of agricultural data as a result of the intricate interactions between environmental variables [18].

TABLE 6.1 Result of the Dunn Test

S. No.	Comparison Pair	Mean Rank Difference
1	10–20 vs. 20–30	−4.838321
2	10–20 vs. 30–40	−9.810467
3	10–20 vs. 40–50	−14.507610
4	20–30 vs. 30–40	−4.972146
5	20–30 vs. 40–50	−9.669289
6	30–40 vs. 40–50	−4.697143

Further studies examined how soil type, temperature, precipitation, and geographical differences affect the amount of water needed. The influence of temperature and meteorological variables on patterns of water use was explained using visual aids, highlighting the necessity of customized water management plans in response to changing weather conditions. In keeping with earlier research emphasizing the significance of regional variability in agricultural water use, the examination of regional differences in water needs also highlighted the significance of taking spatial settings into account when planning water management [19].

Additionally, the investigation of several soil types revealed unique water needs linked to various soil properties, offering insightful information for enhancing irrigation techniques and managing soil moisture. These results support previous research highlighting the crucial impact that soil characteristics play in controlling plant water intake and water availability [20].

Significant differences in water consumption behaviors were also found when the investigation of water usage patterns under various temperature conditions was conducted. The study employed nonparametric statistical methods, including the Kruskal–Wallis test and Dunn post-hoc comparisons, to obtain strong conclusions regarding the impact of temperature variations on patterns of water usage. These findings are consistent with earlier studies that have demonstrated the sensitivity of agricultural water demand to temperature fluctuations [21].

All things considered, this study's results add to a more sophisticated knowledge of the complex variables influencing the amount of water needed for agriculture. This study contributes to the creation of evidence-based water management techniques that are suited to various environmental situations by combining statistical analysis with visual representations. This helps to advance sustainable farming practices and the management of water resources.

6.6 RECOMMENDATIONS

a. **Implement precision irrigation techniques:** Using advanced tools like soil moisture monitors, meteorological information, and remote sensing, you can improve irrigation plans and provide water exactly where and when it is needed. In addition to ensuring the effective use of restricted water resources, this helps reduce the wasteful consumption of water.
b. **Promote water-efficient crop selection:** Encourage crop selection that is water-efficient promote the growth of crop kinds that are suitable for the local agroclimatic—those resistant to drought or requiring less water. In doing so, you can preserve or even increase agricultural productivity while lowering the need for water.
c. **Encourage agroforestry and soil conservation practices:** By integrating trees and shrubs into agroforestry systems, you can enhance soil moisture retention, control water cycles, and reap other advantages like carbon sequestration and biodiversity preservation.
d. **Offer support and monetary incentives:** Give farmers who implement water-efficient practices financial incentives, subsidies, and programs of technical help. As a result, adopting sustainable water management methods and technology may be encouraged, and the initial investment costs may be mitigated.

e. **Policy interventions**
   - **Water pricing and subsidy reforms:** Farmers can be urged to utilize water wisely by putting in place effective water pricing systems. Water-saving technology should be the focus of subsidies.
   - **Water rights and allocation systems:** Rights to water and systems of allocation water resources are more successfully

managed when there are clear water rights and open allocation procedures. By preventing over-extraction, these regulations guarantee fair distribution.

- Agroforestry, precision irrigation, and drought-tolerant crops are examples of CSA techniques. These policies support sustainable water use.

f. **Technological innovations:**

- Direct-to-root (drip and sprinkler) irrigation systems reduce water waste by supplying water to plant roots. They increase the effectiveness of water utilization.
- **Rainwater harvesting:** Harvesting rainfall for agricultural purposes lessens reliance on surface and groundwater resources.
- **Satellite-based irrigation monitoring:** Accurate scheduling of irrigation is made possible by the monitoring of agricultural water requirements through the use of satellite data and remote sensing.
- **Desalination and use of brackish water:** Techniques that transform brackish or saltwater into freshwater can increase the amount of water available for farming.

g) **Changes within institutions:**

- **Community-based water management:** Sustainable practices are fostered when local communities are given the authority to manage their water resources. Participatory methods increase accountability and ownership. By taking into account social, economic, and environmental factors, integrated water resource management strategies improve the distribution and management of water resources.

6.7 FUTURE RESEARCH AND TECHNIQUES

- Techniques for replenishing depleted aquifers through research, such as artificial recharge using managed aquifer recharge systems. Investigate if replenishing aquifers with surplus surface water during rainy seasons is feasible.
- **Innovations in desalination:** Expand the energy and economic efficiency of desalination technology. Look into the localized water supply through decentralized desalination machines.

- **Climate-resilient agriculture:** Develop adaptive methods by researching how climate change affects water supply and practicing climate-resilient agriculture. Examine methods that are climate-aware and improve agricultural water resilience.
- **Policy and governance research:** Evaluate the efficacy of current water policies and governance frameworks through policy and governance research. To support sustainable water management, identify policy gaps and suggest reforms.
- **Capacity building and education:** Investing in educational and capacity-building initiatives will help farmers, extension agents, and legislators learn more about water-efficient techniques.
  Spread the word about how crucial it is for farmers to conserve water.
- **Partnerships and cooperation:** To solve the water crisis, encourage cooperation between academics, decision-makers, nongovernmental organizations, and the corporate sector. Promote the exchange of knowledge and interdisciplinary study.

In brief, a wide range of tactics and initiatives are covered in the advice given in order to support agriculture's sustainable use of water. Future research directions, institutional reforms, policy initiatives, and technological advancements are only a few of the many topics that these recommendations cover. Collectively, the suggestions offer an all-encompassing structure for advocating for the sustainable utilization of water in agriculture, tackling the intricate issues related to water shortages and climate change, all the while building resilience and extended environmental sustainability.

6.8 CONCLUSION

The results of this research are essential in addition to being helpful tools for planning and assessing water resource systems. Provided water-accounting ideas and processes are also helpful for characterizing and summarizing water consumption. They can offer a useful summary and indicate areas that need more in-depth research when it comes to evaluation and performance assessment. Water scarcity, climate change, and food security in agricultural systems can be addressed creatively by researchers and practitioners by combining knowledge from hydrology, agronomy, engineering, economics, and policy.

This work offers crucial insights that guide the development of effective policies for managing water resources and sustainable agricultural practices through an examination of the complex relationships between temperature, weather, and regional variations.

These discoveries are essential to lessening the numerous issues related to water scarcity and enhancing agricultural output in light of the increasingly unpredictable and variable climate. The Comprehensive Assessment of Water Management in Agriculture emphasizes that new investments in water management are essential to agriculture's ability to meet future food demands. This is because water resources are under more stress and unpredictability due to climate change. This work promotes resilience and sustainability in agricultural systems, which safeguards both the long-term sustainability of agricultural livelihoods and the world's food security. It will be essential to maintain multidisciplinary cooperation and a persistent research endeavor in the future to successfully negotiate the ever-changing intricacies of agricultural water management. This chapter can help to address the urgent issues affecting agricultural water supplies and clear the path for future generations to live in a more secure and sustainable future by embracing innovation and using scientific discoveries.

KEYWORDS

- **sustainable development**
- **water management**
- **statistical tools**
- **temperature**
- **policy interventions**

REFERENCES

1. von Braun, J., Afsana, K., Fresco, L., & Hassan, M. (2021). Science for transformation of food systems: Opportunities for the UN Food Systems Summit. In: von Braun, J., Afsana, K., Fresco, L.O., Hassan, M.H.A. (Eds.), *Science and Innovations for Food Systems Transformation*. Springer, Cham.

2. Rockström, J., Karlberg, L., Wani, S. P., Barron, J., Hatibu, N., Oweis, T., Bruggeman, A., Farahani, J., & Qiang, Z. (2010). Managing water in rainfed agriculture—the need for a paradigm shift. *Agricultural Water Management*, 97(4), 543–550.
3. Previati, M., Bevilacqua, I., Canone, D., Ferraris, S., & Haverkamp, R.(2010). Evaluation of soil water storage efficiency for rainfall harvesting on hillslope micro-basins built using time domain reflectometry measurements. *Agricultural Water Management*, 97(3), 449–456.
4. Grafton, R. Q., Williams, J., Perry, C. J., Molle, F., Ringler, C., Steduto, P., Udall, B., Wheeler, S. A., Wang, Y., Garrick, D., & Allen, R. G. (2018). The paradox of irrigation efficiency. *Science*, 361(6404), 748–750.
5. Molden, D., & Sakthivadivel, R. J. I. J. (1999). Water accounting to assess use and productivity of water. *International Journal of Water Resources Development*, 15 (1–2), 55–71.
6. Carlsen, L., & Bruggemann, R. (2022). The 17 United Nations' sustainable development goals: A status by 2020. *International Journal of Sustainable Development & World Ecology*, 29(3), 219–229.
7. Turral, H., Burke, J., & Faurès, J. M. (2011). Climate Change, Water and Food Security No. 36. Food and Agriculture Organization of the United Nations (FAO).
8. Hoekstra, A. Y., & Mekonnen, M. M. (2012). The water footprint of humanity. *Proceedings of the National Academy of Sciences*, 109(9), 3232–3237.
9. Siebert, S., Burke, J., Faures, J. M., Frenken, K., Hoogeveen, J., Döll, P., & Portmann, F. T. (2010). Groundwater use for irrigation—a global inventory. *Hydrology and Earth System Sciences*, 14(10), 1863–1880.
10. Vink, M. J., Boezeman, D., Dewulf, A., & Termeer, C. J. (2013). Changing climate, changing frames: Dutch water policy frame developments in the context of a rise and fall of attention to climate change. *Environmental Science & Policy*, 30, 90–101.
11. Unep, A., & Assessment, I. R. R, (2016). The Rise of Environmental Crime. UNEP: Nairobi.
12. Rockström, J., Falkenmark, M., Karlberg, L., Hoff, H., Rost, S., & Gerten, D. (2009). Future water availability for global food production: The potential of green water for increasing resilience to global change. *Water Resources Research*, 45(7).
13. Garnett, T., Appleby, M. C., Balmford, A., Bateman, I. J., Benton, T. G., Bloomer, P. & Godfray, H. C. J. (2013). Sustainable intensification in agriculture: Premises and policies. *Science*, 341(6141), 33–34.
14. Molden, D., Oweis, T., Steduto, P., Bindraban, P., Hanjra, M. A., & Kijne, J. (2010). Improving agricultural water productivity: Between optimism and caution. *Agricultural Water Management*, 97(4), 528–535.
15. Wichelns, D. (2017). The water-energy-food nexus: Is the increasing attention warranted, from either a research or policy perspective? *Environmental Science & Policy*, 69, 113–123.
16. Kruskal, W. H., & Wallis, W. A. (1952). Use of ranks in one-criterion variance analysis. *Journal of the American Statistical Association*, 47(260), 583–621.
17. Conover, W. J., & Iman, R. L. (1981). Rank transformations as a bridge between parametric and nonparametric statistics. *The American Statistician*, 35(3), 124–129.
18. Stroup, W. W. Non-normal data in agricultural experiments, *Conference on Applied Statistics in Agriculture*. 2013. https://doi.org/10.4148/2475-7772.1018.

19. D'odorico, P., Carr, J. A., Laio, F., Ridolfi, L., & Vandoni, S. Feeding humanity through global food trade. *Earth's Future*, 2(9), 458–469.
20. Haokip, I. C., Premalatha, R. P., Homeshwari Devi, M., Chetan Jangir, B. H., Sunil, S. K., Surekha, K., & Srinivasa Rao, C. (2020). Climate change adaptation and mitigation through soil management. In: *Climate Change and Indian Agriculture: Challenges and Adaptation Strategies* (pp. 105–130). ICAR-National Academy of Agricultural Research Management: Hyderabad.
21. Barnwal, P., & Kotani, K.2013. Climatic impacts across agricultural crop yield distributions: An application of quantile regression on rice crops in Andhra Pradesh, India. *Ecological Economics*, 87, 95–109.

CHAPTER 7

Factor Analysis for Attention Deficit Hyperactivity Disorder Symptoms Questionnaires (Adult ADHD Self-Report Scale V1.1) Among Hei Learners

SACHITANAND SINGH[1,2*], RENU THAKUR[3], and KRISHAN KUMAR[4]

[1]*Department of Optometry, UIAHS, Chandigarh University, Mohali, Punjab, India*

[2]*Department of Optometry, CSHS, Chitkara University, Rajpura, Punjab, India*

[3]*Centre for Research Impact and Outcome, Chitkara University, Rajpura, Punjab, India*

[4]*Department of Psychiatry, Postgraduate Institute of Medical Education & Research (PGIMER), Chandigarh, India*

*Corresponding author

ABSTRACT

Attention-deficit hyperactivity disorder (ADHD) is a neurodevelopmental disorder that adversely affects academic and professional outcomes, family dynamics, and financial stability. It impacts children globally, with increasing recognition of its presence in adults. This study focuses on factor analysis to find out the prevalence of adult ADHD symptoms among undergraduate students aged 18–23 in Punjab, India's higher education institutions. Conducted from May to September 2023, the study used a cross-sectional quantitative survey with the ASRS-v1.1 scale administered

Integrative Approaches to Quality, Data Analysis, and Interdisciplinary Research.
Amir Ahmad Dar and Waseem Z. Lone (Eds.)

DOI: 10.1201/9781779641014-9

via an online form. A total of 330 students participated. The questionnaire assessed inattention, hyperactivity, and impulsivity, with responses categorized into five levels: (1) never, (2) rarely, (3) sometimes, (4) often, and (5) very often. "Sometimes" was the most common response across all categories, suggesting that many students occasionally experience ADHD symptoms. "Very often" was consistently low across categories. Statistical analysis, including Cronbach's alpha, Kaiser–Meyer–Olkin (KMO), Bartlett's test, and factor analysis, confirmed the reliability of the scale for assessing ADHD symptoms. The overall prevalence of ADHD symptoms was 33.23%, with individual rates of 38% for inattention, 42.6% for hyperactivity, and 29% for impulsivity. The study highlights a significant prevalence of ADHD symptoms among undergraduate students in Punjab, India.

7.1 INTRODUCTION

Attention has a limited capacity for receiving stimuli; the number of things a person can concentrate on during a brief exposure is known as attention span [1]. Three facets of human attention are investigated processing speed, selectivity, and awareness. These components may be experimentally isolated, and their interactions can be investigated in the context of comparable tasks [2, 3]. Studies on adults diagnosed with attention-deficit hyperactivity disorder (ADHD) have shown that there are clinical parallels between their characteristics and those of children with ADHD in terms of demographic, psychosocial, psychiatric, and cognitive factors [4, 5]. ADHD persistence is predicted by mental comorbidities, psychosocial difficulties, and a family history of the disorder. Research on the history of ADHD in families has repeatedly demonstrated a significant familial component. Although there is no clear-cut reason for ADHD, data point to neurological and hereditary factors. According to structural and functional imaging studies, the etiology of ADHD includes anomalies in the dopaminergic and noradrenergic systems as well as malfunctions in the fronto-subcortical pathways [6, 7]. The adult ADHD self-report scale (ASRS-v1.1) symptom checklist was a widely used diagnostic tool designed to screen for ADHD in adults. It was created in collaboration with the workgroup on adult ADHD and the World Health Organization. The purpose of the checklist was to give a preliminary assessment of the existence and intensity of adult ADHD symptoms. Based on the Diagnostic and Statistical Manual of Mental Disorders, Fourth Edition (DSM-IV), the ASRS-v1.1 has 18 items that correspond to the symptoms of ADHD. These questions are divided into two parts: Part A: This contains the first six questions which are considered highly predictive of ADHD. These questions focus on core symptoms related to inattention. Part B: This includes the remaining 12 questions, providing additional context and detail about the individual's symptoms of hyperactivity and impulsivity. In every ASRS-v1.1 question, participants are asked to rate, on a scale of 0–4, the frequency of particular behaviors during the previous six months (0: never, 1: rarely, 2: sometimes, 3: often, and 4: very often). The questions include a range of topics related to ADHD as follows: *Inattention*: Inability to maintain focus, prioritize work, obey directions, and forgetfulness in day-to-day activities. *Hyperactivity and impulsivity*: Issues such as fidgeting, difficulty remaining seated, feeling restless, talking excessively, interrupting others, and difficulty waiting one's turn. *Part A scoring*: If a respondent scores a 4 (often) or 5 (very often) on four or more of the six questions, it suggests a high likelihood of ADHD. *Part B scoring*: The responses provide further detail to help clinicians understand the breadth and impact of the symptoms, but Part A is the primary screening tool [8]. The ASRS-v1.1 is intended to identify people who might require a more comprehensive assessment by a healthcare provider; it is not a diagnostic tool in and of itself. The ASRS-v1.1 can be used in both clinical settings (e.g., by psychiatrists, psychologists, and primary care physicians) and nonclinical settings (e.g., workplace assessments, educational environments) to identify individuals who might benefit from a full ADHD diagnostic evaluation [9–12]. It can also be used to monitor symptoms over time and assess the effectiveness of interventions on ADHD symptomatic patients. While the ASRS-v1.1 is a valuable screening tool, a comprehensive assessment for ADHD should include a detailed clinical interview, collateral information from family or close contacts, and potentially other psychological testing [13]. Accurate diagnosis and suitable treatment planning are ensured by this comprehensive approach. Inattentive, hyperactive/impulsive, and a mix of both forms of ADHD are listed in the DSM-5 criteria, which are presently in use. A person must have shown six or more signs of impulsivity, hyperactivity, or inattention for at least six months before turning 12 in order to be diagnosed with ADHD [14–16]. This study aimed to find out the reliability and factor analysis of the ASRS-v1.1 questionnaire among higher educational institutes and undergraduate students and to check any relationship available between ADHD symptoms and multiple history such as age, gender, education level, number of siblings, type of family, mother's and father's education, and if students were hosteller or a day scholar.

7.2 EXPERIMENTAL METHODS AND MATERIALS

In Punjab, India, a cross-sectional quantitative study was carried out from May to September 2023 to determine the prevalence of ADHD among students in higher educational institutes aged from 18 to 23 years. The Punjab Ethical Community at Chitkara University provided the ethical clearance (IHEC/CU/PB/DHR/23/182).

7.2.1 *SAMPLE SIZE CALCULATION*

***Z*-statistic (*Z*):** *Z* value is 1.96 for the customary 95% level of confidence. We used 3% error and 95% confidence intervals in this investigation. The proportion (prevalence) that was obtained from earlier research is known as the expected proportion (*P*). In India, the prevalence of adult ADHD was 7.3% [17, 18]. Thus, p equals 0.073.

Precision (*d*): Investigators must have a thorough understanding of this value. It is possible to infer from the formula that the sample size varies inversely with the precision squared (d^2) [19, 20]. Instead of being a percentage, d in the calculation should be a proportion of one, and for the highest number of samples that Cohen's D suggested was 0.3.

$$n = z2p(1 - p)/d^2$$

$$n = 1.962 \times 0.073(1 - 0.073)/0.032$$

$$= 3.842 \times 0.073 \times 0.927/0.0009$$

$$= 3.842 \times 0.067671/0.0009$$

$$= 0.259992/0.0009$$

$$= 289$$

A total of 330 students were considered for this study from higher educational institutes in Punjab considering that a few of them could leave the questionnaires half-filled or wrongly filled. Students with best corrected visual acuity of 20/20 at distance and N6 at near and students were excluded with a history of any ocular injury, surgery, and infection in the eye, currently taking any medication, diagnosed ADHD patients or any learning or mental disorder, head trauma, received or receiving any kind of psychological, behavioral, occupational or vision therapy, and general health issues. ADHD questionnaire (ASRS-v1.1) [25–27] was constructed in Google Forms along with 18 ADHD questionnaires and basic history. After obtaining approval from the higher educational institute and informed consent from students, questionnaires were circulated, and responses were taken from undergraduate students. The data were analyzed using SPSS 20 and Excel.

7.3 RESULTS

The age range was 18–23 years with a mean of 18.95 ± 1.13 years. Out of 330 students, 203 were female and 127 were male, which is 61.5% and 38.5%, respectively, as shown in Figure 7.1. In this study, 31 students were single children with no siblings, 188 students had one sibling, two students had more than 5 and 16 students had equal or more than four siblings. This study had a maximum number of students from nuclear families and extended families; very few students were from single-parent and step-families. Student's parents' education levels were three uneducated fathers and eight uneducated mothers among the population. This questionnaire likely assesses various aspects related to inattention, hyperactivity, and impulsivity. The responses were categorized into five levels: never, rarely, sometimes, often, and very often.

Table 7.1 shows that the maximum number of students was from age group between 18 and 19 years and four students were from 23 years old. Of 330 undergraduate students, 11 were studying diplomas and 319 were studying graduation courses. In this study, many demographic data were taken such as age, gender, number of siblings, type of family, father's and mother's education level, and the last one was students were staying in a hostel or their residence these data were taken to make the correlation between attention issues and different demographic data. Out of 330 students, 31 students were single children with no siblings, 2 students had more than five, and 16 students had equal or more than four siblings here in this research maximum is 188 students have one sibling.

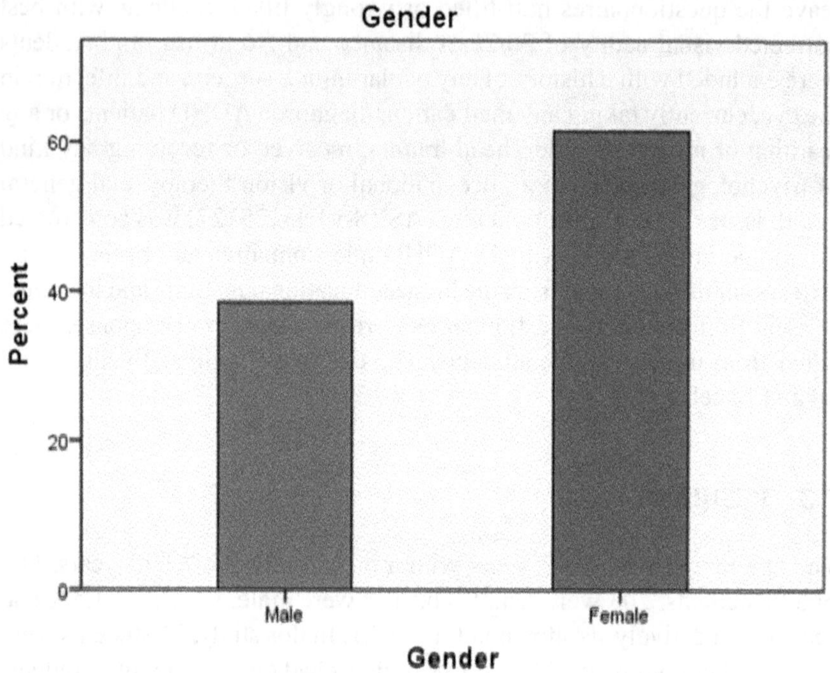

FIGURE 7.1 Gender distribution where female was higher than male students.

TABLE 7.1 The Distribution of Students by Age

Age	Frequency
18	146
19	103
20	49
21	18
22	10
23	4
Total	330

Family types typically refer to the composition of a family unit based on the relationships between its members. Table 7.2 shows the study has categorized families into several types. The maximum number of students was from nuclear family and extended family. Very few students were from single-parent and step-families.

TABLE 7.2 Different Types of Family as Per Student Distribution

Family Type	Frequency
Joint/Extended family	107
Nuclear family	175
Single-parent family	11
Grandparent family	35
Step-family	2
Total	330

This questionnaire likely assesses various aspects related to inattention, hyperactivity, and impulsivity. Table 7.3 shows responses are categorized into five levels: "never," "rarely," "sometimes," "often," and "very often."

Columns (AT1–AT6, HA1–HA6, IM1–IM6): These columns represent different sets of questions or items within the ADHD questionnaire. Each set was focused on a specific aspect of ADHD, such as inattention (AT), hyperactivity (HA), and impulsivity (IM). There are six questions in each category, labeled from 1 to 6.

1. *Row categories (never, rarely, sometimes, often, and very often)*: These categories represent the response options provided by individuals taking the ADHD questionnaire. Each row indicates how many respondents selected a particular response for the questions in each category. These categories likely represent the frequency of symptoms associated with ADHD.
2. *Frequency data*: The numbers in each cell of the table represent the count or frequency of individuals who responded with the corresponding level for each set of questions.

The bottom of Table 7.3 shows the cumulative count for each set of question responses and the total of 330 respondents who completed this ADHD questionnaire, and this row provides an overview of the distribution of their responses. To determine which response categories are showing high or low responses according to the three categories.

In the AT category, the "sometimes" response has the highest count (132), while the "very often" response has the lowest count (10).

In the HA category, the "sometimes" response has the highest count (128), while the "never" response has the lowest count (33).

TABLE 7.3 Number of Responses as Per the Different Categories of Questions from ADHD Questionnaires

	AT1	AT2	AT3	AT4	AT5	AT6	HA1	HA2	HA3	HA4	HA5	HA6	IM1	IM2	IM3	IM4	IM5	IM6
Never	50	52	80	58	44	51	33	34	87	51	29	143	29	68	66	56	60	137
Rarely	105	102	101	86	71	78	105	55	111	104	62	86	74	115	98	109	99	103
Sometimes	132	135	106	136	126	134	129	128	94	93	117	69	144	100	108	113	116	67
Often	33	29	33	36	59	51	45	79	23	56	76	24	57	33	39	42	38	14
Very often	10	12	10	14	30	16	18	34	15	26	46	8	26	14	19	10	17	9
Total	330	330	330	330	330	330	330	330	330	330	330	330	330	330	330	330	330	330

In the IM category, the "sometimes" response has the highest count (144), while the "never" response has the lowest count (29).

Overall, "sometimes" has the highest count across all three categories, which may indicate that many respondents experience these ADHD-related symptoms occasionally. "Very often" has consistently low counts in all three categories, suggesting that few respondents reported experiencing symptoms at a very high frequency. "Sometimes" might be considered a moderate level of symptom frequency, while "very often" represents a high frequency.

Table 7.4 shows 330 student's parents how is the education patterns, the education levels of both fathers and mothers, along with the corresponding frequencies. *Education level*: This column represents the different educational levels, which are typically categorized into "uneducated," "10th grade," "12th grade," "undergraduate," and "Masters." Each row corresponds to a specific education level. *Frequency of father and mother*: Indicates how many fall into each education level category. *Uneducated*: There were three uneducated fathers and eight uneducated mothers among the population. *10th grade*: In this category, there are 49 fathers and 67 mothers who have completed their education up to the 10th-grade level. *12th grade*: This category includes parents who have completed their education up to the 12th grade. There are 70 fathers and 83 mothers in this group.

TABLE 7.4 The Education Level of the Father and Mother

Education Level	Frequency of Father	Frequency of Mother
Uneducated	3	8
10	49	67
12	70	83
Undergraduate	151	115
Masters	57	57
Total	330	330

Undergraduate: Parents in this category have completed an undergraduate degree. There are 151 fathers and 115 mothers with undergraduate degrees.

Masters: This category represents parents who have attained a master's degree. There are 57 fathers and 57 mothers with master's degrees.

Factors such as age, gender, education level, parent education level, family type, siblings, and whether the student was staying in a hostel or their home and as per the result. Perfect positive associations are represented by a value of plus one, and perfect negative correlations by a value of minus one for Pearson's *r*. Zero denotes the complete absence of linear correlation. Table 7.5 shows in a few column that correlation was weak; still the data were significant, which means that due to its high sample size, this study has sufficient statistical power to detect even extremely modest effects. Correlation was done between all related factors such as age, gender, education level, parent education level, family type, siblings, and whether the student is staying in a hostel or their home and ADHD symptom responses and results show that there was no such correlation among them, so these all factors do not impact ADHD symptoms among students.

Table 7.6 shows there was no correlation between the 18 questions; it shows that each individual item or question was different and finding the different answer can be used to construct in questionnaires.

Model: Table 7.7 is likely providing information about the model used for the regression analysis. Regression analysis involves building a model on the basis of one or more independent variables to forecast or explain changes in a dependent variable.

R: The "*R*" value represents the correlation coefficient of the model dependent and independent variables. Here, it is labeled as "a," which suggests it might be a partial correlation coefficient, meaning it reflects the relationship after controlling for other variables.

R square: The percentage of the dependent variable's variation that the independent variables account for is shown by the *R*-squared value. With an *R*-squared of 0.106, the independent factors account for 10.6% of the variation in the dependent variable.

Adjusted R square: An alternative form of *R*-squared that accounts for the quantity of independent variables in the model is called adjusted *R*-squared. It makes the necessary adjustments for the degrees of freedom. A higher adjusted *R*-squared is generally better, as it penalizes models with too many predictors that may not add much explanatory power. Here adjusted *R*-squared is 0.054.

Std. error of the estimate: This statistic represents the standard error of the residuals. This represented the way the data points were distributed or dispersed around the regression line. A lower value indicates a better fit of the model. The standard error is 1.099.

TABLE 7.5 The Pearson Correlation between Each Category of Attention Six Questions to All Related Factors

Correlations		Age	Gender	Qualification	No. of Siblings	Family Type	Father's Education Level	Mother's Education Level	Hosteler/Day Scholar
AT1	Pearson correlation	−0.053	−0.55	−0.01	−0.11	−0.14	0.015	0.015	−0.53
	Sig. (2-tailed)	0.341	0.321	0.983	0.845	0.793	0.781	0.781	0.342
AT2	Pearson correlation	0.014	−0.26	0.033	0.002	−0.21	−0.15	0.002	−0.119
	Sig. (2-tailed)	0.802	0.635	0.553	0.967	0.700	0.787	0.971	0.031
AT3	Pearson correlation	0.099	−0.53	0.082	0.089	−0.27	−0.26	−0.103	0.031
	Sig. (2-tailed)	0.073	0.336	0.139	0.107	0.622	0.639	0.063	0.579
AT4	Pearson correlation	0.075	−0.90	0.121*	−0.80	−0.46	.039	0.058*	−0.05
	Sig. (2-tailed)	0.176	0.104	0.028	0.145	0.403	0.480	0.296	0.931
AT5	Pearson correlation	−0.76	−0.147	0.040	−0.65	−0.81	0.004	0.002	−0.33
	Sig. (2-tailed)	0.171	0.008	0.471	0.239	0.144	0.942	0.975	0.552
AT6	Pearson correlation	0.052	−0.110	0.012	0.033	−0.22	−0.57	−0.40	−0.42
	Sig. (2-tailed)	0.343	0.046	0.825	0.556	0.696	0.299	0.464	0.445

*Correlation is statistically significant at the 0.05 level ($p < 0.05$). This means there is less than a 5% probability that the correlation happened by random chance.

**Correlation is statistically significant at the 0.01 level ($p < 0.01$). This means there is less than a 1% probability that the correlation is due to chance—it is stronger evidence against randomness.

TABLE 7.6 The Pearson Correlation between Each 18 Questions from ADHD Questionnaires

	AT1	AT2	AT3	AT4	AT5	AT6	HA1	HA2	HA3	HA4	HA5	HA6	IM1	IM2	IM3	IM4	IM5	IM6
AT1	1	0.495	0.282	0.326	0.326	0.197	0.363	0.363	0.366	0.28	0.294	0.111	0.37	0.263	0.199	0.219	0.276	0.164
AT2	0.495	1	0.312	0.315	0.234	0.132	0.391	0.289	0.334	0.318	0.261	0.095	0.335	0.252	0.154	0.172	0.259	0.223
AT3	0.282	0.312	1	0.299	0.294	0.128	0.322	0.254	0.32	0.306	0.261	0.239	0.299	0.193	0.166	0.302	0.216	0.263
AT4	0.326	0.315	0.299	1	0.273	0.251	0.303	0.318	0.252	0.193	0.306	0.151	0.329	0.238	0.135	0.23	0.228	0.135
AT5	0.326	0.234	0.294	0.273	1	0.275	0.333	0.385	0.293	0.261	0.281	0.117	0.36	0.148	0.153	0.206	0.148	0.067
AT6	0.197	0.132	0.128	0.251	0.275	1	0.128	0.246	0.216	0.142	0.271	0.095	0.224	0.158	0.269	0.273	0.232	0.171
HA1	0.363	0.391	0.322	0.303	0.333	0.128	1	0.404	0.395	0.424	0.319	0.247	0.279	0.231	0.2	0.328	0.192	0.233
HA2	0.363	0.289	0.254	0.318	0.385	0.246	0.404	1	0.337	0.337	0.346	0.148	0.342	0.306	0.205	0.199	0.272	0.186
HA3	0.366	0.334	0.32	0.252	0.293	0.216	0.395	0.337	1	0.344	0.304	0.249	0.266	0.264	0.187	0.168	0.289	0.28
HA4	0.28	0.318	0.306	0.193	0.261	0.142	0.424	0.337	0.344	1	0.327	0.322	0.322	0.241	0.25	0.225	0.253	0.245
HA5	0.294	0.261	0.261	0.306	0.281	0.271	0.319	0.346	0.304	0.327	1	0.072	0.259	0.195	0.201	0.181	0.214	0.071
HA6	0.111	0.095	0.239	0.151	0.117	0.095	0.247	0.148	0.249	0.322	0.072	1	0.134	0.286	0.153	0.293	0.208	0.333
IM1	0.37	0.335	0.299	0.329	0.36	0.224	0.279	0.342	0.266	0.322	0.259	0.134	1	0.346	0.232	0.183	0.233	0.078
IM2	0.263	0.252	0.193	0.238	0.148	0.158	0.231	0.306	0.264	0.241	0.195	0.286	0.346	1	0.096	0.234	0.221	0.182
IM3	0.199	0.154	0.166	0.135	0.153	0.269	0.2	0.205	0.187	0.25	0.201	0.153	0.232	0.096	1	0.306	0.331	0.245
IM4	0.219	0.172	0.302	0.23	0.206	0.273	0.328	0.199	0.168	0.225	0.181	0.293	0.183	0.234	0.306	1	0.28	0.244
IM5	0.276	0.259	0.216	0.228	0.148	0.232	0.192	0.272	0.289	0.253	0.214	0.208	0.233	0.221	0.331	0.28	1	0.329
IM6	0.164	0.223	0.263	0.135	0.067	0.171	0.233	0.186	0.28	0.245	0.071	0.333	0.078	0.182	0.245	0.244	0.329	1

TABLE 7.7 The Relationship between One or More Independent Variables (Predictors) and a Dependent Variable

Model	R	Adjusted R^2	R Square	Std. Error	Change Statistics				
					R Square Change	F Change	df1	df2	Sig. F Change
1	0.326[a]	0.054	0.106	1.099	0.106	2.051	18[a]	311	0.008

[a]List of predictors (independent variables).

[b]Dependent variable (age).

[a]Predictors (constant): IM6, AT5, IM2, IM3, AT4, AT6, HA6, AT2, HA5, IM4, IM5, AT3, HA3, HA4, HA2, IM1, AT1, HA1.

[b]Dependent variable: age.

Change statistics: This section provides information about changes in the model and how they affect the model's performance.

R square change: This is the change in *R*-squared compared to a previous model. In your summary, it increased by 0.106, indicating that the current model added explanatory power compared to a previous model.

F change: The model's significance was evaluated using the *F*-statistic. The *F* change value of 2.051 suggests that the current model's predictors are collectively significant in explaining the variance in the dependent variable.

Sum of squares (SS): Table 7.8 starts with the splitting the whole variance in the dependent variable "age" into regression and residual components.

TABLE 7.8 The ANOVA Summary Provided in the Analysis Is Used to Evaluate the Significance of the Regression Model in Predicting the Dependent Variable, "Age," Based on the Independent Variables Used in the Analysis

ANOVA	Sum of Squares	df	Mean Square	F	Sig.
Regression	44.600	18	2.478	2.051	0.008[a]
Residual	375.719	311	1.208		
Total	420.318	329			

Note: [a]Dependent variable: age.

Regression SS: This dependent variable was 44.600.

Residual SS: This represents the unexplained or error variation in the dependent variable. In the analysis, it is 375.719.

7.3.1 DEGREES OF FREEDOM (DF)

Regression df: This is the number of independent variables used in the regression model. In the analysis, it is 18.

Residual df: This is the degrees of freedom associated with the error term; this was the sum of the data points in the model less the number of independent variables. In the analysis, it is 311.

Mean square (MS): To compute this, divide the total squares by the number of degrees of freedom. It represents the average variation for each component.

- Regression MS: 44.600/18 = 2.478
- Residual MS: 375.719/311 = 1.208

F-statistic (F): The regression model's explained variance divided by the variance that was not explained yields the *F*-statistic. It is calculated by dividing the regression MS by the residual MS. In the analysis, it is 2.051.

Significance (Sig.): This is the *p*-value that corresponds to the *F*-statistic. The regression model is statistically significant if the *p*-value is low (usually less than 0.05), which suggests that at least one of the independent variables in the model significantly affects the dependent variable.

Conclusion: Table 7.8 shows the *F*-statistical analysis is 2.051, and its associated *p*-value (sig.) is 0.008 (denoted as 0.008), indicating that the regression model was statistically significant at the 0.05 significance level. In other words, at least one of the independent variables was significantly related to the dependent variable "age."

R-squared (R^2): *R*-squared represented the percentage of the dependent variable's variation that the independent variables in the model could account for. In the analysis, the *R*-squared value was 0.106, meaning that approximately 10.6% of the variance in "age" can be explained by the independent variables.

Adjusted R-squared: The adjusted *R*-squared value takes into account the number of independent variables in the model and offers a more cautious estimation of the percentage of variation that is explained. In the analysis, the adjusted *R*-squared is 0.054.

This ANOVA summary suggests that the regression model is statistically significant, and it explains a certain amount of the dependent variable's fluctuation "age." However, the adjusted *R*-squared indicates that the model may not be explaining a very high proportion of the variance.

Model: Table 7.9 specifies the model or equation for which the coefficients are reported.

Unstandardized coefficients (B): These are the estimated coefficients for each independent variable in the units of the dependent variable.

Standardized coefficients (beta): These coefficients represent the estimated change in the dependent variable in standard deviation units (*z*-scores) for a one-standard-deviation change in the independent variable. Standardized coefficients allow for a comparison of the relative importance of each independent variable in the model.

TABLE 7.9 The Coefficients Associated with Each Independent Variable (Predictors) in the Regression Model

Model	Unstandardized Coefficients		Standardized Coefficients	*t*	Sig.
	B	**Std. Error**	**Beta**		
(Constant)	1.384	0.181		7.626	0.000
AT1	−0.20	0.076	−0.18	−0.256	0.798
AT2	−0.07	0.075	−0.06	−0.92	0.926
AT3	.098	0.066	0.096	1.498	0.135
AT4	−0.133	0.066	−0.128	−2.015	0.045
AT5	−0.110	0.062	−0.116	−1.790	0.074
AT6	0.033	0.063	0.033	0.525	0.600
HA1	−0.08	0.075	−0.08	−0.108	0.914
HA2	0.088	0.065	0.091	1.344	0.180
HA3	0.011	0.066	0.011	0.163	0.871
HA4	0.060	0.062	0.065	0.965	0.335
HA5	0.034	0.060	0.036	0.568	0.570
HA6	0.010	0.063	0.010	0.161	0.873
IM1	−0.59	0.070	−0.57	−0.851	0.396
IM2	−0.121	0.064	−0.119	−1.886	0.060
IM3	−0.33	0.060	−0.34	−0.553	0.581
IM4	0.107	0.068	0.101	1.563	0.119
IM5	0.087	0.064	0.087	1.360	0.175
IM6	0.034	0.067	0.032	0.505	0.614

Note: The table provides information about their standardization, *t* values, and significance levels.

t-Value (t): The *t*-value is a measure of how many standard errors the coefficient is away from zero. It is used to test the hypothesis that coefficient to "0." Larger absolute *t*-values indicate more significant relationships between the independent variable and the dependent variable.

Significance (sig.): This column reports the *p*-value associated with each *t*-value. It displays the likelihood that the random chance independent and dependent variables will be observed. Lower *p*-values (typically less than 0.05) suggest that the relationship is statistically significant.

Table 7.9 shows the regression model and extracted the information:

- The value of the dependent variable is represented by the intercept term in the regression model, which is represented by the "Constant" row, when there are zero independent variables.
- The other rows represent the coefficients for specific independent variables (e.g., AT1, AT2, AT3, AT4, etc.).
- For each independent variable, you have information about the unstandardized coefficient (*B*), standardized coefficient (beta), the *t*-value (*t*), and the significance level (sig.).
- The standardized coefficients (beta) are useful for comparing the relative importance of the dependent variable's variance that may be explained by the independent factors.
- The *t*-values and associated *p*-values (sig.) can help you determine whether each independent variable has a statistically significant impact on the dependent variable. In general, if the *p*-value is less than a chosen significance level (commonly 0.05), you may consider the relationship as statistically significant.
- For example, in the table, you can see that AT4 has a significant impact on the dependent variable as its *p*-value (sig.) is 0.045, which is less than 0.05.
- Other independent variables, such as AT1, AT2, and HA1, do not appear to have a significant impact on the dependent variable, as their *p*-values are greater than 0.05.

The information in this table is crucial for understanding the correlations between the independent variables, including their strengths and directions, and the dependent variable in your regression model.

Plot points fall into nearly a straight line. Figure 7.2 shows that there is a positive or direct relationship, and a good illustration of what a linear relationship looks like. It is called a positive relationship because the line has a positive or upward slope.

Table 7.10 represents the KMO value 0.833 that further confirms that ASRS-v1.1 questionnaires were useful for checking ADHD in students of higher educational institutes. Bartlett's test of sphericity has an approximate chi-square value of 1804.178, with 325 degrees of freedom. The *p*-value (sig.) associated with Bartlett's test is 0.000. This result indicates that the correlations between variables are significantly different from zero, supporting the idea that data were suitable for factor analysis. The KMO value of 0.833 reinforces this conclusion.

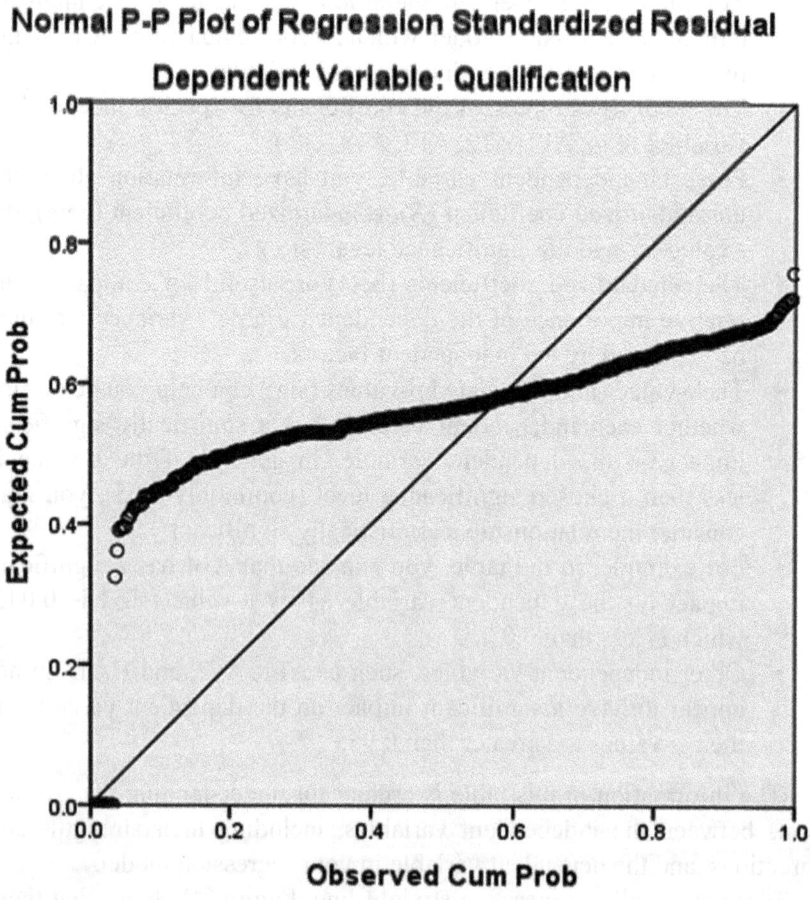

FIGURE 7.2 The normal P–P plot of regression standard residual values.

TABLE 7.10 KMO and Bartlett's Test of Sphericity

KMO and Bartlett's Test[a]		
Kaiser–Meyer–Olkin measure of sampling adequacy		0.833
Bartlett's test of sphericity	Approx. chi-square	1804.178
	df	325
	Sig.	0.000

[a]Way of representing the result in SPSS.

Figure 7.3 and Table 7.11 contain the eigenvalue for 26 questions, and as per the formation of the components for factor analysis, eigenvalue more than 1 is considered as a factor component. Figure 7.3 and Table 7.11 show a total of eight component values is more than 1.

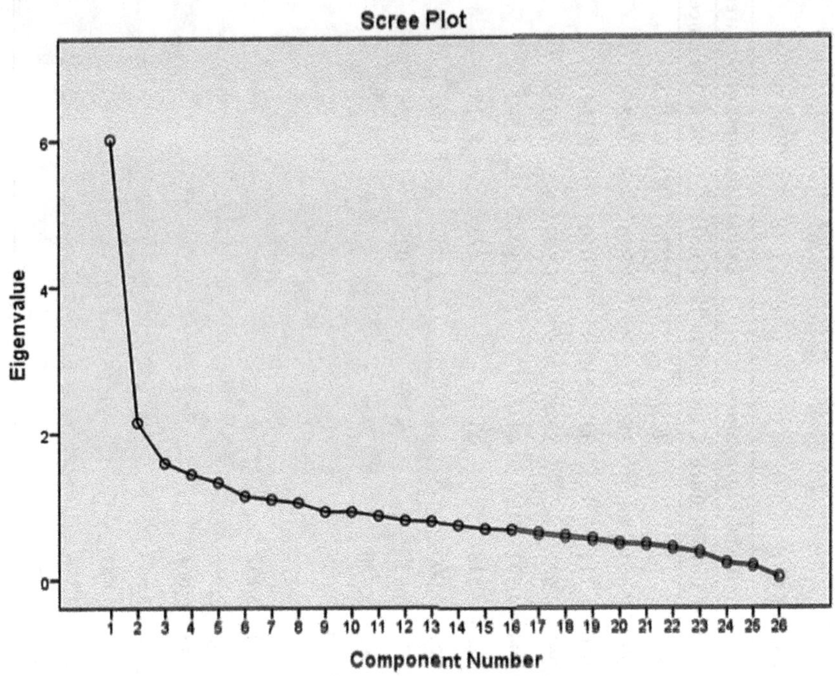

FIGURE 7.3 The eigenvalue value and here the eight components were above 1.

TABLE 7.11 The Eigenvalue and as Per the Formation of the Components for Factor Analysis

Total Variance Explained

Component	Initial Eigenvalues			Extraction Sums of Squared Loadings		Extraction Sums of Squared Loadings
	Total	% of Variance	Cumulative %	Total	% of Variance	Cumulative %
1	5.376	20.678	20.678	5.376	20.678	20.678
2	1.990	7.655	28.333	1.990	7.655	28.333
3	1.616	6.214	34.547	1.616	6.214	34.547
4	1.267	4.875	39.422	1.267	4.875	39.422
5	1.194	4.592	44.014	1.194	4.592	44.014
6	1.123	4.318	48.332	1.123	4.318	48.332
7	1.057	4.065	52.396	1.057	4.065	52.396
8	1.029	3.956	56.352	1.029	3.956	56.352
9	0.967	3.720				
10	0.959	3.688				
11	0.851	3.274				
12	0.814	3.132				
13	0.768	2.955				
14	0.754	2.901				
15	0.694	2.669				
16	0.647	2.487				
17	0.618	2.376				
18	0.593	2.279				

TABLE 7.11 *(Continued)*

Component	Initial Eigenvalues			Extraction Sums of Squared Loadings		Extraction Sums of Squared Loadings
	Total	% of Variance	Cumulative %	Total	% of Variance	Cumulative %
19	0.576	2.215				
20	0.561	2.159				
21	0.489	1.882				
22	0.456	1.753				
23	0.438	1.686				
24	0.421	1.619				
25	0.412	1.585				
26	0.329	1.266				

Table 7.12 shows the commonalities values and as the data suggest, the maximum value is higher than 0.5 only, and it suggests a value less than 0.5 can be extracted from factors.

TABLE 7.12 The Commonalities Values

Communalities					
Variable	**Initial**	**Extraction**	**Variable**	**Initial**	**Extraction**
Age	1.000	0.632	**HA1**	1.000	0.560
Gender	1.000	0.491	**HA2**	1.000	0.478
Qualification	1.000	0.622	**HA3**	1.000	0.473
No. of Siblings	1.000	0.553	**HA4**	1.000	0.585
Family Type	1.000	0.742	**HA5**	1.000	0.497
Father's education level	1.000	0.724	**HA6**	1.000	0.483
Mother's education level	1.000	0.782	**IM1**	1.000	0.519
Hosteler/Day scholar	1.000	0.614	**IM2**	1.000	0.580
AT1	1.000	0.577	**IM3**	1.000	0.609
AT2	1.000	0.589	**IM4**	1.000	0.478
AT3	1.000	0.441	**IM5**	1.000	0.494
AT4	1.000	0.490	**IM6**	1.000	0.586
AT5	1.000	0.474			
AT6	1.000	0.579			

Table 7.13 shows the component matrix and its loading and above 0.5 is considered good for factor analysis, so all the below 0.5 loading data was deleted from this table.

Table 7.14 shows all 26 items that include 18 questions and eight other factors that can influence attention and related symptoms. Here, Cronbach's alpha value is 0.792, which shows reliability.

Table 7.15 shows a total of 26 questions item-wise for each question of Cronbach's alpha, and if the item is deleted from the matrix, what will be the next value of Cronbach's alpha.

Table 7.16 shows the pattern matrix and the data below 0.5 loadings was deleted; it also shows only three-factor matrices are formed by these 18 questionnaires so three factors can be predicted through these data.

TABLE 7.13 Component Matrix and Its Loading

	Component Matrix							
	Component							
	1	**2**	**3**	**4**	**5**	**6**	**7**	**8**
Age					0.597			
Gender			0.557					
Qualification						−0.542		
No. of siblings		−0.546						
Family type							0.609	
Father's education level		0.602	0.545					
Mother's education level		0.735						
Hosteler/Day scholar					0.622			
AT1	0.619							
AT2	0.587							
AT3	0.567							
AT4	0.545							
AT5	0.536							
AT6								
HA1	0.647							
HA2	0.626							
HA3	0.615							
HA4	0.603							
HA5	0.536							
HA6								
IM1	0.586							
IM2								
IM3				−0.523				
IM4	0.505							
IM5	0.524							
IM6			0.526					

TABLE 7.14 Cronbach's Alpha Value for All the 26 Items

	Reliability Statistics	
Cronbach's Alpha	**Cronbach's Alpha Based on Standardized Items**	**No. of Items**
0.792	0.771	26

TABLE 7.15 The Total Item-Wise Cronbach's Alpha

	Scale Mean If Item Deleted	Scale Variance If Item Deleted	Corrected Item-Total Correlation	Squared Multiple Correlation	Cronbach's Alpha If Item Deleted
Age	41.72	106.958	0.055	0.117	0.800
Gender	59.28	110.289	−0.98	0.183	0.797
Qualification	58.70	109.115	0.102	0.078	0.793
No. of siblings	59.19	108.418	−0.02	0.188	0.802
Family type	58.73	110.094	−0.73	0.101	0.802
Father's education level	58.03	108.561	0.002	0.395	0.800
Mother's education level	58.23	109.726	−0.60	0.459	0.804
Hosteler/Day scholar	59.27	109.663	−0.36	0.086	0.796
AT1	59.13	98.734	0.513	0.382	0.776
AT2	59.13	99.241	0.478	0.372	0.777
AT3	59.30	98.417	0.480	0.301	0.777
AT4	59.09	99.017	0.458	0.285	0.778
AT5	58.79	99.017	0.410	0.316	0.780
AT6	58.96	100.929	0.352	0.235	0.784
HA1	58.94	97.866	0.538	0.401	0.774
HA2	58.60	96.564	0.539	0.372	0.773
HA3	59.37	97.700	0.503	0.347	0.775
HA4	58.97	96.549	0.513	0.370	0.774
HA5	58.52	98.171	0.443	0.296	0.778
HA6	59.68	101.010	0.341	0.292	0.784
IM1	58.74	99.044	0.459	0.370	0.778
IM2	59.25	99.803	0.408	0.272	0.781
IM3	59.13	100.517	0.349	0.252	0.784
IM4	59.15	99.868	0.426	0.303	0.780
IM5	59.12	99.087	0.434	0.300	0.779
IM6	59.72	100.466	0.394	0.313	0.781

Table 7.17 shows Cronbach's alpha value for 18 items, and the value was 0.856, which is the reliability of these questionnaires as shown in

Table 7.14. The Cronbach's alpha value for the 26 items—which included 18 questions and eight additional factors that may influence attention and related symptoms—was 0.792, indicating an acceptable level of reliability.

TABLE 7.16 The Pattern Matrix for 18 Questionnaires

Pattern Matrix[a]			
	Component		
	1	2	3
AT1	0.704		
AT2	0.700		
AT3			
AT4	0.545		
AT5	0.598		
AT6			0.736
HA1	0.644		
HA2	0.621		
HA3	0.552		
HA4	0.500		
HA5	0.541		
HA6		0.715	
IM1	0.630		
IM2			
IM3			0.698
IM4			
IM5			
IM6		0.660	

[a]Means extraction method: Principal axis factoring. Rotation Method: Oblimin with Kaiser normalization.

TABLE 7.17 Cronbach's Alpha Value for 18 Items

Reliability Statistics		
Cronbach's Alpha	**Cronbach's Alpha Based on Standardized Items**	**No. of Items**
0.856	0.857	18

Table 7.18 shows 18-question item-wise Cronbach's alpha and if the item was deleted from the matrix, what will be the next value of Cronbach's alpha; the same data are shown in Table 7.15 for 26-question item-wise Cronbach's alpha value if the item is deleted.

TABLE 7.18 Total Item-Wise Cronbach's Alpha

Item-Total Statistics					
	Scale Mean If Item Deleted	**Scale Variance If Item Deleted**	**Corrected Item-Total Correlation**	**Squared Multiple Correlation**	**Cronbach's Alpha If Item Deleted**
AT1	26.93	95.044	0.533	0.371	0.846
AT2	26.93	95.600	0.495	0.359	0.848
AT3	27.10	95.039	0.484	0.279	0.848
AT4	26.89	95.595	0.463	0.261	0.849
AT5	26.59	94.844	0.450	0.294	0.850
AT6	26.76	97.239	0.368	0.223	0.853
HA1	26.74	94.192	0.559	0.393	0.845
HA2	26.40	93.231	0.541	0.344	0.845
HA3	27.17	93.845	0.531	0.323	0.846
HA4	26.77	93.043	0.524	0.337	0.846
HA5	26.32	94.657	0.452	0.271	0.850
HA6	27.48	97.484	0.349	0.259	0.854
IM1	26.54	94.924	0.501	0.333	0.847
IM2	27.05	96.335	0.415	0.247	0.851
IM3	26.93	96.628	0.375	0.225	0.853
IM4	26.95	96.308	0.437	0.282	0.850
IM5	26.92	95.391	0.453	0.266	0.849
IM6	27.52	97.570	0.370	0.264	0.853

Table 7.19 shows eigenvalues for 18 questions and formed three components for factor analysis; Figure 7.3 and Table 7.11 show eigenvalues as per 26 questions and formed eight components for factor analysis.

Figure 7.4 shows how the items are related to each other; all the points are close to each other; it means that all the questions are interconnected and few points were far, which shows that the question was different and can formed different components.

TABLE 7.19 The Eigenvalue and as Per the Formation of the Components for Factor Analysis

Total Variance Explained							
Component	**Initial Eigenvalues**			**Extraction Sums of Squared Loadings**			**Rotation Sums of Squared Loadings**[a]
	Total	**% of Variance**	**Cumulative %**	**Total**	**% of Variance**	**Cumulative %**	**Total**
1	5.325	29.583	29.583	5.325	29.583	29.583	4.874
2	1.451	8.059	37.642	1.451	8.059	37.642	2.145
3	1.179	6.551	44.193	1.179	6.551	44.193	2.632
4	0.971	5.395	49.588				
5	0.950	5.278	54.865				
6	0.874	4.855	59.720				
7	0.822	4.565	64.286				
8	0.766	4.255	68.541				
9	0.734	4.080	72.622				
10	0.677	3.760	76.381				
11	0.647	3.592	79.974				
12	0.621	3.451	83.424				
13	0.595	3.303	86.727				
14	0.545	3.026	89.753				
15	0.502	2.790	92.543				
16	0.470	2.613	95.156				
17	0.455	2.529	97.685				
18	0.417	2.315	100.000				

Notes: Extraction method: principal component analysis.
[a]The sum of squared loadings cannot be summed to determine the overall variance when the components are correlated.

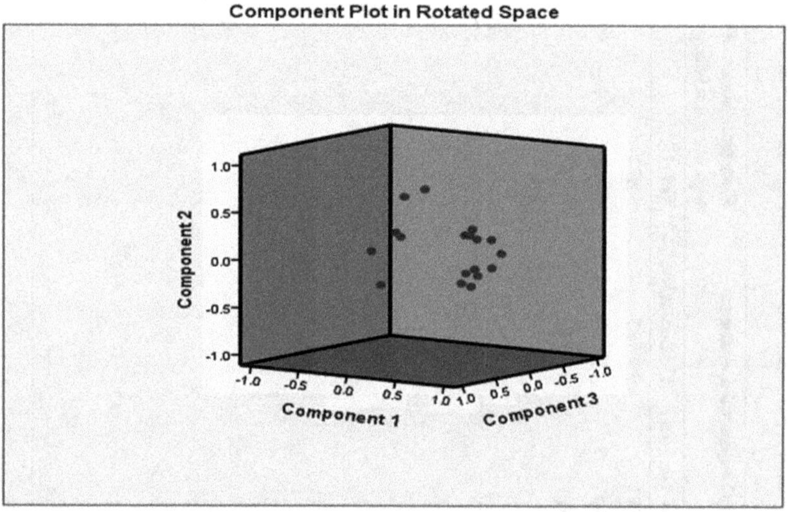

FIGURE 7.4 How items are related to each other.

As per Table 7.20, the current study suggests that out of 330 students, 114 students had moderate symptoms of attention, 128 students had hyperactive symptoms, and 87 students had impulsivity symptoms; so as per these data, the prevalence rate of attention deficit symptomatic students was 38.78%.

TABLE 7.20 The Number of Responses from Each Category of Question Attention, Hyperactive, and Impulsivity

	Mean No_ATT	Mean No_HYPER	Mean No_IMP
Never	41	40	55
Rarely	175	162	188
Sometime	108	117	83
Often	5	9	3
Very Often	1	2	1
Total	330	330	330

Note: As per this table, maximum responses were from rarely and sometime. Very few responses were from very often in all three categories.

Figure 7.5 shows the mean of responses as per inattention, hyperactivity, and impulsivity on the basis of response categories: never, rarely, sometime, often, and very often. Figure 7.5 also shows that most of the

responses were from rarely and sometime category, which means many students have at least 2–3 symptoms of ADHD.

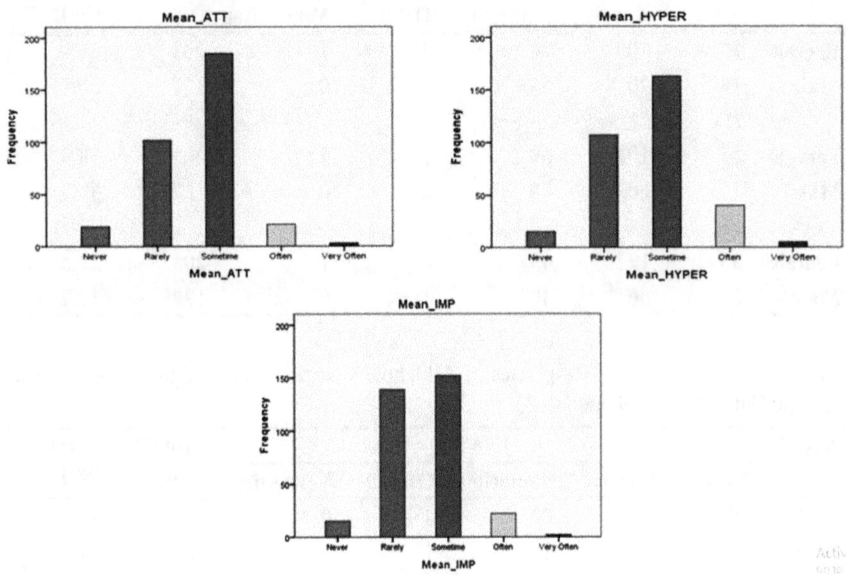

FIGURE 7.5 Mean value of all the inattention, hyperactivity, and impulsivity 1–3 category responses wise.

Table 7.21 shows that inattention was more prevalent in females compared to males. Hyperactivity levels were nearly equal, with males reporting slightly more responses. However, impulsivity symptoms were more pronounced in males than in females.

Table 7.22 shows that inattention was the same in both age category but hyperactivity and impulsivity symptoms were slightly higher in 18–19 age category compared to 20–23. Table 7.22 shows that as age increases, the responses come down to never and rarely, and in age below 20, responses were more often and very often.

7.4 DISCUSSION

The present study included age group from 18 to 23 years both male and female students from higher educational institute. All the students pursuing their undergraduates' courses and for checking the prevalence,

TABLE 7.21 Number of Responses of All Three Categories of Question Responses as Per Gender

Gender	INAT					Total No	Total (%)
	Never	Rarely	Sometime	Often	Very Often		
Female	23	105	70	4	1	203	36.9
Male	18	70	38	1	0	127	30.7
	HT						
Female	23	102	69	7	2	203	38.4
Male	17	60	48	2	0	127	39.3
	IM						
Female	35	122	43	2	1	203	22.6
Male	20	66	40	1	0	127	32.2

TABLE 7.22 Number of Responses of All Three Categories of Question Responses as Per Age Category 18–19 and 20–23

Age	INAT					Total No.	Total (%)
	Never	Rarely	Sometime	Often	Very Often		
18–19	29	134	82	4	0	249	34.5
20–23	12	41	26	1	1	81	34.5
	HT						
18–19	31	120	91	6	1	249	39.3
20–23	9	42	26	3	1	81	37
	IM						
18–19	43	139	65	2	0	249	26.9
20–23	12	49	18	1	1	81	24.6

this study used self-report scale for ADHD (ASRS-v1.1) questionnaires, which contain 18 questions. This study found that the prevalence of ADHD symptomatic students overall was 33.23%, where inattention was 38%, hyperactivity was 42.6%, and impulsivity was 29%. A study by Meng Shi in China in 2019 looked into the connection between internet addiction and personality traits in Chinese medical students. The study revealed that 44.7% of medical students had inattention, and that 35.5%, 8.6%, and 0.6% of students in the 17–26 age range had mild, moderate, and severe symptoms of ADHD, respectively [21]. Researchers also discovered that people with internet addiction were more likely than those without it to experience indications of ADHD [22]. Internet addiction among students was not examined in the current study. In 2019, Takashi Ohnishi conducted a study in Japan with the goal of determining the prevalence and patterns of psychiatric comorbidities in adult ADHD in a routine clinical setting and the study's mean age was 33.07, SD 9.79 years, and the findings showed that 336 (58.43%) of the patients were inattentive, 40 (6.96%) were hyperactive-impulsive, and 301 (52.35%) were patients with comorbidities [23]. In order to determine how informative self-reported adult ADHD symptoms were, Michael J. Silverstein conducted a study in 2018 in New York City, the study titled "An Examination of the Agreement Between the Adult Attention-Deficit/Hyperactivity Disorder Self-Report Scale V1.1 and Adult Attention-Deficit/Hyperactivity Disorder Investigator Symptom Rating Scale" revealed that inattention was more common than hyperactivity, with the combination of both being 36.8% and hyperactivity being 1.2%. The combination of both, with ADHD along with a few other factors, making up 2.9%, and the mean age group was 28.8, SD 8.6 years [24]. Michael J. Silverstein's 2019 study in Philadelphia, USA, was carried out in continuation with the goal of validating the expanded versions of the Adult ADHD Investigator Symptom Rating Scale and the Adult ADHD Self-Report Scale v1.1 Symptom Checklist; here they consider age group 32, SD 10.5 years, and they also find out the prevalence of ADHD was 57.20% [25]. In the current study, researcher tried to find out the correlation between age, gender, education, number of sibling, family type, education of mother and father, and hostel or day scholar with ADHD symptoms, and this current study found out that there was no huge difference between the age groups but as per each question-wise data, it shows that as the age increases, the symptoms decreases. Female students were showing higher symptoms compared to male students. This may be because more female students participated in this study. Roberta Waite [26] carried out a study in 2020 in Wynnewood, USA, to evaluate the symptoms of ADHD in young adults attending universities using the ASRS v1.1 and looked at associations with social anxiety and self-efficacy in those between the ages of 19–20 and found out 10.80% prevalence of ADHD, and there was another study conducted by Michael J. Silverstein to test–retest reliability of the adult ADHD self-report scale. The 2018 Boston primary care practice used the ASRS-v1.1 screener in non-ADHD controls, in age group 38.1, SD 10.8, and they found that the prevalence of ADHD was 11.25% [27]. ADHD was a complex neurocomplication, and many advanced imaging-based diagnostics tools were under research to make it simple for diagnosis and management [28]. ADHD prevalence was higher than required all kinds of support to reduce ADHD symptoms to improve all kinds of skill education, work-life, and personal-social relationships [12, 29].

7.5 CONCLUSION

The present study found that the adult ADHD self-report scale (ASRS) v1.1 questionnaire was a well-established tool for checking ADHD symptoms among the adult population in higher educational institutions. The prevalence rate of ADHD symptoms among higher educational institutes was high, and the overall prevalence was lower at 33.23%, but if we find out the prevalence of ADHD symptomatic students individually, as per inattention it was 38%, for hyperactivity it was 42.6%, and for impulsivity it was 29%. This study also found out that many other factors were thought to be related to attention, but it did not show such a relationship as age, gender, education level, parent education level, family type, number of siblings, and whether the student is staying in a hostel or their home.

KEYWORDS

- **attention**
- **attention-deficit hyperactivity disorder**
- **attention-deficit hyperactivity disorder symptoms**
- **higher educational institution**
- **learning difficulty**
- **factor analysis**
- **adult attention-deficit hyperactivity disorder self-report scale**

REFERENCES

1. Binder, M. D., Hirokawa, N., & Windhorst, U. (Eds.). (2009). *Encyclopedia of Neuroscience* (Vol. 3166). Springer: Berlin, Germany.

2. Broman, A. T., West, S. K., Munoz, B., Bandeen-Roche, K., Rubin, G. S., & Turano, K. A. (2004). Divided visual attention as a predictor of bumping while walking: The Salisbury Eye Evaluation. *Investigative Ophthalmology & Visual Science, 45*(9), 2955–2960.
3. Kirk, H. E., Gray, K., Riby, D. M., Taffe, J., & Cornish, K. M. (2017). Visual attention and academic performance in children with developmental disabilities and behavioural attention deficits. *Developmental Science, 20*(6), e12468.
4. Allport, A. (1989). *Visual Attention: Foundations of Cognitive Science* (pp. 631–682).
5. Biederman, J. (2005). Attention-deficit/hyperactivity disorder: A selective overview. *Biological Psychiatry, 57*(11), 1215–1220.
6. Joseph, J. K., & Devu, B. K. (2019). Prevalence of attention-deficit hyperactivity disorder in India: A systematic review and meta-analysis. *Indian Journal of Psychiatric Nursing, 16*(2), 118–125.
7. Lecendreux, M., Konofal, E., & Faraone, S. V. (2011). Prevalence of attention deficit hyperactivity disorder and associated features among children in France. *Journal of Attention Disorders, 15*(6), 516–524.
8. Kessler, R. C., Adler, L., Ames, M., Demler, O., Faraone, S., Hiripi, E. V. A., Howes, M. J., Jin, R., Secnik, K., Spencer, T., Ustun, T. B., & Walters, E. E. (2005). The World Health Organization adult ADHD Self-Report Scale (ASRS): A short screening scale for use in the general population. *Psychological Medicine, 35*(2), 245–256.
9. Wei, C. C., & Ma, M. Y. (2017). Influences of visual attention and reading time on children and adults. *Reading & Writing Quarterly, 33*(2), 97–108.
10. Ball, K., Owsley, C., Sloane, M. E., Roenker, D. L., & Bruni, J. R. (1993). Visual attention problems as a predictor of vehicle crashes in older drivers. *Investigative Ophthalmology & Visual Science, 34*(11), 3110–3123.
11. Zametkin, A. J., & Ernst, M. (1999). Problems in the management of attention-deficit–hyperactivity disorder. *New England Journal of Medicine, 340*(1), 40–46.
12. Pellow, J., Solomon, E. M., & Barnard, C. N. (2011). Complementary and alternative medical therapies for children with attention-deficit/hyperactivity disorder (ADHD). *Alternative Medicine Review, 16*(4), 323.
13. Thakur, R., Jayakumar, J., & Pant, S. (2019). A comparative study of visual attention in hearing impaired and normal school going children. *Indian Journal of Otology, 25*(4), 192–195.
14. Edition, F. (2013). Diagnostic and statistical manual of mental disorders. *American Psychiatric Association, 21*(21), 591–643.
15. Martel, M. M., Schimmack, U., Nikolas, M., & Nigg, J. T. (2015). Integration of symptom ratings from multiple informants in ADHD diagnosis: A psychometric model with clinical utility. *Psychological Assessment, 27*(3), 1060.
16. Epstein, J. N., & Loren, R. E. (2013). Changes in the definition of ADHD in DSM-5: Subtle but important. *Neuropsychiatry, 3*(5), 455.
17. Khan, N. T., & Khan, K. (2018). Prevalence of adult Attention Deficit Hyperactivity Disorder (ADHD) among undergraduates at BUITEMS. *Journal of Biomolecular Research and Therapeutics, 7*(2), 165.
18. Shashi, B., Shobhit, P., & Bheemsain, T. (2018). Adult ADHD in health science students of India. *International Journal of Scientific Study, 6*(5), 47–51.

19. Naing, L., Winn, T. B. N. R., & Rusli, B. N. (2006). Practical issues in calculating the sample size for prevalence studies. *Archives of Orofacial Sciences*, *1*, 9–14.
20. Charan, J., & Biswas, T. (2013). How to calculate sample size for different study designs in medical research. *Indian Journal of Psychological Medicine*, *35*(2), 121–126.
21. Shi, M., & Du, T. J. (2019). Associations of personality traits with internet addiction in Chinese medical students: The mediating role of attention-deficit/hyperactivity disorder symptoms. *BMC Psychiatry*, *19*, 1–8.
22. Bisht, B., Kaur, N., & Goyal, S. K. (2021). Prevalence of internet gaming disorder (IGD) in university students and its relationship with depression. *Indian Journal of Forensic Medicine & Toxicology*, *15*(4), 921–927.
23. Ohnishi, T., Kobayashi, H., Yajima, T., Koyama, T., & Noguchi, K. (2019). Psychiatric comorbidities in adult attention-deficit/hyperactivity disorder: Prevalence and patterns in the routine clinical setting. *Innovations in Clinical Neuroscience*, *16*(9–10), 11.
24. Silverstein, M. J., Faraone, S. V., Alperin, S., Biederman, J., Spencer, T. J., & Adler, L. A. (2018). How informative are self-reported adult attention-deficit/hyperactivity disorder symptoms? An examination of the agreement between the adult attention-deficit/hyperactivity disorder self-report scale V1. 1 and adult attention-deficit/hyperactivity disorder investigator symptom rating scale. *Journal of Child and Adolescent Psychopharmacology*, *28*(5), 339–349.
25. Silverstein, M. J., Faraone, S. V., Alperin, S., Leon, T. L., Biederman, J., Spencer, T. J., & Adler, L. A. (2019). Validation of the expanded versions of the adult ADHD self-report scale v1. 1 symptom checklist and the adult ADHD investigator symptom rating scale. *Journal of Attention Disorders*, *23*(10), 1101–1110.
26. Waite, R., Buchanan, T., & Leahy, M. (2022). Assessing ADHD symptoms among young adults in the university with the ASRS v1. 1: Examining associations with social anxiety and self-efficacy. *International Journal of Disability, Development and Education*, *69*(5), 1631–1644.
27. Silverstein, M. J., Alperin, S., Faraone, S. V., Kessler, R. C., & Adler, L. A. (2018). Test–retest reliability of the adult ADHD Self-Report Scale (ASRS) v1. 1 Screener in non-ADHD controls from a primary care physician practice. *Family Practice*, *35*(3), 336–341.
28. Khullar, V., Salgotra, K., Singh, H. P., & Sharma, D. P. (2021). Deep learning-based binary classification of ADHD using resting state MR images. *Augmented Human Research*, *6*(1), 5.
29. Jin, P., Li, X., Ma, B., Guo, H., Zhang, Z., & Mao, L. (2020). Dynamic visual attention characteristics and their relationship to match performance in skilled basketball players. *PeerJ*, *8*, e9803.

CHAPTER 8

History of Mathematics in Africa, from Ancient Mathematics to Modern Data Science: Africa's Legacy and Future

ARSHAD AHMAD KHAN[1*], SANI HALIRU RINI[2], YAKUBU IBRAHIM BARGA[3], BASHAR SULEIMAN ARGUNGU[4], and ABBAS YUSUF BALARABE[5]

[1]*Department of Mathematics, Guru Nanak University Hyderabad, India*

[2]*Department of Mathematics, School of Chemical Engineering and Physical Sciences, Lovely Professional University, Phagwara, Punjab, India*

[3]*Department of Mathematics, Federal University Birnin Kebbi, Kebbi State, Nigeria*

[4]*Department of General Studies, Adamu Augie College of Education, Argungu, Kebbi State, Nigeria*

[5]*Department of Mathematics, Kebbi State University of Science and Technology, Aliero, Kebbi State, Nigeria*

*Corresponding author

ABSTRACT

This chapter explores the rich history of mathematics in Africa, shedding light on its contributions from ancient African civilizations, Islamic scholars, and modern mathematicians. However, this historical journey also uncovers the challenges faced by African mathematicians, including colonialism, limited access to education and resources, and the marginalization of indigenous mathematical knowledge. The chapter also examines the recent

Integrative Approaches to Quality, Data Analysis, and Interdisciplinary Research.
Amir Ahmad Dar and Waseem Z. Lone (Eds.)

DOI: 10.1201/9781779641014-10

advancements in the field, highlighting the efforts of African mathematicians to reclaim and revitalize traditional mathematical practices, as well as the growing recognition of African scholars in the global mathematical community.

8.1 INTRODUCTION

Mathematics is a universal language that has played a vital role in the development of human civilization. Its origins date back thousands of years, with various regions contributing to its evolution. Africa, in particular, has a rich history of mathematical contributions, despite facing numerous challenges throughout the years.

The mathematical history in Africa is rich, spanning millennia and encompassing a multitude of cultures and civilizations across the continent. Often overshadowed by the more widely known mathematical achievements of ancient Greece and Mesopotamia, the mathematical traditions of Africa have made significant contributions to the development of numerical systems, geometry, algebra, and applied mathematics.

In ancient Egypt, the Nile Valley civilization flourished as one of the earliest centers of mathematical inquiry [16]. The Egyptians demonstrated advanced knowledge in practical mathematics, essential for tasks such as surveying, architecture, and agriculture. The pyramid's construction remains a powerful testament to their mastery of geometry and engineering, showcasing an understanding of mathematical concepts that surpassed mere practical applications [19].

Moving across the continent, in ancient Carthage (modern-day Tunisia), scholars and mathematicians engaged in sophisticated mathematical thinking. Carthaginian mathematicians were known for their contributions to theoretical mathematics, as well as their practical applications in trade, navigation, and astronomy. The Carthaginian civilization played a crucial role in the transmission of mathematical knowledge between Africa and the Mediterranean world [7].

Further south, in regions like Timbuktu in Mali, the empires of West Africa became centers of learning and commerce. The scholars of Timbuktu, in particular, were renowned for their advanced knowledge and skills in the field of astronomy, mathematics, and medicine. The University of Sankore, a prominent center of learning, attracted scholars from across the Islamic world, fostering the exchange of mathematical ideas and advancements [16].

In East Africa, the Swahili city–states were hubs of trade and intellectual exchange. The maritime activities of the Swahili people required advanced knowledge of navigation, leading to developments in mathematical concepts related to mapping, distances, and timekeeping [16].

Although a significant portion of the historical record was lost or overlooked, ongoing research is shedding light on the intricate mathematical traditions of various African societies. These traditions not only contributed to the practical needs of their respective civilizations but also laid the groundwork for broader mathematical principles that continue to impact the field today. The history of mathematics in Africa is a story of diverse cultures, each contributing its unique perspective to the global development of mathematical thought. As scholars uncover more about Africa's mathematical heritage, it becomes increasingly evident that the continent played a vital role in shaping the foundations of this universal language of science and discovery.

This chapter is organized in the following manner. Section 8.2 provides a review of the literature. Section 8.3 focuses on the early mathematical contributions and the mathematical artifacts found in Africa. Section 8.4 discusses the challenges faced by African mathematicians. Section 8.5 mentions the advancement of mathematics in Africa and the creation of some initiatives to promote African mathematics. Finally, Section 8.6 concludes this chapter.

8.1.1 OBJECTIVE

The objective of this chapter is to provide a comprehensive understanding of the history of mathematics in Africa and its significance in the global mathematical community, focusing on the contributions of African mathematicians from ancient civilization to the present day in the field. It will discuss the challenges faced by African mathematicians in the discipline, as well as the impact of colonization on the study and teaching of mathematics on the continent. The chapter will finally discuss the advancement and current efforts aimed at promoting the study and application of mathematics in Africa, and highlight the potential for future advancements in the field.

8.1.2 SCOPE

This chapter will unveil in a structured manner, starting with an exploration of historical contributions to mathematics from different regions of Africa. It will address the challenges faced by African mathematicians throughout history and analyze the advancements of mathematics in the continent.

8.1.3 RESEARCH QUESTIONS

The research questions are as follows:

1. What were the significant mathematical achievements in various regions of Africa?
2. How did historical challenges impact the development of mathematics in Africa?
3. What are the recent advancements and initiatives shaping the future of mathematics in Africa?

8.2 REVIEW OF LITERATURE

Mathematics is often considered as a universal language that exceeds cultural and geographical boundaries. However, the history of mathematics is not a monolithic narrative that traces its origins and development from one source. Rather, it is a rich and diverse culture that reflects the contributions of many civilizations and peoples across the globe. One of the regions that has made significant and yet often overlooked contributions to the history of mathematics is Africa.

Among the challenges of studying the history of mathematics in Africa is the lack and diversity of sources that document the mathematical practices and knowledge of various African peoples. Unlike other regions, such as Europe or Asia, where written records and manuscripts have been preserved and transmitted for centuries, most of the mathematical sources in Africa are oral, material, or archaeological, these include oral traditions, myths, proverbs, songs, games, rituals, calendars, art, architecture, artifacts, and inscriptions [6]. As such, they require different methods of analysis and interpretation than the conventional textual sources used in the history of mathematics. Some scholars who have pioneered the study of African mathematics using these alternative sources and methods include Zaslavsky, Gerdes, Joseph, and Zulu [7, 20].

Zaslavsky [20] was one of the first to explore the mathematical aspects of the cultural and social practices of various ethnic groups in Africa, such as the Hausa, the Igbo, the Yoruba (all in present day Nigeria), the Nubians (Northern Sudan and Southern Egypt), and the Basotho (Lesotho and South Africa). She examined how these groups used mathematics in their daily life, such as counting, measuring, estimating, dividing, trading, weaving, carving, and building. She also showed how their mathematical concepts and systems were embedded in their languages, symbols, cosmologies, and worldviews [20].

Gerdes [7] focused on the geometrical and combinatorial aspects of the African mathematical heritage, especially in relation to the art and design of different cultures, such as the Lunda, Chokwe, Makonde, and Ndebele. He analyzed the patterns, symmetries, transformations, and algorithms that underlie the creation and interpretation of various forms of African art, such as basketry, pottery, textiles, sculptures, paintings, and murals. He also demonstrated how these forms of art can be used as pedagogical tools to teach and learn mathematics in a culturally relevant and engaging way [7].

Joseph [9] provided a comprehensive and comparative overview of the history of mathematics in Africa, spanning from ancient to modern times. He traced the origins and development of mathematical ideas and practices in various regions and civilizations of Africa, such as Egypt, Nubia, Ethiopia, Mali, Ghana, Songhai, Morocco, and Zimbabwe. He also examined the interactions and influences between African mathematics and other mathematical traditions, such as Greek, Arabic, Indian, and European. He argued that African mathematics has a distinct and original character that deserves recognition and appreciation in the global history of mathematics [7, 9].

Zulu proposed an Africa-centered approach to the history of mathematics, based on the philosophy and epistemology of the Basotho people of Southern Africa. He argued that the Basotho, like other African peoples, had a sophisticated mathematical lexicon and system that predated the European colonization and modernization of Africa. He also claimed that the Basotho mathematics is based on a holistic and relational worldview that differs from the dualistic and analytical worldview of Western mathematics. He suggested that the Basotho mathematics can offer alternative and complementary perspectives and insights to the current mathematical problems and challenges [18].

The history of mathematics in Africa is not a homogeneous or linear story, but rather a mosaic of diverse and dynamic stories that reflect the mathematical achievements and innovations of different African cultures and regions. Some of the examples of these achievements and innovations are as follows:

- The Egyptian mathematics, which is one of the oldest and most influential mathematical traditions in the world, dates back to 3000 BCE [18]. The Egyptians developed a decimal system of numeration, a system of fractions, a method of solving linear and quadratic equations, and a body of geometrical knowledge that included the calculation of areas, volumes, angles, and the famous Pythagorean theorem [13]. The Egyptians also used mathematics for practical purposes, such as surveying, astronomy, engineering, and administration [17]. Their mathematical knowledge was recorded and transmitted in various papyri, such as the Rhind papyrus, the Moscow papyrus, and the Berlin papyrus [11, 15, 19].
- The Nubian mathematics, which is closely related to the Egyptian mathematics, but also has some distinctive features, dates back to 1000 BCE. The Nubians, who ruled over Egypt for some time, adopted and adapted the Egyptian system of numeration, fractions, and geometry, but also developed their system of metrology, based on the cubit, the palm, and the finger. The Nubians also used mathematics for astronomical purposes, such as predicting eclipses, solstices, and equinoxes. Their mathematical knowledge was inscribed on various monuments, temples, and pyramids, such as the Gebel Barkal, the Meroe, and the Nuri [2, 16].
- The Ethiopian mathematics, which is influenced by both the Egyptian and the Greek mathematics, but also has some original contributions, dates back to 300 BCE. The Ethiopians, who were part of the Axumite kingdom, developed a system of numeration that used both alphabetic and ideographic symbols, a system of fractions that used both unit and binary fractions, and a system of algebra that used both symbolic and rhetorical methods. The Ethiopians also used mathematics for religious and calendrical purposes, such as computing the dates of Easter and other festivals, and determining the direction of prayer. Their mathematical knowledge

was preserved and transmitted in various manuscripts, such as the Liber Abaci, the Kitab al-Fusul, and the Bahra Hasab [2, 9, 16].

- The Islamic mathematics, which is a synthesis of the Greek, the Indian, and the Persian mathematics, but also has some significant innovations, dates back to 800 CE. The Islamic mathematicians, who spread their influence across North Africa and West Africa, developed a system of numeration that used the Arabic numerals and the decimal place value, a system of algebra that introduced the concept of polynomials, equations, and functions, and a system of geometry that extended the Euclidean geometry to include trigonometry, conic sections, and spherical geometry. The Islamic mathematicians also used mathematics for scientific and technological purposes, such as astronomy, optics, mechanics, and navigation. Their mathematical knowledge was written and disseminated in various books, such as the *Al-Jabr wa al-Muqabala* (The Compendious Book on Calculation by Completion and Balancing), and the *Al-Tafhim li-Awail Sina'at al-Tanjim* (Book of Instruction in the Elements of the Art of Astrology) [1, 2, 20].
- The West African mathematics, which is influenced by both the Islamic and the indigenous mathematics, but also has some unique features, dates back to 1200 CE. The West Africans, who were part of the Mali, Ghana, and Songhai empires, developed a system of numeration that used both the Arabic numerals and the indigenous symbols, such as the cowries, the knots, and the beads. They also developed a system of arithmetic that used both the decimal and the duodecimal bases, and a system of geometry that used both the Euclidean and the non-Euclidean concepts, such as fractals and symmetry. The West Africans also used mathematics for artistic and architectural purposes, such as creating patterns, designs, and structures, such as the Great Mosque of Djenné, the Sankore University, and the Timbuktu Manuscripts [9, 16, 20].
- The Southern African mathematics, which is based on the indigenous mathematics, but also has some modern adaptations, dates back to 1500 CE. The Southern Africans, who belong to various ethnic groups, such as the Zulu, the Xhosa, the Sotho, and the Ndebele, developed a system of numeration that used both the oral and the written forms, a system of fractions that used both the rational and the irrational numbers, and a system of geometry that used both the planar and the

spatial concepts, such as angles, shapes, and transformations. The Southern Africans also used mathematics for cultural and educational purposes, such as expressing their identity, values, and beliefs, and teaching and learning mathematics in a contextualized and meaningful way [20].

8.3 EARLY MATHEMATICAL AND DATA SCIENCE REPRESENTATION CONTRIBUTIONS IN AFRICA

8.3.1 THE SOURCES OF ETHNOMATHEMATICS IN AFRICA [6]

There are various sources of ethnomathematics information in Africa, such as:

1. *Texts and manuscripts*: Texts and manuscripts contain mathematical information and knowledge from various ancient African civilizations, like ancient Egyptian texts.
2. *Oral traditions knowledge*: Knowledge passed down through generations, like stories, proverbs, and rituals that contain mathematical concepts.
3. *Indigenous knowledge system*: Indigenous knowledge of various African communities that contains mathematics in their daily activities, which has been passed down from generation to generation till today. Such knowledge includes counting, measuring, and problem-solving.
4. *Astronomy and calendars*: Many ancient African cultures have developed astronomical knowledge to track time, seasons, and celestial events like the Sothic calendar of ancient Egyptians.

8.3.2 ANCIENT EGYPT

Ancient Egypt is among the earliest and most significant contributors to mathematics in Africa. Egyptian mathematics was highly developed and is one of the foundations of modern mathematics [10]. They made advancements in arithmetic, algebra, trigonometry, geometry, and the concept of pi. Ancient Egyptians used a decimal system, which laid the groundwork for our current base-10 number system [3, 8, 17].

8.3.2.1 EGYPTIAN NUMBERS

The Ancient Egyptians used the hieroglyphic system to represent their numbers, which was based on the 10 scale. The picture below shows how the Ancient Egyptians represented their numbers by using symbols and markings as shown in Figure 8.1 [3, 4, 17].

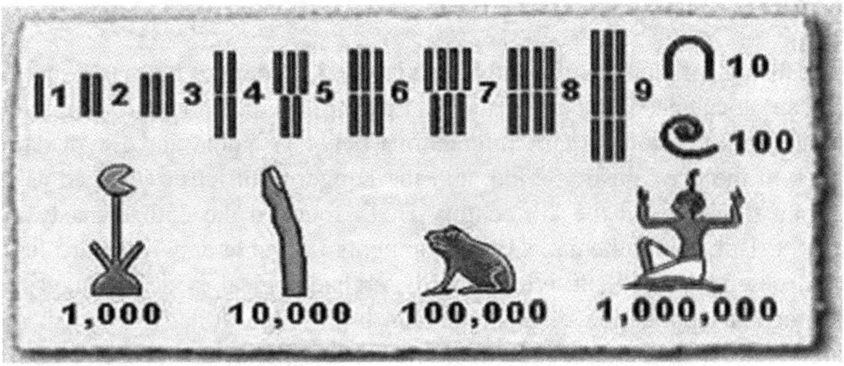

FIGURE 8.1 Egyptian numbers.

8.3.2.2 ASTRONOMY AND CALENDAR DEVELOPMENT

Early 4800 BCE, ancient Egyptians had created a calendar. Their knowledge of mathematics and astronomy helps them to develop a 365-day calendar containing 12 months of 30 days each and 5 feast days [17].

8.3.2.3 LAND SURVEYING AND TAXATION

In 3100 BCE, during the era of the Egyptian mace, numerous agricultural communities along the River Nile banks were unified under a Nubian ruler, King Menes. He established a dynasty of 32 Pharaohs that endured for 3000 years. To govern this vast dynasty effectively, the Egyptians developed an efficient administration system for tax collection, conducting censuses, and maintaining a large army. Mathematics was essential for these tasks. Initially, the Egyptians used to count glyphs. The Pharaoh divided the land into equal-sized plots, granting each man a square piece from which an annual tax was levied. If a farmer reported that his land had been damaged by the river's encroachment, the Pharaoh would send inspectors and surveyors to measure the extent of the damage and assess the loss. This data would then be used to adjust his property tax accordingly. This process may have led to the invention of Geometry, which later influenced Greek mathematics [10, 13, 17].

8.3.3 MATHEMATICS IN ANCIENT NUBIA AND THE KINGDOM OF KUSH

The history of mathematics in Nubia and the Kingdom of Kush (presently Sudan), located to the south of ancient Egypt, is less documented compared to its northern counterpart. Interactions between Nubia and Egypt date back to the predynastic period, and the Kingdom of Kush emerged as a strong state around the 8th century BCE, founded the 25th Dynasty in Egypt. But the mathematical developments in Nubia and Kush are less clear due to limited surviving records; archaeological evidence suggests a practical application of mathematical knowledge in activities such as architecture, agriculture, and trade. The cultural exchange between Nubia, Kush, and Egypt likely facilitated the transfer of mathematical concepts, although the details remain less well-documented compared to the mathematical history of ancient Egypt [2, 16].

8.3.4 MATHEMATICS IN THE SWAHILI COAST

The Swahili Coast, located in Eastern Africa, forms dynamic commerce cities along the eastern shores of Africa, such as Kilwa, Mombasa, and Zanzibar, and has a historical legacy of mathematical practice and innovation intertwined with its flourishing maritime trade. The Swahili Coast, as a key link in the Indian Ocean trade network, participated in extensive trade with diverse cultures, such as the Arab world, Persia, India, and China. While direct evidence of specific mathematical advancements is limited, the coastal inhabitants likely applied practical mathematical skills in navigation, trade, and construction. The region's architectural marvels, including coral stone buildings and mosques, show the application of geometric principles and measurement in construction. Cultural exchanges with different civilizations may have led to the adoption and adaptation of various mathematical techniques, fostering a dynamic mathematical environment that supported the Swahili Coast's prominence in trade and cultural exchange [16].

8.3.5 MATHEMATICS IN HAUSA LAND

Hausa is a language spoken primarily in West Africa, most especially in the northern part of Nigeria and the southeastern part of the Niger Republic. The Hausa people's occupations are trading, architecture, engineering, agriculture, weaving, metal work, leather work, and dyeing. If we consider the mentioned occupations of Hausa people, we will grasp that they must have some mathematical skills and thinking to enable them to carry out such tasks successfully.

The Hausa people have a system of counting in their language. The numbers can be combined to represent higher numbers. For instance, 11 is Goma sha daya, meaning you will add 10 and 1. Hausa numeral from 1 to 10e is shown in Table 8.1.

TABLE 8.1 Hausa Counting

Hausa	English
Daya	1
Biyu	2
Uku	3
Hudu	4
Biyar	5
Shida	6
Bakwai	7
Takwas	8
Tara	9
Goma	10

8.3.6 MATHEMATICAL ARTIFACTS FOUND IN AFRICA

8.3.6.1 THE LEBOMBO BONE (35,000 BC)

The Lebombo bone is a baboon fibula with 29 incised markings used as a mathematical instrument used as a measuring device, and was discovered in the Lebombo Mountains located between South Africa and Eswatini. The device is at least 35,000 years old, and it could be used to either track menstrual or lunar cycles, as shown in Figure 8.2 [11].

FIGURE 8.2 Lebombo bone.

8.3.6.2 ISHANGO BONE (20,000 BC)

The Ishango bone is considered the world's oldest evidence of advanced mathematics. Ishango bone was a baboon fibula discovered Democratic Republic of Congo, dating to at least 20,000 BC. The bone is now in the Museum of Natural Science in Brussels. The Ishango bone is a measuring device and tally stick. The inscriptions on the bone are clearly separated into clusters of markings that represent various quantities, as shown in Figure 8.3 [9, 11, 15].

8.3.6.3 MOSCOW PAPYRUS (2000 BC)

Moscow papyrus is among the most well-known historical mathematical documents found in ancient Egyptian civilization. The papyrus contains mathematical texts written in the hieratic script of the ancient Egyptian writing system. The document contains 25 mathematical problems and their solutions on different topics, including arithmetic, geometry, and algebra. The Moscow papyrus was written in the Middle Kingdom of ancient Egypt around 1850 BCE or even earlier. It is currently kept in the Pushkin State Museum of Fine Arts in Moscow, Russia, as shown in Figure 8.4 [19].

8.3.6.4 RHIND MATHEMATICAL PAPYRUS

The Rhind mathematical papyrus, also called the Ahmes papyrus, is one of the most mathematical documents from ancient Egypt. It dates back to around 1550 BCE. The papyrus was written in hieratic script, a flowing script of ancient Egyptian writing. The Rhind papyrus covers a wide range of topics such as arithmetic, algebra, and geometry. It also contains mathematical solutions of many problems and applications related to the calculations of the area of fields, volume of granaries, and the method of distributing food and drinks among workers. The Rhind papyrus is currently kept in the British Museum in London, as shown in Figure 8.5 [3, 5].

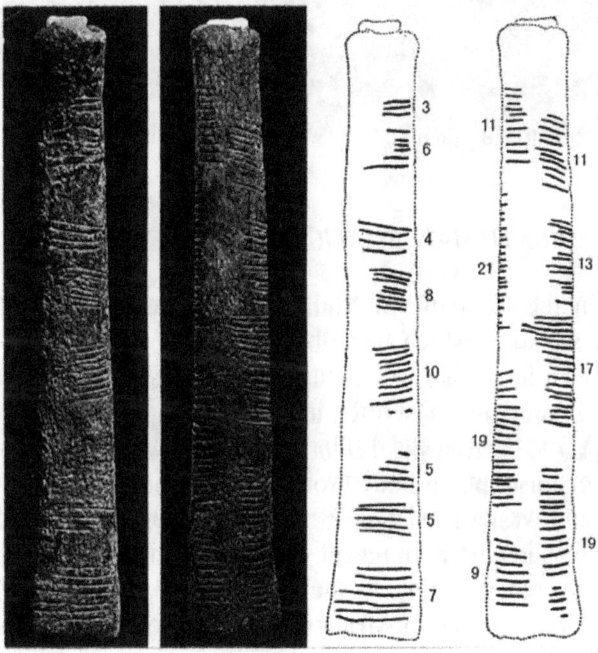

FIGURE 8.3 The Ishango bone.

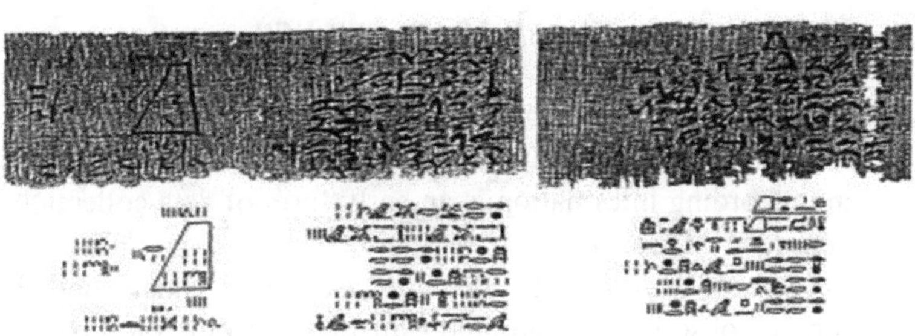

FIGURE 8.4 Moscow papyrus.

FIGURE 8.5 The Rhind papyrus.

8.3.6.5 TIMBUKTU MATHEMATICAL MANUSCRIPTS (12000S AD)

Timbuktu in the Republic of Mali is the home of the world's oldest University, Sankore, which had libraries full of manuscripts written in Ajami (African languages, particularly those of Songhai, Mandé, Hausa, Swahili, and many others, written in their languages but using Arabic) in the 1200s AD [2]. From the 1300s to 1800s AD, the Malians started to hide some manuscripts in underground, basements, and attics for fear of Europeans and western Asian destruction and theft, as they did in Kemet and many areas in Africa. In recent years, more than 700,000 scripts have been rediscovered, attesting to the continuous knowledge of advanced mathematics and science in Africa well before colonization, as shown in Figure 8.6 [2, 16].

8.3.7 RELEVANCE TO MODERN DATA SCIENCE

1. *Data collection and recording:* The use of tools like tally sticks and bones, such as the Lebombo bone and Ishango bone, for counting and recording information is an early form of data collection and storage in Africa.
2. *Statistical analysis:* The development of calendars and astronomical observations required statistical reasoning to predict and understand patterns over time.

3. *Geometric and spatial analysis:* The application of geometry in construction and land measurement reflects early forms of spatial data analysis.
4. *Numerical systems:* The development of various numerical systems showcases an understanding of data representation and manipulation, foundational in data science.

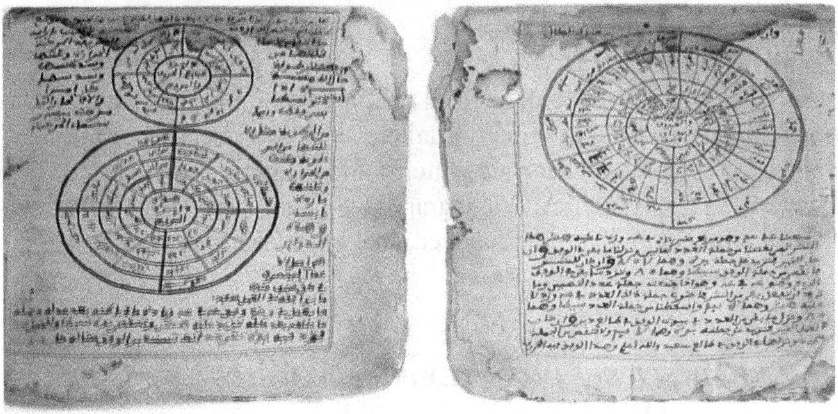

FIGURE 8.6 Timbuktu scripts contained mathematics and astronomy.

8.3.7.1 MODERN DATA SCIENCE

Data science is a field that uses scientific methods, processes, algorithms, and systems to extract knowledge and insight from structured and unstructured data. Data science puts together aspects of statistics, computer science, expertise, and information theory to analyze and interpret complex data sets. The processed data can be presented in graphs, tables, charts, and visual images to give a piece of meaningful information for decision-making [21].

8.3.7.2 DATA ANALYSIS TOOLS

1. *Spreadsheets*: Tools like Microsoft Excel have become widely used for data analysis due to their accessibility and ease of use.
2. *Statistical software*: Programs like Python, Stata, Excel, MATLAB, SPSS, SAS, and R provided more advanced statistical analysis capabilities.

8.3.7.3 BIG DATA AND MACHINE LEARNING

Big data is an extremely large dataset that cannot be easily by human to managed, processed, and analyzed using traditional data processing tools. Examples of big data sources are sensors, social media, transactions, and logs.

8.3.7.4 DATA VISUALIZATION

Data visualization can be defined as the process of representing information and data graphically using visual elements such as charts, maps, and graphs to help users understand patterns and insights. Tools like Tableau, Power BI, Zoho Analytics, Whatagraph, Qlik, and many more have revolutionized the way data is visualized, making it easier to derive insights and communicate findings.

8.3.8 DATA SCIENCE IN CONTEMPORARY AFRICA

African data scientists are increasingly using modern tools like Python, R, and SQL, along with cloud-based platforms like Google Cloud, AWS, and Azure, to tackle local problems in health, agriculture, finance and banking, Market access, education, urban planning and development, and more.

8.4 CHALLENGES FACED BY AFRICAN MATHEMATICIANS

African mathematicians have faced a lot of challenges in various aspects. Some of the challenges faced by African mathematicians include the following:

1. *Colonialism:* The colonization of Africa by Western powers had drawn Africans back from advancing in their indigenous mathematical system of education. Western colonizers introduced Western mathematical methods and curricula, disregarding or dismissing the mathematical traditions and contributions of African societies, which caused the loss of much mathematical traditional knowledge [14].

2. *Language barriers:* As a result of colonialization in Africa, mathematical education is being taught in foreign languages (English and French) instead of local languages. This language barrier can cause a lack of understanding of mathematics to the students and sometimes even the teachers [14].
3. *Lack of funding:* The lack of funding for research and education in Africa is among the challenges that African mathematicians are facing, which results in their inability to conduct innovative research and publish their findings [12].
4. *Brain drain and loss of skilled mathematicians:* Due to the lack of funding and resources in Africa has led to a shortage of qualified mathematicians and restricted opportunities for professional development. As a result, many African mathematicians have been compelled to seek research and academic opportunities abroad, leading to a brain drain and the loss of valuable intellectuals on the continent [12].
5. *Insufficient recognition:* Lack of recognition from the international community is among the challenges African mathematicians face despite their potential contribution to scientific research and societal development [12].

8.4.1 WAY OUT OF THESE CHALLENGES

To address these challenges, it needs serious efforts from various stakeholders such as governments, funding organizations, academic institutions, and international organizations. Providing adequate access to resources, enhancing mathematical education, and starting to teach mathematics in local languages. Also, increasing recognition of African mathematicians from the international community can help overcome the challenges faced by African mathematicians and promote their advancement in the field.

8.5 ADVANCEMENT OF MATHEMATICS IN AFRICA

In recent years, there have been various advancements in the mathematics field in Africa. Some major advancements are as follows:

1. *Establishment of research institutions:* African countries have established research institutions and centers for promoting and developing mathematical studies. This institution creates a platform for mathematicians to conduct research and contribute to the global mathematical community. Examples of some mathematical institutions and centers in Africa are the National Mathematical Center in Nigeria, the Centre for the Advancement of Non-Traditional Mathematics at the University of South Africa, the Institute for Mathematical and Physical Sciences and Computation (IS2M) in Morocco.
2. *Increase in research output*: African mathematicians have been making contributions to various branches of mathematics. They have made a lot of research publications and conference presentations within and outside Africa, which shows their expertise and advancement in the field of mathematics.
3. *Increased access to education*: The number of students pursuing mathematics education at all levels in Africa has been increasing in recent years as a result of the expansion of educational institutions and the availability of scholarships and financial aid.
4. *Applying mathematics in technology:* African mathematicians are applying their knowledge in areas like computer science, engineering, and telecommunications, which contribute to the development of technology in Africa and beyond.
5. *International collaborations*: African mathematicians are increasingly collaborating with researchers from all over the world to exchange knowledge and enhance the visibility of African mathematicians within the global mathematical community [12].

8.5.1 INITIATIVES TO PROMOTE AFRICAN MATHEMATICS [12]

The following are the initiatives to promote African Mathematics.

1. *African Institute for Mathematical Sciences (AIMS):* AIMS is a Pan-African network of centers of excellence enabling Africa's gifted students to become innovators leading the continent toward scientific, educational, and economic self-sufficiency.
2. *African Mathematics Millennium Science Initiative (AMMSI):* An organization created in 2008 that promotes the development

of African mathematics. It focuses on developing mathematical research, education, and application in Africa.

3. *International Centre for Theoretical Physics (ICTP):* African Mathematical School: ICTP organizes the African Mathematical School, which brings together young mathematicians from across Africa to learn from world-renowned mathematicians. This program aims to enhance research and teaching capacities in mathematics in Africa.
4. *African Women in Mathematics Association (AWMA)*: AWMA is established in 2013. The main aims of the association are to promote women and young girls in the field of mathematics in Africa. AWMA is a nonprofit, international, and nongovernmental organization.

8.5.2 NOTABLE AFRICAN MATHEMATICIANS AND THEIR CONTRIBUTIONS [1]

Notable African mathematicians and their contributions are as follows:

1. *Abu'l-Hasan Ali ibn Abd al-Rahman ibn Yunus* (c. 950–1009) was a prominent Arab mathematician and astronomer of the Islamic golden age. He is known for his significant contributions to the development of mathematical and astronomical sciences.
2. *Al-Marrakushi ibn al-Banna, also known as Ibn al-Banna al-Marrakushi* (c. 1256–1321), was a notable Moroccan mathematician, astronomer, and philosopher.
3. *Grace Awani Alele-Williams* (December 16, 1932–March 25, 2022) was a distinguished Nigerian mathematician and academic. She is known for her pioneering contributions to mathematics and education in Nigeria.
4. *Francis Kofi Ampenyin Allotey* (August 9, 1932–November 2, 2017) was a renowned Ghanaian mathematician and physicist known for his significant contributions to mathematical physics and his role in advancing education in Ghana.
5. *Fatma Moalla* (January 14, 1939) is a notable Tunisian mathematician known for her contributions to mathematics and her role in advancing education in Tunisia.

8.6 CONCLUSION

In conclusion, the history of mathematics in Africa is a complex and multifaceted story that encompasses contributions, challenges, and advancements. African mathematicians have made good contributions to the field of mathematics throughout history, from ancient civilizations to the present day. Ancient African mathematics demonstrates early forms of data collection, recording, and analysis, which are central to modern data science. By recognizing and understanding these contributions, we see that the principles of data science have deep historical roots, reflecting humanity's long-standing quest to understand and manipulate the world through data. However, they have also faced many challenges, including inadequate funding, a lack of recognition from the international community, and the negative impact of colonization by Western powers. Despite these challenges, African mathematicians have continued to make advancements in various fields of mathematics, and there is a growing movement to promote mathematics education and research in Africa. With continued support and recognition, African mathematicians have the potential to make even greater contributions to the field of mathematics in the future.

KEYWORDS

- **African mathematics**
- **data science**
- **early African mathematics**
- **challenges faced by African mathematicians**
- **advancement of African mathematics**

REFERENCES

1. African mathematician Biographies. Retrieved January 9, 2024 from https://mathshistory.standrews.ac.uk/Biographies/category-african/
2. Ancient African Mathematics. Retrieved January 4, 2024 from https://www.taneter.org/math.html

3. Burton, D. M. (2011). *The History of Mathematics: An Introduction* (pp.1–37), 7th edn., University of New Hampshire.
4. Cajori, F. (1919). *A History of Mathematics* (pp. 9–14), 2nd edn., The Macmillan Company.
5. Chace, A. B., Bull, L. S., Manning, H. P., & Archibald, R. C. (1927). *The Rhind Mathematical Papyrus Volume 1* (pp. 3–5). Oberlin: Ohio, USA.
6. Dirk, H. (2006). Mathematics in (central) Africa before colonization. *117*, 135–162. Retrieved from https://www.researchgate.net/publication/265872061
7. Gerdes, P. (1994). On mathematics in the history of Sub-Saharan Africa. *Historia Mathematica, 21*, 345–376.
8. Gillings, R. J. (1971). *Mathematics in the Time of the Pharaohs* (pp. 1–8). Dover Publications, Inc.: New York.
9. Joseph, G. G. (2009). *The Crest of the Peacock, Non-European Roots Mathematics*, 3rd edn., University of Manchester (pp. 30–35). Princeton University Press: Princeton & Oxford.
10. Katz, V. J. (2008). *A History of Mathematics, An Introduction* (pp. 1–10), 3rd edn., University of the District of Columbia
11. Mamokgethi, S., & Bangura, A. (2011). *African Mathematics from Bones to Computers* (pp. 11–15). Lanham, Maryland 20706 UPA Acquisitions Department (301) 459–3366
12. Mathematics in Africa: Challenges and opportunities. In: *A Summary Report Prepared for the International Congress of Mathematicians (ICM)*, In Seoul, Korea August 13–21, 2014 by the International Mathematics Union (IMU).
13. O'Connor, J. J., & Robertson, E. F. (2000). *An Overview of Egyptian Mathematics*. School of Mathematics and Statistics, University of St Andrews: Scotland. Retrieved from https://mathshistory.st-andrews.ac.uk/HistTopics/Egyptian_mathematics/
14. Ocheni, S., & Nwankwo, B. C. (2012). *Analysis of Colonialism and Its Impact in Africa*, Vol 8 No. 3 (pp. 46–54).
15. Pletser, V., & Dirk, H. (2008). *An Interpretation of the Ishango Rods* (pp. 139–150).
16. Stephen, O. (2023). From the Nile to the Niger: Tracing the development of African mathematics. Retrieved from https://www.oriire.com/article/from-the-nile-to-the-niger-tracing-the-development-of-african-mathematics
17. Uta, C. M., & Carl, B. B. (2010). *A History of Mathematics* (pp. 8–20), 3rd edn., John Wiley & Sons, Inc.
18. Veroustraete, F. (2023). *A History of Mathematics: From Ancient Origins to the Modern Era* (pp. 1–2). https://doi.org/10.13140/RG.2.2.18860.33926
19. Wendrich, W. (1996). Ancient Egyptian rope and knots. In: *History and Science of Knots* (pp. 43–68).
20. Zaslavsky,C.(1999).*AfricaCountsNumberandPatterninAfricanCultures*(pp.25–200), 3rd edn., Published by Lawrence Hill Books. Retrieved from https://www.everand.com/read/161284343/Africa-Counts-Number-and-Pattern-in-African-Cultures#
21. Alex, C. (2021). *Data Science for Beginners, Comprehensive Guide to Most Important Basics in Data Science* (pp. 9–15)

CHAPTER 9

Exploring Decentralized Inventory Strategies: A Study

PRERNA JAIN[1], NITIN KUMAR MISHRA[1,*], RENUKA NAMWAD[1], and RANU[2]

[1]*Department of Mathematics, Lovely Professional University, Phagwara, Punjab, India*

[2]*Department of Mathematics, NIILM University, Kaithal, Haryana, India*

*Corresponding author

ABSTRACT

Amid the disruptions to global supply chains caused by the COVID-19 pandemic, the need for decentralized inventory management has become evident. This chapter examines decentralized supply chain inventory models to enhance resilience and efficiency. Analyzing 50 research papers, we explore various decentralized strategies and their impact on managerial decision-making, focusing on Stackelberg's mechanisms for cost savings and service improvements. Using Excel and Python, we conducted a detailed data analysis. We identified significant positive correlations, such as between decentralized and inventory management, and negative correlations, such as between blockchain implementation and inventory management. Heatmaps and advanced visualizations were used to illustrate these relationships. Our review highlights the importance of further research on decentralized supply chain models incorporating blockchain technology and multiperiod inventory frameworks. By identifying research gaps and potential improvements, this chapter aims to inform strategic decision-making in supply chain management, contributing to cost minimization, enhanced insights, and better coordination across the supply chain.

Integrative Approaches to Quality, Data Analysis, and Interdisciplinary Research.
Amir Ahmad Dar and Waseem Z. Lone (Eds.)

DOI: 10.1201/9781779641014-11

9.1 INTRODUCTION

The emergence of the COVID-19 pandemic has rocked the global economy, with its most significant impact felt on supply chains. This pandemic has exposed vulnerabilities in traditional centralized supply chain structures, necessitating the urgent need for adaptive and resilient systems to mitigate disruptions [1].

In response to this challenging situation, the concept of decentralized supply chain management has garnered significant attention. Decentralization offers the potential to distribute decision-making authority and resources across multiple nodes within the supply chain network, thereby enhancing flexibility and responsiveness in the face of unforeseen events [2].

The COVID-19 pandemic has highlighted the limitations of traditional centralized supply chain models, such as limited flexibility and delayed decision-making during supply chain disruptions. These vulnerabilities underscore the critical need for innovative approaches to supply chain management that can better adapt to dynamic and uncertain environments [3].

Centralized supply chain management is a traditional approach where decision-making authority and operational control are concentrated in a single central location or department. Key decisions regarding inventory management, production scheduling, and distribution are made at the centralized level shown in Figure 9.1. While this approach promotes efficiency and consistency, it can also be rigid and inflexible. During disruptive events such as natural disasters or pandemics, centralized supply chain systems struggle to respond rapidly and adapt, as decision-making is centralized [4]. The primary limitation of centralized supply chain management is its rigidity and inflexibility, especially during disruptive events such as pandemics or natural disasters. Due to centralized decision-making authority, responses can be slow, and adaptability can be compromised, exacerbating the impact of supply chain disruptions [5].

Decentralized supply chain management emphasizes decentralized decision-making and operational control. Decision-making authority and resources are distributed across multiple nodes or locations. Decentralization allows for greater agility and responsiveness, as decisions can be made quickly at the local level and resources can be dynamically allocated based on local demand and conditions. This approach provides better adaptability during disruptions and enables customized responses at the local level [6].

Decentralized supply chain management is crucial during disruptions, as decision-making is decentralized, and resources are dynamically allocated based on local conditions. This approach enhances supply chain flexibility and responsiveness, helping minimize disruptions' impact [3].

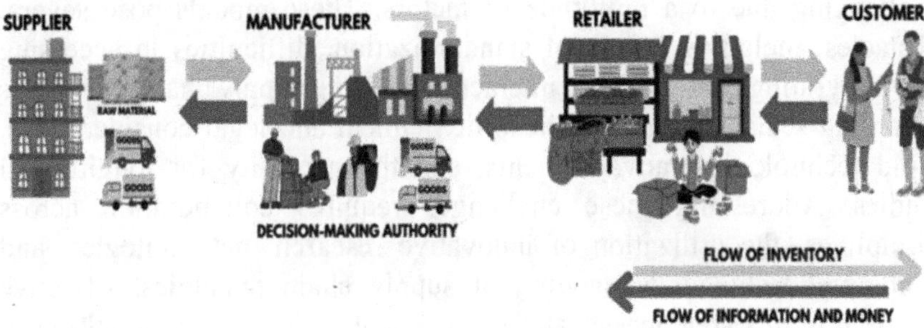

FIGURE 9.1 Centralized supply chain management.

In the current business landscape, decentralized supply chain models offer unique solutions to the challenges and complexities faced by organizations. These models come with several key advantages. First, they enable organizations to swiftly adapt to market fluctuations and changes in demand, fostering flexibility and responsiveness. By distributing decision-making authority, decentralized models empower members to make informed and timely decisions, thereby enhancing agility.

Moreover, decentralization mitigates disruptions and uncertainties within the supply chain by encouraging risk sharing among participants. This collaborative approach allows organizations to maintain business continuity by collectively navigating unforeseen events. Additionally, decentralized models foster a culture of trust, cooperation, and information sharing among participants, leading to increased efficiency, innovation, and overall supply chain performance.

Technological advancements such as blockchain and the Internet of Things further enhance decentralized supply chains by improving coordination, visibility, and efficiency through seamless data sharing, transparency, and real-time insights [7]. Furthermore, decentralized supply chains promote environmental sustainability, waste reduction, and ethical sourcing, thus contributing to sustainable development and social responsibility.

By leveraging emerging technologies and adapting swiftly to changing circumstances, decentralized supply chains offer organizations a competitive edge, resulting in improved customer satisfaction, cost savings, and product differentiation [8]. In today's dynamic and interconnected business environment, embracing decentralization empowers organizations to thrive and stay ahead of the curve.

Researching decentralized supply chain models can be particularly challenging due to a multitude of factors. These models pose several obstacles, including a lack of standardization, difficulties in accessing and integrating data, intricate interactions among supply chains, concerns regarding scalability and applicability, ethical and legal considerations, rapid technological advancements, and the necessity for longitudinal studies. Addressing these challenges requires collaboration across disciplines, the utilization of innovative research methodologies, and a comprehensive understanding of supply chain dynamics. Effective research in this area necessitates engagement with industry practitioners and staying abreast of industry advancements. By overcoming these challenges, a better understanding and implementation of decentralized supply chain models can be achieved.

In this chapter, we delve into different aspects of inventory decentralization, ranging from theoretical frameworks to practical implementations. Our focus extends to understanding the underlying principles, challenges, and opportunities presented by decentralization in inventory management. By examining a wide array of literature, we aim to provide insights into the potential benefits and limitations of decentralization strategies in optimizing inventory processes.

In Section 9.2, we outline our data collection process and present descriptive statistics, including the use of academic databases (e.g., Google Scholar, Scopus), keyword selection, and inclusion/exclusion criteria. We also provide statistics on the distribution of papers by journals, year, country, and author affiliations. In Section 9.3, we review the literature on decentralized inventory management, covering methodologies, practical applications, advantages and risks, empirical studies, and emerging trends.

Section 9.4 identifies research gaps and opportunities by critically evaluating existing literature and providing insights for further investigation. We introduce data analysis techniques, explain our correlation analysis, and present results using visualizations. Section 9.5 synthesizes key findings, reflecting on themes, challenges, and opportunities. We propose future research directions to encourage further inquiry and innovation in decentralized inventory management.

9.2 METHODOLOGY

9.2.1 DATA COLLECTION

In this chapter, our objective was to conduct a comprehensive literature review on decentralized inventory management within supply chain management. To achieve this, we employed academic databases and search engines like Google Scholar, Scopus, and Web of Science. We carefully selected keywords such as "decentralized inventory management" and "supply chain decentralization" to guide our search process. Utilizing Boolean operators (AND, OR, NOT), we formulated a systematic search strategy to retrieve relevant literature. Subsequently, we applied inclusion and exclusion criteria to screen the retrieved literature based on its alignment with our research topic. By reviewing titles and abstracts, we identified articles of interest and retrieved full-text versions for further evaluation if necessary. From these articles, we extracted pertinent data, including author details, publication years, journal sources, research methodologies employed, key findings, and conclusions.

9.2.2 DESCRIPTIVE STATISTICS

9.2.2.1 PAPERS DISTRIBUTION BY JOURNALS

The distribution of papers across various journals provides insights into the academic landscape of research on decentralized inventory strategies. Among the prominent publishers, IEEE and Springer stand out with nine papers each, reflecting their significant contribution to this field. Elsevier follows closely with four papers, while other notable publishers include MDPI, Taylor & Francis, and Inderscience Online shown in Figure 9.2. Interestingly, a substantial portion of the literature, comprising 16 papers, is published in journals not categorized under the listed publishers, highlighting the diverse sources contributing to this body of knowledge.

9.2.2.2 DISTRIBUTION OF PAPERS BY YEAR

The geographic distribution of research papers offers insights into global engagement with the topic of decentralized inventory strategies.

China emerges as a dominant contributor, with 20 papers originating from researchers based in the country. India follows closely with 12 papers, reflecting substantial research activity from this region as shown in Figure 9.3. Additionally, contributions from Europe and the USA are notable, with five and eight papers, respectively. Australia and Southeast Asia also make significant contributions, indicating the global relevance and interest in this research area.

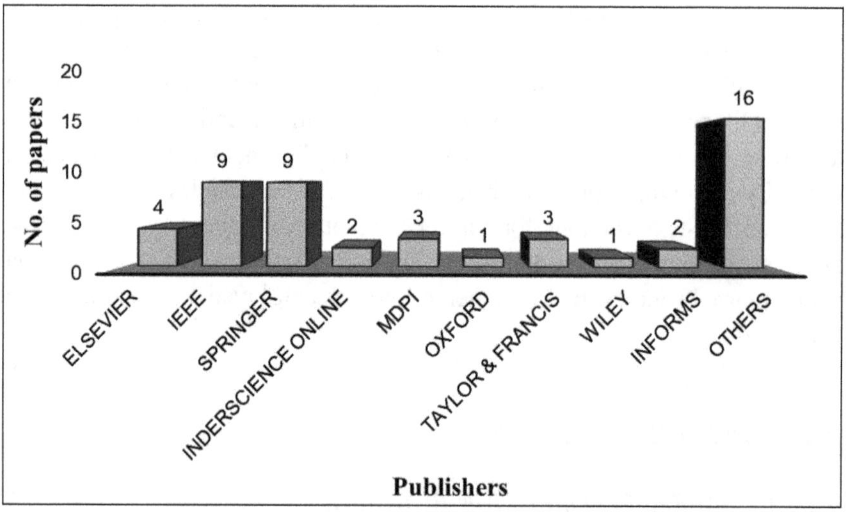

FIGURE 9.2 Paper distribution by publishing houses.

9.2.2.3 COUNTRY-WISE CLASSIFICATION

The geographic distribution of research papers offers insights into global engagement with the topic of decentralized inventory strategies. China emerges as a dominant contributor, with 20 papers originating from researchers based in the country shown in Figure 9.4. India follows closely with 12 papers, reflecting substantial research activity from this region. Additionally, contributions from Europe and the USA are notable, with five and eight papers, respectively. Australia and Southeast Asia also make significant contributions, indicating the global relevance and interest in this research area.

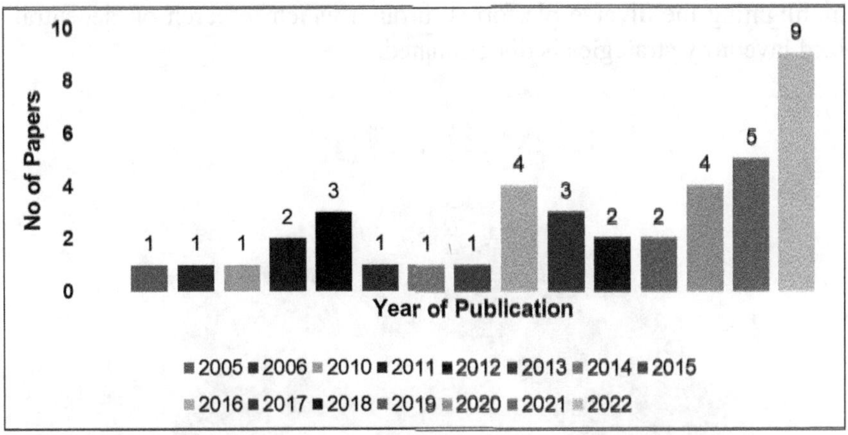

FIGURE 9.3 Distribution of papers by years.

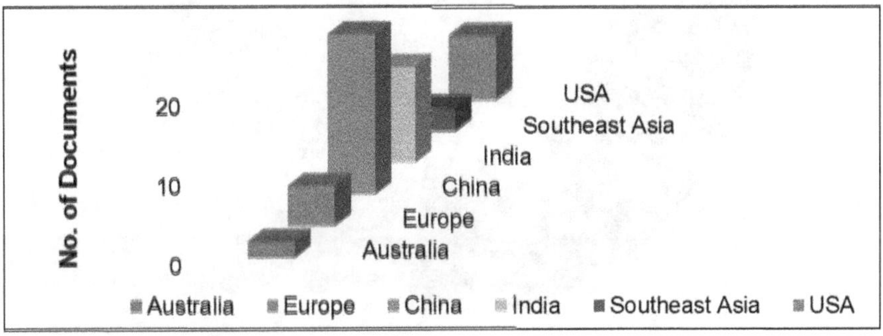

FIGURE 9.4 Country-wise classification.

9.2.2.4 AFFILIATION OF JOURNALS

Analyzing the affiliation of authors provides insights into the institutional landscape driving research on decentralized inventory strategies. Scopus, a prominent academic database, is associated with 13 papers, indicating the involvement of researchers shown in Figure 9.5 affiliated with institutions indexed in this database. A substantial portion of the literature, comprising 24 papers, involves authors affiliated with SCI Scopus-indexed institutions and other affiliations. Furthermore, contributions from conferences and book chapters are noteworthy, with nine and four papers, respectively, highlighting the diverse platforms through which research on decentralized inventory strategies is disseminated.

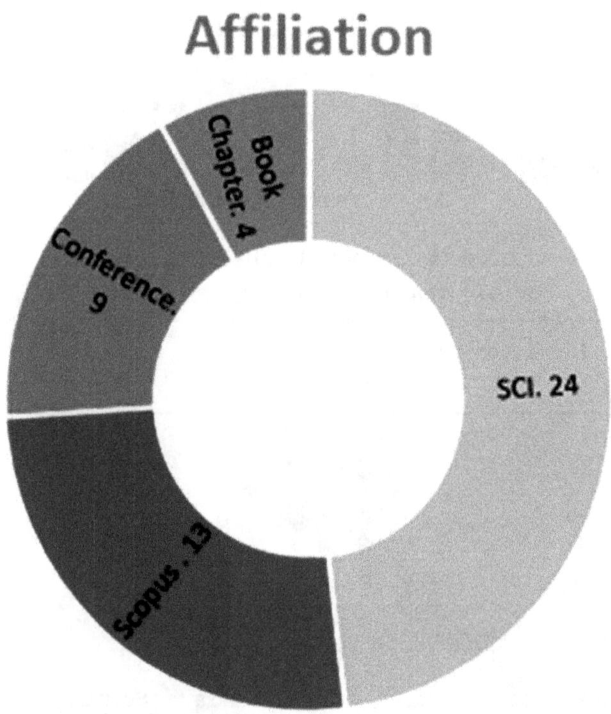

FIGURE 9.5 Affiliation of journals.

9.3 LITERATURE REVIEW

Our analysis delves into a comprehensive examination of decentralized inventory strategies within the domain of supply chain management. In this chapter, we meticulously scrutinized 50 papers, each offering valuable insights into the multifaceted aspects of supply chain operations, with a particular focus on decentralized inventory management practices. Through our thorough examination, we aimed to uncover the underlying trends, emerging technologies, and innovative methodologies that collectively contribute to the advancement of decentralized inventory strategies.

In Table 9.1, we present a summary of the key methodologies and technologies explored by various authors in their research on decentralized and centralized inventory management within the realm of supply chain management. This table serves as a reference point for understanding the diverse approaches and solutions proposed by scholars in addressing the challenges and opportunities associated with inventory management in decentralized supply chains.

Throughout our chapter, we aim to provide a comprehensive overview of the current state of research in decentralized inventory management, shedding light on the historical evolution, significant milestones, and key contributors in this field. By synthesizing findings from a wide range of scholarly works, we endeavor to offer valuable insights and perspectives that can inform future research directions and practical applications in supply chain management.

9.3.1 ANALYSIS OF DIFFERENT METHODOLOGIES

Our chapter has synthesized various methodologies and common themes prevalent in the selected studies. Researchers, including [9–12], have extensively explored the implications of centralized and decentralized approaches in supply chain management. These studies delineate the advantages and disadvantages associated with each approach. Several papers, such as those by [13–15], among others, utilize optimization techniques to address inventory management, production allocation, pricing decisions, and overall supply chain performance. Certain studies, exemplified by the works of [9, 10] and others employ game theory frameworks, like Stackelberg games, to analyze decision-making processes and coordination mechanisms within supply chains.

Mathematical models play a pivotal role in formulating supply chain problems and deriving analytical solutions. These models, as demonstrated in studies by [11, 12] and others, consider various factors such as demand, pricing, inventory costs, and coordination mechanisms. Simulation techniques are employed to mimic real-world supply chain scenarios, enabling researchers to evaluate the performance of different strategies and decision-making approaches. Researchers like [10, 13], among others, utilize simulation methodologies. Certain methodologies incorporate blockchain technology to enhance transparency, traceability, and information sharing in supply chains. This trend is observed in studies by [9, 10], and others. Agent-based methodologies, particularly for analyzing decentralized supply chains, are employed in studies by [14], and others.

These methodologies consider the behavior and interactions of individual agents within the system.

Various coordination mechanisms, such as revenue-sharing contracts, are explored in studies by [15, 16], among others, to align incentives among supply chain members and improve overall profitability and efficiency. Some methodologies address environmental concerns, such as carbon taxation, recycling activities, and green supply chain management. This reflects a growing emphasis on sustainability in supply chain decision-making, evident in studies by [16, 17], and others.

9.3.2 PRACTICAL APPLICATIONS OF DECENTRALIZED INVENTORIES

In this chapter, we have observed various types of decentralized inventory strategies that have been studied. These strategies are proposed to optimize inventory management and streamline operations. Here are some prominent types of decentralized inventory strategies, each with examples illustrating their practical application:

1. *Vendor-managed inventory (VMI):* VMI involves the supplier or vendor taking responsibility for controlling inventory levels at customer locations based on predetermined agreements and requirements [18]. For example, Procter and Gamble collaborates with Walmart for VMI, where P&G monitors and replenishes inventory levels at Walmart's distribution centers and stores.
2. *Consignment inventory:* Consignment inventory entails the supplier retaining ownership of the inventory until it is consumed or sold by the customer [19]. Boeing employs a consignment inventory model with its suppliers, where Boeing pays for parts only upon their use in aircraft assembly, thus reducing inventory carrying costs.
3. *Cross-docking:* Cross-docking entails the direct transfer of goods from inbound transportation vehicles to outbound vehicles with minimal or no storage in between, reducing the need for warehouse storage [20]. Walmart employs a cross-docking strategy, where incoming goods are sorted and immediately loaded onto outbound trucks for delivery to stores, minimizing inventory holding costs.
4. *Drop shipping*: Drop shipping involves fulfilling customer orders by directly shipping products from manufacturers or wholesalers to end customers, eliminating the need for retailers to hold inventory [21]. An example is Amazon's third-party seller program, where

independent sellers list their products on Amazon's platform, and Amazon handles order fulfillment and shipping directly to customers.

5. *Just-in-time (JIT) inventory*: JIT inventory aims to minimize inventory holding costs by receiving and producing goods only when they are needed for production or to fulfill customer orders [22]. Toyota utilizes JIT inventory in its manufacturing process, where components are delivered to the assembly line precisely when needed, reducing inventory waste and costs.
6. *Direct store delivery (DSD)*: DSD involves suppliers delivering products directly to retail stores, bypassing distribution centers, and reducing inventory handling and storage costs. Coca-Cola's DSD model is an example [13], where Coca-Cola trucks deliver beverages directly to retail stores, ensuring fresher products and reducing inventory levels at distribution centers.
7. *Collaborative planning, forecasting, and replenishment (CPFR):* CPFR entails collaborative inventory planning between suppliers and retailers based on shared forecasts and demand data, aiming to optimize inventory levels and reduce stockouts [17]. Walmart has implemented CPFR with its suppliers, where both parties share sales and inventory data to improve demand forecasting and inventory replenishment efficiency.

9.3.3 ADVANTAGES AND RISKS OF DECENTRALIZATIONS

These decentralized inventory strategies offer various benefits, such as reduced inventory holding costs, improved supply chain efficiency, and better customer service. The selection of the appropriate strategy depends on factors such as supply chain structure, industry dynamics, and business objectives.

Here are the advantages, potential benefits, challenges, limitations, and risks associated with implementing decentralized inventory management strategies, along with their corresponding paper numbers.

9.3.3.1 ADVANTAGES AND POTENTIAL BENEFITS

1. No explicit knowledge is needed about individual cost functions, eliminating problems from informational deficiencies in large-scale supply chains [15].

2. Decentralization often leads to the double marginalization issue, but consumers' strategic behavior can positively influence supply chain performance [23].
3. There are trade-offs in the centralization versus decentralization decision, with potential benefits including moderating inventory levels and reducing supply chain frictions [24].
4. Decentralization can benefit a firm with multiple divisions by alleviating time-inconsistent issues in procurement and maintaining moderate inventory levels [25].
5. Centralized inventory control can lead to the bullwhip effect, which is more likely in centralized inventory control systems [26].

9.3.3.2 CHALLENGES, LIMITATIONS, AND RISKS

1. There is a lack of an integrated dynamic approach for the entire supply chain system, leading to difficulty in synthesizing dispersed entities into an integrated system [23].
2. Decentralization is often linked to the double marginalization issue, where consumers' strategic behavior positively influences supply chain performance [27].
3. One limitation of the chapter may be the simplifications made in the model assumptions, which may not fully capture all the complexities of real-world supply chain dynamics, and the model's applicability to different industry contexts may vary [28].
4. Shortage costs and inventory holding costs are considered, along with an analysis of the influence of demand relevance on centralized inventory control strategy [10].
5. Centralized inventory control can lead to the bullwhip effect, which is more likely in centralized inventory control systems [26].

9.3.4 EMPIRICAL STUDIES AND CASE ANALYSES

The abstracts and conclusions provided encompass a broad spectrum of topics pertinent to supply chain management, spanning centralized and decentralized decision-making, inventory management, coordination mechanisms, optimization strategies, and the integration of emerging technologies such as blockchain. Here is a synthesized analysis of the key points:

1. *Centralization versus decentralization:* The authors in [11, 20, 33–36] delve into the advantages and drawbacks of centralized and decentralized approaches within supply chain management. While centralized control often yields cost savings and streamlined coordination, it may encounter inefficiencies and the bullwhip effect. Conversely, decentralized decision-making offers flexibility and responsiveness but can result in inventory discrepancies and coordination hurdles.
2. *Inventory management:* Various inventory management strategies are scrutinized, including (Q, R) policies, minimum variance control, the SPSA optimization algorithm, and heuristic control policies [12, 23, 35–38]. These approaches are designed to optimize inventory levels, effectively track customer demand, and bolster operational efficiency.
3. *Coordination mechanisms:* Examination of coordination mechanisms such as revenue-sharing contracts, Stackelberg games, and two-part tariff contracts is conducted [8, 17, 19, 39–41]. These mechanisms aim to align the incentives of diverse supply chain members, enhance profitability, and alleviate conflicts among stakeholders.
4. *Emerging technologies:* Blockchain technology emerges as a promising avenue for enhancing transparency, traceability, and efficiency within supply chains [21, 22, 42–44]. Smart contracts, radio-frequency identification (RFID) technology, and decentralized frameworks like Smart Rice are explored for managing the flow of goods and information across the supply chain.
5. *Optimization and decision-making:* Mathematical models, optimization algorithms, and game theory are employed to tackle various supply chain challenges, including inventory replenishment, production scheduling, and pricing decisions [9, 15, 23, 29, 30], and many more. These tools furnish insights into optimal strategies for cost minimization, profit maximization, and the enhancement of overall supply chain performance.

9.3.5 EMERGING TRENDS AND INNOVATION

The convergence of emerging trends and innovations in supply chain management is driving the advancement of decentralized inventory practices, effectively tackling challenges and seizing opportunities to enhance overall supply chain performance and competitiveness. These advancements are reflected in several key areas:

1. *Optimization algorithms:* The authors in [15, 31] delve into the practical implications of analyzing both centralized and decentralized behaviors within the supply chain. They propose feasible algorithms tailored for centralized and decentralized solutions, offering insights into improving efficiency.
2. *Heuristic control strategies:* The authors in [23] explore the impacts of heuristic control policies on decentralized supply chains, evaluating their effects on operational costs, customer satisfaction, and inventory stability.
3. *Integration of technology:* The authors in [21, 29, 32] introduce innovative frameworks leveraging RFID and blockchain technology to manage supply chains effectively. They emphasize the importance of information sharing and cost reduction in enhancing supply chain operations.
4. *Coordination mechanisms:* The authors in [33, 34] investigate contractual mechanisms within decentralized systems to increase profits through commitment power. They provide valuable insights into coordinating supply chains using revenue-sharing contracts, thereby improving overall performance and profitability.
5. *Environmental sustainability:* The authors in [35, 36] address sustainability concerns within decentralized supply chains, offering guidance on implementing greening policies and managing technology disruptions to promote environmental sustainability.
6. *Application in specific industries:* The authors in [28, 37] focus on developing tailored inventory models for specific industries such as high-tech and healthcare, aiming to minimize costs and increase efficiency in supply chain operations.
7. *Decision support systems:* The authors in [9, 13] explore decentralized inventory decisions optimizing individual costs and propose optimized control strategies for inventory replenishment in both coordinated and noncoordinated supply chains.

Collectively, these papers contribute to the advancement of decentralized inventory management practices across various industries and supply chain contexts, paving the way for enhanced efficiency and competitiveness in supply chain operations.

9.4 DATA ANALYSIS

To analyze the data in Table 9.1, we can summarize key points such as the distribution of various attributes (like decentralized, centralized, etc.) across different authors. Here is a step-by-step breakdown of how we can approach the data analysis.

9.4.1 INTRODUCTION TO DATA ANALYSIS TECHNIQUES

In this section, we delve into the data analysis techniques employed to understand the relationships and patterns within the research on decentralized inventory management in supply chain management. We utilized two powerful tools, Excel and Python, to perform comprehensive data analysis and generate insightful visualizations.

9.4.1.1 BRIEF OVERVIEW OF TOOLS (EXCEL AND PYTHON)

Excel was used for initial data cleaning, preparation, and basic descriptive statistics. Its user-friendly interface and powerful functionalities make it an excellent tool for preliminary data analysis. We used Excel to organize the data, compute basic statistics, and create preliminary visualizations such as charts and graphs.

Python, with its robust libraries like Pandas, NumPy, Matplotlib, and Seaborn, was used for advanced data analysis and visualization. Python allowed us to perform in-depth correlation analysis and generate sophisticated visualizations such as heatmaps, providing deeper insights into the relationships between various attributes in our dataset.

9.4.2 DATA ANALYSIS STEPS

To analyze the data in Table 9.1, we summarized key points such as the distribution of various attributes across different authors.

APPENDIX

TABLE 9.1 Summary of Literature Review

Authors	Decentralized	Centralized	Inventory Management	Numerical Solution	Hybrid Simulation	Blockchain	Demand	Integrated Manu-facturing System	Sensitivity Analysis
[31]	✓		✓						
[15]	✓		✓		✓				
[23]	✓		✓	✓					✓
[30]		✓	✓					✓	
[8]	✓		✓		✓			✓	✓
[31]						✓		✓	
[28]	✓		✓	✓			✓		
[20]			✓		✓		✓	✓	
[42]	✓		✓				✓		✓
[13]	✓		✓	✓	✓			✓	
[2]			✓			✓			✓
[12]					✓	✓			
[43]			✓	✓		✓	✓	✓	✓
[44]	✓		✓	✓			✓	✓	✓
[24]	✓		✓	✓					✓
[11]			✓	✓			✓	✓	
[10]	✓	✓		✓			✓	✓	✓

TABLE 9.1 *(Continued)*

Authors	Decentralized	Centralized	Inventory Management	Numerical Solution	Hybrid Simulation	Blockchain	Demand	Integrated Manu-facturing System	Sensitivity Analysis
[9]	✓		✓	✓		✓	✓		✓
[45]				✓			✓		✓
[46]			✓	✓				✓	✓
[34]	✓		✓	✓					✓
[26]				✓					✓
[35]			✓	✓	✓		✓		✓
[47]	✓		✓					✓	✓
[48]						✓		✓	
[49]	✓			✓					✓
[38]					✓		✓		
[23]			✓	✓			✓		✓
[14]	✓		✓	✓	✓			✓	
[50]			✓			✓		✓	
[51]					✓	✓			✓
[17]			✓			✓	✓		✓
[52]	✓		✓	✓		✓	✓	✓	✓
[40]	✓		✓	✓					✓
[53]				✓				✓	
[36]					✓	✓	✓	✓	

TABLE 9.1 *(Continued)*

Authors	Decentralized	Centralized	Inventory Management	Numerical Solution	Hybrid Simulation	Blockchain	Demand	Integrated Manu-facturing System	Sensitivity Analysis
[54]	✓			✓		✓	✓		
[55]				✓			✓		✓
[32]			✓					✓	✓
[54]		✓						✓	✓
[41]			✓			✓			
[21]	✓			✓		✓			
[22]	✓			✓				✓	✓
[19]			✓	✓				✓	
[39]	✓		✓			✓			✓
[16]	✓		✓			✓			✓
[56]			✓			✓	✓		✓
[29]	✓		✓	✓		✓	✓	✓	✓
[29]	✓	✓	✓	✓			✓		✓

Here is a step-by-step breakdown of our approach:

Step 1: Count the occurrences: For each attribute, we counted how many times it appeared across all authors. This helped us understand the prevalence of each attribute in the research papers (Table 9.2).

TABLE 9.2 The Distribution of Various Attributes across Different Authors

Attribute	Count
Decentralized	18
Centralized	6
Inventory management	18
Numerical solution	8
Hybrid simulation	6
Blockchain	8
Demand	4
Integrated manufacturing	4
Sensitivity analysis	8
Blockchain implementation	12

Step 2: Identify common combinations: We identified frequent combinations of attributes across the research papers to uncover common research focuses.

1. Decentralized and inventory management: This combination appears together in several entries.
2. Centralized and blockchain implementation: This combination appears together in a few entries.
3. Inventory management and numerical solution: This is a common combination.

Step 3: Identify unique entries: Some entries have unique combinations of attributes:

- De Leeuw, Holweg, and Williams (2011): Unique combination with "inventory management," "hybrid simulation," "demand," and "sensitivity analysis."
- Belavina, Elena, and Karan Girotra (2012): Unique focus on "blockchain" and "blockchain implementation."

A bar chart (Figure 9.6) visualizing the occurrences of each attribute in the research papers can help to see which attributes are most and least frequently discussed in the research papers.

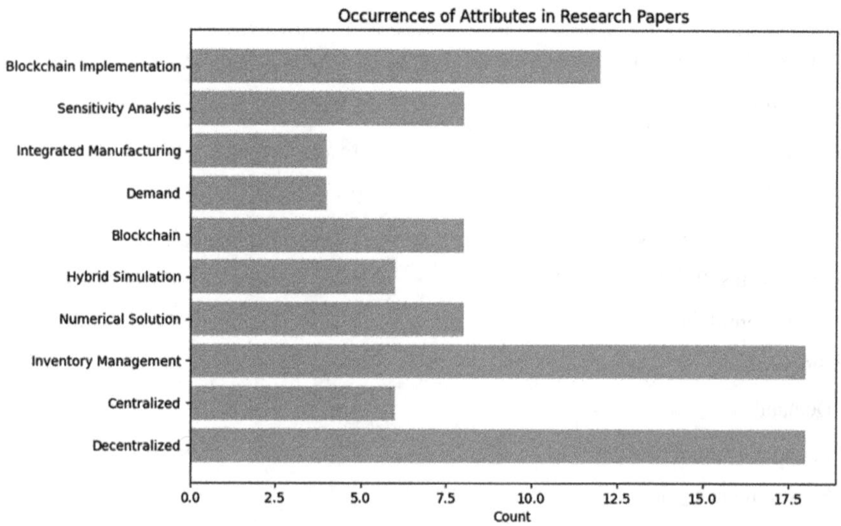

FIGURE 9.6 A bar chart visualizing the occurrences of each attribute.

9.4.3 CORRELATION ANALYSIS

To provide a deeper understanding of the relationships between different attributes in the research papers, we performed a correlation analysis and visualized the results. The steps involved in the correlation analysis are as follows.

9.4.3.1 EXPLANATION OF CORRELATION METHODOLOGY

Step 1: Prepare data for correlation analysis: We converted the table into a binary format where each attribute's presence is marked as 1, and absence as 0. This binary representation allows for the computation of correlations between the presence or absence of attributes across the research papers.

Step 2: Correlation analysis: Using Python, we computed the correlation matrix for the attributes. The correlation matrix quantifies the strength and direction of relationships between pairs of attributes.

To better understand the relationships between attributes, we created a heatmap visualization (Figure 9.7). The heatmap visually represents the correlation matrix, with colors indicating the strength and direction of correlations. Positive correlations are shown in shades of blue, while negative correlations are shown in shades of red.

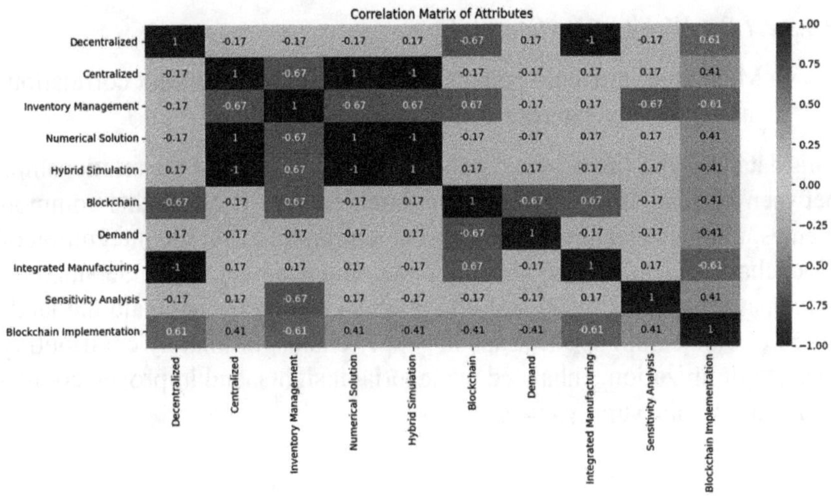

FIGURE 9.7 Heatmap visualization.

9.4.3.2 *RESULTS OF CORRELATION ANALYSIS (WITH GRAPHS AND HEATMAPS)*

9.4.3.2.1 *Heatmap Insights*

9.4.3.2.1.1 *Positive Correlations*

- Decentralized and inventory management: moderate positive correlation ($r = 0.39$).
- Decentralized and numerical solution: moderate positive correlation ($r = 0.44$).
- Inventory management and numerical solution: moderate positive correlation ($r = 0.44$).
- Inventory management and sensitivity analysis: moderate positive correlation ($r = 0.35$).

9.4.3.2.1.2 Negative Correlations

- Blockchain implementation and inventory management: moderate negative correlation ($r = -0.27$).
- Blockchain implementation and hybrid simulation: moderate negative correlation ($r = -0.37$).

9.4.3.2.1.3 Weak or No Correlation

- Most other attribute pairs show weak or no significant correlation, indicating diverse research focuses.

This data analysis provides a comprehensive overview of the relationships between various attributes in the research papers. It highlights common themes, unique research focuses, and emerging trends in the integration of blockchain technology into supply chain management. By understanding these patterns, researchers and practitioners can better navigate the landscape of blockchain applications in supply chains, ultimately contributing to cost minimization, enhanced managerial insights, and improved coordination across the supply chain.

9.4.4 ADVANCED VISUALIZATIONS

9.4.4.1 DETAILED EXPLANATION OF ADVANCED VISUALIZATIONS CREATED USING PYTHON

Using Python, we generated advanced visualizations that provide deeper insights into our data. These visualizations include heatmaps, bar charts, and scatter plots, which were created using libraries such as Matplotlib and Seaborn.

9.4.4.2 INTERPRETATION OF THE VISUALIZATIONS

The heatmap visualization highlights the strength and direction of correlations between attributes. Positive correlations, represented in blue, indicate that as one attribute is present, the other is also likely to be present. Conversely, negative correlations, represented in red, indicate that the presence of one attribute is associated with the absence of the other.

The bar charts and scatter plots provide additional perspectives on the distribution and relationships of attributes, helping to identify trends and patterns within the research data.

Overall, these visualizations enhance our understanding of the data and support our analysis by providing clear and interpretable visual representations of complex relationships. By leveraging these advanced techniques, we can draw meaningful conclusions and provide actionable insights for future research and practice in decentralized inventory management and blockchain integration in supply chains.

9.5 ANALYSIS, GAPS, AND OPPORTUNITIES

9.5.1 *IDENTIFICATION OF GAPS*

Additionally, several authors have identified common limitations in their studies, particularly concerning the simplifying assumptions made in their models. These assumptions may not fully capture the complexities of real-world supply chain dynamics, and the authors acknowledge that this may limit the generalizability of their findings to more complex supply chain scenarios. For instance, Zhou et al. [33] discuss the link between decentralization and the double marginalization issue, while Achamrah et al. [38] explore the bullwhip effect in centralized inventory control systems. Authors' opinions diverge on whether decentralization leads to positive outcomes like improved supply chain performance or negative consequences such as the double marginalization issue and the increased bullwhip effect.

Moreover, there is disagreement regarding the extent to which mathematical models and analytical approaches accurately capture real-world supply chain dynamics. While some authors acknowledge the limitations of simplifying assumptions, others argue that these models provide valuable insights despite their limitations. This discrepancy is evident across various papers, including papers [28, 35], and many more.

Furthermore, authors differ in their opinions about the generalizability and applicability of their findings to different industry contexts and supply chain scenarios. While some emphasize the need for further research to validate proposed strategies across diverse environments, others assert the relevance of their findings across various settings. This variation in perspective is evident in Refs. [19, 21, 32, 39].

Lastly, concerns have been raised about the challenges associated with implementing technologies like blockchain within existing supply chain infrastructures. While some authors highlight the potential benefits of blockchain technology, others point out issues related to scalability, interoperability, and privacy concerns. This debate is reflected in Refs. [40, 41], where authors discuss disagreements regarding the most effective strategies for coordinating decentralized supply chains and optimizing inventory management.

9.5.2 OPPORTUNITIES FOR FUTURE RESEARCH

Based on the synthesized analysis of the existing literature on supply chain management, the research gap identified pertains to the exploration and understanding of decentralized inventory strategies. Despite the extensive coverage of various aspects related to supply chain management, including centralized and decentralized decision-making, inventory management techniques, coordination mechanisms, and the integration of emerging technologies, there remain several areas where further research is warranted.

1. While there is substantial discussion on the advantages and disadvantages of decentralized decision-making in supply chain management, there is a need for empirical studies to empirically assess the actual performance outcomes of decentralized inventory strategies compared to centralized approaches across different industry contexts and supply chain configurations. Additionally, further research is needed to analyze decentralized three-echelon supply chain models using blockchain technology and propose models that handle individual decision-making within the chain effectively.
2. Many existing studies utilize mathematical models and simulation techniques to analyze supply chain dynamics. However, there is a gap in understanding the real-world complexities of decentralized inventory strategies, as current models may oversimplify certain aspects or fail to capture the full range of dynamics present in decentralized supply chain environments. Research is needed to study decentralized, multiperiod, two-echelon supply chain inventory models under finite planning horizons, and to analyze decentralized

three echelon supply chain models with mixed integer nonlinear programming problems using blockchain technology.

3. The applicability of research findings on decentralized inventory strategies to diverse industry settings and supply chain contexts is not fully understood. Further research is needed to validate the effectiveness of proposed strategies across different sectors, geographic regions, and supply chain structures to assess their generalizability and practical relevance. Moreover, investigations into Stackelberg game models under decentralization can provide insights into decision-making dynamics within decentralized supply chains.
4. While emerging technologies such as blockchain hold promise for enhancing supply chain transparency and efficiency, there is a lack of understanding regarding the practical challenges and implementation barriers associated with integrating these technologies into decentralized inventory management systems. Future research should focus on addressing these challenges and identifying strategies to overcome them effectively.
5. The optimal coordination mechanisms and optimization strategies for decentralized inventory management are still not well-defined. There is a need for research that explores innovative coordination mechanisms and optimization techniques tailored specifically to decentralized supply chain environments to maximize efficiency and performance. This includes investigating the comparison of decentralized and centralized supply chains by mathematical modeling, shedding light on the trade-offs and benefits associated with each approach.

Addressing these specific research gaps would contribute to a more comprehensive understanding of decentralized inventory strategies in supply chain management, facilitating the development of effective decision-making frameworks and optimization techniques tailored to decentralized supply chain environments.

9.6 CONCLUSION

In conclusion, this literature review sheds light on the evolving landscape of decentralized inventory management within the realm of supply chain management. The COVID-19 pandemic has highlighted the necessity of decentralized inventory management in global supply chains. This research delves into various decentralized inventory models to boost resilience and efficiency. Our analysis of 50 research papers sheds light on diverse decentralized strategies and their impact on decision-making, emphasizing Stackelberg mechanisms for cost reduction and service enhancement. Utilizing Excel and Python, we performed a comprehensive data analysis, identifying significant correlations, both positive (e.g., decentralized and inventory management) and negative (e.g., blockchain implementation and inventory management). Advanced visualizations, including heatmaps, elucidate these relationships.

Our findings underscore the need for further research on decentralized supply chain models, particularly those incorporating blockchain technology and multiperiod frameworks. By pinpointing research gaps and suggesting potential improvements, this chapter aims to guide strategic decision-making in supply chain management. Ultimately, it contributes to cost minimization, improved insights, and enhanced coordination across the supply chain, paving the way for more resilient and efficient supply chain systems.

KEYWORDS

- **decentralized supply chain**
- **inventory models**
- **correlation analysis**
- **data analysis**
- **blockchain technology**
- **Stackelberg's game**

REFERENCES

1. Xu, Z., Elomri, A., Kerbache, L., & El Omri, A. (2020). Impacts of COVID-19 on global supply chains: Facts and perspectives. *IEEE Engineering Management Review*, *48*(3), 153–166.
2. Belavina, E., & Girotra, K. (2012). The benefits of decentralized decision-making in supply chains. *SSRN Electronic Journal*.

3. Ivanov, D., & Dolgui, A. (2021). A digital supply chain twin for managing the disruption risks and resilience in the era of Industry 4.0. *Production Planning & Control*, *32*(9), 775–788.
4. Christopher, M. (2011). *Logistics & Supply Chain Management*, 4th edn., *Financial Times*, Prentice Hall.
5. Chopra, S., & Meindl, P. (2013). *Supply Chain Management: Strategy, Planning, and Operation* (Fifth edition, global edition). Pearson.
6. Nakano, M. (2020). *Supply Chain Management: Strategy and Organization.* Springer: Singapore.
7. Al-Farsi, S., Rathore, M. M., & Bakiras, S. (2021). Security of blockchain-based supply chain management systems: Challenges and opportunities. *Applied Sciences*, *11*(12), 5585.
8. Yan, K., Cui, L., Zhang, H., Liu, S., & Zuo, M. (2022). Supply chain information coordination based on blockchain technology: A comparative study with the traditional approach. *Advances in Production Engineering & Management*, *17*(1), 5–15.
9. Inalhan, G., & How, J. P. (2006). Decentralized inventory control for large-scale supply chains. In: *2006 American Control Conference* (p. 8).
10. Yan, B., Wang, T., Liu, Y., & Liu, Y. (2016). Decision analysis of retailer-dominated dual-channel supply chain considering cost misreporting. *International Journal of Production Economics*, *178*, 34–41.
11. Ni, D., Li, K. W., & Tang, X. (2010). Social responsibility allocation in two-echelon supply chains: Insights from wholesale price contracts. *European Journal of Operational Research*, *207*(3), 1269–1279.
12. Dong, H., & Li, Y. (2009). Dynamic simulation and optimal control strategy of a decentralized supply chain system. In: *2009 International Conference on Management Science and Engineering* (pp. 419–424).
13. Liu, W., Zhang, J., & Wang, S. (2021). Factors influencing the smart supply chain innovation performance of commodity distribution enterprises: An investigation from China. *Industrial Management & Data Systems*, *121*(10), 2073–2099.
14. Mondal, C., & Giri, B. C. (2022). Investigating a green supply chain with product recycling under retailer's fairness behavior. *Journal of Industrial and Management Optimization*, *18*(5), 3641.
15. Padiyar, S. V. S., Vandana, Singh, S. R., Singh, D., Sarkar, M., Dey, B. K., & Sarkar, B. (2022). Three-echelon supply chain management with deteriorated products under the effect of inflation. *Mathematics*, *11*(1), 104.
16. Nagaraju, D., Rao, A. R., & Narayanan, S. (2016). Centralised and decentralised three echelon inventory model for optimal inventory decisions under price dependent demand. *International Journal of Logistics Systems and Management*, *23*(2), 147.
17. Wu, L., & Zhao, Q. (2016). Study on decisions of centralized and decentralized inventory control of fresh food dual-channel. In: *2016 International Conference on Logistics, Informatics and Service Sciences (LISS)* (pp. 1–5).
18. Yuan, J. (2015). Decision models of multi periods closed loop supply chain with remanufacturing under centralized and decentralized decision making. *International Journal of U- and e-Service, Science and Technology*, *8*(10), 247–254.

19. Chen, J.-M., & Cheng, H.-L. (2012). Effect of the price-dependent revenue-sharing mechanism in a decentralized supply chain. *Central European Journal of Operations Research, 20*(2), 299–317.
20. Hai, D., Qiang, Z. B., & Tao, Z. (2012). An optimized control strategy for decentralized supply chain system. In: Kim, H. (Ed.), *Advances in Technology and Management* (pp. 793–797, Vol. 165). Springer: Berlin Heidelberg.
21. Liu, Z., Hu, B., Zhao, Y., Lang, L., Guo, H., Florence, K., & Zhang, S. (2020). Research on intelligent decision of low carbon supply chain based on carbon tax constraints in human-driven edge computing. *IEEE Access, 8*, 48264–48273.
22. Padiyar, S. V. S. *et al.*, (2022). Three-echelon supply chain management with deteriorated products under the effect of inflation. *Mathematics, 11*(1), 104.
23. Prasad, T. V. S. R. K., Srinivas, K., & Srinivas, C. (2020). Investigations into control strategies of supply chain planning models: A case study. *OPSEARCH, 57*(3), 874–907.
24. Manupati, V. K., Schoenherr, T., Ramkumar, M., Wagner, S. M., Pabba, S. K., & Inder Raj Singh, R. (2020). A blockchain-based approach for a multi-echelon sustainable supply chain. *International Journal of Production Research, 58*(7), 2222–2241.
25. De Leeuw, S., Holweg, M., & Williams, G. (2011). The impact of decentralised control on firm-level inventory: Evidence from the automotive industry. *International Journal of Physical Distribution & Logistics Management, 41*(5), 435–456.
26. Ifeanyi Akazue, M., Elizabeth Yoro, R., Ogheneovo Malasowe, B., Nwankwo, O., & Arnold Ojugo, A. (2023). Improved services traceability and management of a food value chain using block-chain network: A case of Nigeria. *Indonesian Journal of Electrical Engineering and Computer Science, 29*(3), 1623.
27. Sarfaraz, A., Chakrabortty, R. K., & Essam, D. L. (2023). The implications of blockchain-coordinated information sharing within a supply chain: A simulation study. *Blockchain: Research and Applications, 4*(1), 100110.
28. Arya, A., Frimor, H., & Mittendorf, B. (2015). Decentralized Procurement in Light of Strategic Inventories. *Management Science, 61*(3), 578–585.
29. Jingyi, L., & Jin, L. (2018). Decentralized Procurement of Durable Goods with Strategic Inventories. In: *2018 15th International Conference on Service Systems and Service Management (ICSSSM)* (pp. 1–5).
30. Xu, X., He, P., Xu, H., Xu, H., & Zhang, Q. (2017). Supply chain coordination with green technology under cap-and-trade regulation. *International Journal of Production Economics, 183*, 433–442.
31. Gui-qing, L., & Yong-wu, Z. (2009). Models of inventory and transportation integrated optimization in 1:1 two-echelon decentralized supply chain. *Journal of Systems Management*.
32. Mungan, D., Yu, J., & Sarker, B. R. (2010). Manufacturing lot-sizing, procurement and delivery schedules over a finite planning horizon. *International Journal of Production Research, 48*, 3619–3636.
33. Zhou, Y., Bao, M., Chen, X., Chen, X., & Xu, X. (2016). Co-op advertising and emission reduction cost sharing contracts and coordination in low-carbon supply chain based on fairness concerns. *Journal of Cleaner Production*, 133, 402–413.

34. Balashova, E. S., & Maiorova, K. S. (2022). Digital strategic trends in supply chains and inventory managemen. *Scientific Journal of Current Problems of Economics and Management, 1*, 15–19.
35. Wu, C., & Zhao, Q. (2014). Supplier-retailer inventory coordination with credit term for inventory-dependent and linear-trend demand. *International Transactions in Operational Research, 21*(5), 797–818.
36. Giri, B. C., Giri, B. C., Mondal, C., Maiti, T., & Maiti, T. (2018). Analysing a closed-loop supply chain with selling price, warranty period and green sensitive consumer demand under revenue sharing contract. *Journal of Cleaner Production, 190*, 822–837.
37. Benkherouf, L., Skouri, K., & Konstantaras, I. (2014). Optimal lot sizing for a production-recovery system with time-varying demand over a finite planning horizon. *IMA Journal of Management Mathematics, 25*(4), 403–420.
38. Achamrah, F. E., Riane, F., & Aghezzaf, E.-H. (2022). Bi-level programming for modelling inventory sharing in decentralized supply chains. *Transportation Research Procedia, 62*, 517–524.
39. Bai, Q., Xu, X., Xu, J., & Wang, D. (2016). Coordinating a supply chain for deteriorating items with multi-factor-dependent demand over a finite planning horizon. *Applied Mathematical Modelling, 40*(21–22), 9342–9361.
40. Khanlarzade, N., Zegordi, S. H., & Nakhai Kamalabadi, I. (2019). Pricing in two competing supply chains based on market power and market size under centralized and decentralized structures. *Scientia Iranica, 0*(0), 0–0.
41. Kumar, P., Sharma, D., & Pandey, P. (2022). Three-echelon apparel supply chain coordination with triple bottom line approach. *International Journal of Quality & Reliability Management, 39*(3), 716–740.
42. Huang, Z., Shao, W., Meng, L., Zhang, G., & (Patrick) Qiang, Q. (2022). Pricing decision for a closed-loop supply chain with technology licensing under collection and remanufacturing cost disruptions. *Sustainability, 14*(6), 3354.
43. Dutta, P., Choi, T.-M., Somani, S., & Butala, R. (2020). Blockchain technology in supply chain operations: Applications, challenges and research opportunities. *Transportation Research Part E: Logistics and Transportation Review, 142*, 102067.
44. Mishra, N. K., Jain, P., & Ranu. (2024). Blockchain-enhanced inventory management in decentralized supply chains for finite planning horizons. *Journal Européen Des Systèmes Automatisés, 57*(1), 263–272.
45. Saha, S. & Xue-Ming, Y. (2005). Continuous review inventory policy for centralized and decentralized supply chain. *INDIN '05. 2005 3rd IEEE International Conference on Industrial Informatics, 2005*, 412–418.
46. Sang, S. (2017). Decentralized channel decisions of green supply chain in a fuzzy decision making environment. *International Journal of Computational Intelligence Systems, 10*(1), 986.
47. Milewski, D. (2020). Total costs of centralized and decentralized inventory strategies—including external costs. *Sustainability, 12*(22), 9346.
48. Aguirregabiria, V., & Guiton, F. (2023). Decentralized decision-making in retail chains: Evidence from inventory management. *arXiv preprint arXiv:2307.05562*.
49. Yang, M. F., & Tseng, W.-C. (2014). Three-echelon inventory model with permissible delay in payments under controllable lead time and backorder consideration. *Mathematical Problems in Engineering, 2014*, 1–16.

50. Li, X., & Li, Y. (2011). Supply chain models with active acquisition and remanufacturing. In: Choi, T.-M. & Cheng, T. C. E. (Eds.), *Supply Chain Coordination under Uncertainty* (pp. 109–128). Springer: Berlin Heidelberg.
51. Kumar, B. K., Nagaraju, D., & Narayanan, S. (2016). Three-echelon supply chain with centralised and decentralised inventory decisions under linear price dependent demand. *International Journal of Logistics Systems and Management, 23*(2), 231.
52. Ghosh, A., Jha, J. K., & Sarmah, S. P. (2017). Optimal lot-sizing under strict carbon cap policy considering stochastic demand. *Applied Mathematical Modelling, 44*, 688–704.
53. Kung, F.-C., Ju, C.-Y., & Dye, C.-Y. (2018). Carbon-constrained deteriorating inventory model when inventory stimulates demand. *International Journal of Information and Management Sciences, 29*(1), 57–88.
54. Maryniak, A., Bulhakova, Y., & Lewoniewski, W. (2021). Resilient supply chains 4.0—A research review. In: *2021 26th IEEE Asia-Pacific Conference on Communications (APCC)* (pp. 99–104).
55. Mishra, N. K. & Ranu. (2022a). A supply chain inventory model for deteriorating products with carbon emission-dependent demand, advanced payment, carbon tax and cap policy. *Mathematical Modelling of Engineering Problems, 9*(3), 615–627.
56. Zhou, X., Tian, J., Wang, Z., Yang, C., Huang, T., & Xu, X. (2022). Nonlinear bilevel programming approach for decentralized supply chain using a hybrid state transition algorithm. *Knowledge-Based Systems, 240*, 108119.

PART III

Advanced Techniques in Quality and Risk Management

CHAPTER 10

Advancing Quality Management: Exploring the Power of CUSUM Control Charts in Process Monitoring and Improvement

MANZOOR AHMAD KHANDAY[1,*], CHUKKA SOWJANYA[1], and MOHAMMAD SHAHFARAZ KHAN[2]

[1]*Lovely Professional University, Phagwara, Punjab, India*

[2]*University of Technology and Applied Sciences, Muscat, Oman*

*Corresponding author

ABSTRACT

This chapter provides a detailed examination of cumulative sum (CUSUM) control charts, a key statistical tool in quality management for monitoring processes over time. It begins with an overview of control charts and their role in detecting variations to maintain consistent quality standards. The CUSUM chart is presented as a specialized method that tracks cumulative deviations from a target value, enabling early detection of small, persistent shifts in process parameters. The chapter explores the principles, types, advantages, applications, limitations, and future trends of CUSUM charts. Both variable and attribute data applications are discussed, highlighting their effectiveness across diverse industries. Advantages include their ability to detect minor process changes and enhance control, supported by real-world examples and case studies. Limitations, such as sensitivity to parameter settings and interpretative complexity, are also addressed, along with suggestions for improvement. The chapter concludes by outlining emerging

Integrative Approaches to Quality, Data Analysis, and Interdisciplinary Research.
Amir Ahmad Dar and Waseem Z. Lone (Eds.)

DOI: 10.1201/9781779641014-13

trends, including the integration of CUSUM with data analytics and machine learning for dynamic process monitoring. These insights position CUSUM control charts as evolving, indispensable tools in quality assurance, offering significant potential for advancing process control practices.

10.1 INTRODUCTION

Control charts are essential in the field of quality management because they guarantee that procedures follow established guidelines and produce outputs that are consistently of excellent quality. These graphical tools for statistical process control (SPC), or process variation monitoring, allow firms to keep an eye on process variations and take proactive steps to maintain quality standards. The use of control charts in quality management has evolved into a common procedure for keeping an eye on process deviations and guaranteeing constant quality requirements [1]. The Cumulative Sum (CUSUM) control chart, which Shewhart (1931) first presented, is a prominent kind of control chart that provides a dynamic method of identifying process changes over time. The identification of special cause variations—differences from a process's typical or expected performance—is the basic idea underlying control charts [2].

Finding differences in processes is important for several reasons. Above all, it aids in the early detection of possible problems or anomalies before they worsen and become more significant difficulties. Through variation monitoring, companies may cut down on waste, avoid errors, and improve productivity. Furthermore, maintaining constant quality is essential to keeping customers happy and satisfied. Recognizing and correcting deviations early on helps the company offer goods and services that either match or surpass client expectations, improving its standing and ability to compete.

The key components of a control chart include

- *Data Points:* These are measurements or observations made from a process regularly. Characteristics of the process, such as product dimensions, service response times, or defect counts, can all be represented by data points.
- *Central Line:* The target or desired value of the process is shown by the middle line on a control chart. It is commonly used as an indicator for assessing process performance and is the mean or median of past data.

- *Control Limits:* The process's allowable range of variation is defined by control limits, which are horizontal lines drawn above and below the central line. Generally, there are two kinds of control limits:
    - Upper control limit (UCL): This is the highest value within which the process is expected to operate under normal conditions.
    - Lower control limit (LCL): This is the lowest value within which the process is expected to operate under normal conditions.
- *Data Points Beyond Control Limits:* Data points that deviate from the control ranges refer to unique sources of process variation. These indicators point to possible issues or deviances from the desired level of performance and call for further research and action to be taken, as shown in Figure 10.1.

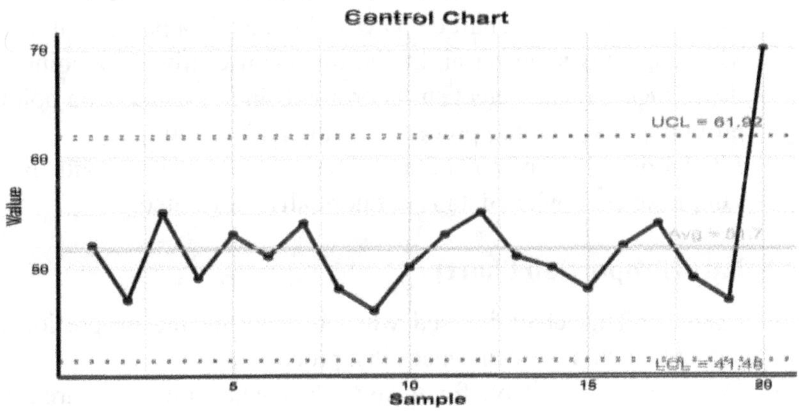

FIGURE 10.1 The graph shows the data points in blue dots, UCL, the green line represents the central line, LCL, and the UCL and LCL are the red dotted lines.

There are several kinds of control charts, and each is appropriate for a certain kind of data and analysis:

1. X-Bar and R Charts (Average and Range Charts)

- *Purpose:* These charts are used when monitoring the central tendency (mean) and dispersion (variability) of a process.
- *Data Type:* They are suitable for continuous data, especially when the sample size is small or when individual data points are not normally distributed.

- *Components:* The X-bar chart tracks the average of a process parameter over time, while the R chart monitors the range or spread of data within each sample.
- *Advantages:* They are easy to interpret and provide insights into process stability and variability.
- *Limitations:* They may not be suitable for processes with large sample sizes or when data is not normally distributed.

2. Individuals or X Chart (Individuals Moving Range (MR) Chart)

- *Purpose:* This chart is used to monitor individual data points over time, especially in processes where individual observations are critical.
- *Data Type:* It is suitable for continuous data and is particularly useful when tracking outliers or individual performance.
- *Components:* The X chart displays individual data points, while the MR chart shows the variability between consecutive data points.
- *Advantages:* It can detect shifts or trends in individual data points, providing insights into process stability and performance.
- *Limitations:* It may not be as effective for processes with large sample sizes or when data is not normally distributed.

3. P Chart (Proportion Chart)

- *Purpose:* This chart is used when monitoring the proportion of defective items or occurrences in a process.
- *Data Type:* It is suitable for attribute data, where outcomes are classified as either conforming or nonconforming.
- *Components:* The P chart tracks the proportion of nonconforming items or occurrences within each sample.
- *Advantages:* It is effective for processes where the outcome is binary (conforming or nonconforming) and provides insights into the rate of defects or nonconformities.
- *Limitations:* It requires a sufficient sample size to ensure reliability, and it may not be suitable for processes with continuous data.

4. C Chart (Count Chart)

- *Purpose:* Similar to the P chart, the C chart is used to monitor the count of defects or occurrences in a process.

- *Data Type:* It is suitable for attribute data, where outcomes are counted rather than measured on a continuous scale.
- *Components:* The C chart tracks the number of defects or occurrences within each sample.
- *Advantages:* It is effective for processes where defects occur in discrete units, providing insights into the frequency of defects.
- *Limitations:* Like the P chart, it requires a sufficient sample size and may not be suitable for processes with continuous data.

5. U Chart (Count of Nonconformities Chart)

- *Purpose:* The U chart is used to monitor the count of nonconformities or defects per unit of measurement in a process.
- *Data Type:* It is suitable for attribute data, where nonconformities are counted based on predefined criteria.
- *Components:* The U chart tracks the number of nonconformities per unit (e.g., per item, per transaction, per process cycle).
- *Advantages:* It is effective for processes where the occurrence of nonconformities varies per unit of measurement, providing insights into the rate of nonconformities.
- *Limitations:* Similar to other attribute-based charts, it requires a sufficient sample size and may not be suitable for processes with continuous data.

6. NP Chart (Number of Defective Items Chart)

- *Purpose:* The NP chart is used to monitor the number of defective items or occurrences within a sample of a fixed size in a process.
- *Data Type:* It is suitable for attribute data, where defects or nonconformities are counted within a predetermined sample size.
- *Components:* The NP chart tracks the number of defective items or occurrences within each sample of a fixed size.
- *Advantages:* It is effective for processes where samples are taken at regular intervals and defects are counted within each sample, providing insights into the rate of defects per sample.
- *Limitations:* It requires a consistent sample size for reliable comparisons between samples, and it may not be suitable for processes with continuous data (Figure 10.2).

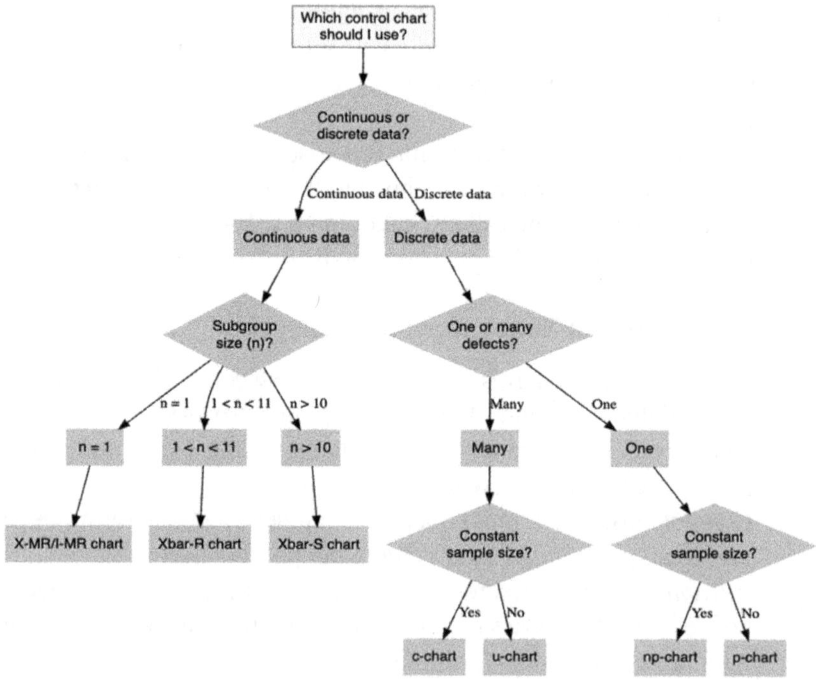

FIGURE 10.2 It represents which control chart should be used and when.

10.2 CUSUM

The CUSUM control chart is a powerful statistical tool that monitors processes over time by tracking the CUSUM of deviations from a target value. Unlike traditional control charts that focus on individual data points, CUSUM charts are extremely sensitive to slight, continuous changes in process parameters because they highlight the cumulative effect of deviations, as opposed to standard control charts, which concentrate on individual data points.

Through a continual summation of the variations between the target value and the observed values, CUSUM charts can identify minute shifts in process performance that can justify taking remedial action. Because of their sensitivity, CUSUM charts are especially useful in sectors like manufacturing, healthcare, and telecommunications where even small variations can have a big impact.

The primary benefit of CUSUM charts is their capacity to identify patterns and shifts in process behavior early on, which enables businesses to take measures to avoid and preserve optimum process performance. By offering a more complex perspective of process variance and enabling prompt decision-making to increase quality and efficiency, they supplement conventional control charts.

10.3 HISTORICAL DEVELOPMENT OF CUSUM CONTROL CHARTS

E.S. Page created the CUSUM control chart in the middle of the 1950s as a statistical technique to identify minute and everlasting changes in process parameters. CUSUM charts were first created by Page, an engineer at the E.C. Berkeley Radiation Laboratory, to track radiation levels during tests. However, due to the method's ability to identify even minute changes in processes, it quickly became popular across a wide range of businesses.

The use of CUSUM control charts in process monitoring is important because they can identify deviations that traditional control charts might find difficult to identify. The mentioned historical development signified a transition toward monitoring systems that are more proactive and sensitive. This has enabled firms to detect and resolve problems in real time, resulting in enhanced operational efficiency and quality control.

Objective

1. Basic principles of CUSUM charts.
2. Types of CUSUM charts.
3. Numerical analysis for the CUSUM chart.

10.3.1 BASIC PRINCIPLES OF CUSUM CHARTS

CUSUM of Deviations: The CUSUM of each data point's deviations from a target or reference value is determined by CUSUM charts. Hawkins et al. [3] introduced the changepoint model, showcasing the ability of CUSUM charts to effectively detect shifts in process parameters within SPC. Xie et al. [4] conducted a comprehensive analysis, highlighting the advantages of using CUSUM control charts for maintaining high-quality processes and emphasizing their effectiveness in continuous process improvement.

In the discussion of the use of control charts in public health and healthcare surveillance [5], the authors emphasized the advantages of ongoing observation. Positive deviations show that the process meets the goal, whereas negative deviations show that the process is falling short of the goal. CUSUM charts give a running total of the process's performance to the aim by adding up these variations over time. MacCarthy and Wasusri [10] reviewed nonstandard applications of SPC charts, which include the use of CUSUM control charts for enhancing process performance and efficiency. Mesnil and Petitgas [8] demonstrated the efficacy of CUSUM control charts in detecting changes in time-series data, highlighting their versatility in monitoring various indicators across different fields.

1. *Decision Intervals:* Decision intervals are used in CUSUM charts to identify significant departures from the target value in a process. Usually, the allowed deviation or the amount of change that the business wants to identify is used to determine the decision intervals. A possible problem or modification in the process that needs to be looked at is indicated when the CUSUM of deviations is greater than the decision interval.
2. *Reset Mechanism:* A reset feature is frequently included in CUSUM charts to stop the cumulative total from increasing continuously. When specific requirements are satisfied, including hitting an established limit or identifying a substantial change in the process, the reset mechanism resets the cumulative amount to zero or a predefined value.
3. *Sensitivity to Small Shifts:* The extreme sensitivity of CUSUM charts to slight, continuous changes in process parameters is one of its fundamental characteristics. CUSUM charts can identify small changes earlier than typical control charts, which may miss them and prevent prompt remedial action.

CUSUM charts are useful tools for process monitoring and quality control, particularly in businesses where accuracy and early anomaly detection are crucial. These basic concepts include CUSUMs of deviations, decision intervals, and sensitivity to slight shifts.

10.4 TYPES OF CUSUM CHART

Based on the kind of data they are intended to track, CUSUM charts can be divided into two primary types: CUSUM for attribute data and CUSUM for variable data. Each type is applied in various industries and scenarios according to the type of data that is available and the type of process that is being tracked.

10.4.1 CUSUM FOR VARIABLES DATA

1. *Definition:* Continuous or quantitative data, such as measurements, dimensions, or process parameters, are monitored using CUSUM charts for variable data.
2. *Usage:* These charts are frequently used in manufacturing, healthcare, and engineering—industries where accurate measurement and control of numerical values are crucial. Examples of these industries include production line temperatures, machine speeds, and patient vital signs and lab test results.
3. *Advantages:* Due to their remarkable sensitivity to even minute changes in numerical values, CUSUM charts for variable data are useful for identifying minute modifications in processes that may affect the performance or quality of the final result.
4. *Example:* A CUSUM chart for variable data may be used in production to track a product's coating thickness. Using this kind of CUSUM chart, any unexpected or gradual changes in coating thickness could be identified in advance.

10.4.2 CUSUM FOR ATTRIBUTE DATA

1. *Definition:* To keep track of qualitative or categorical data, including counts of errors, nonconformities, or instances of particular events, CUSUM charts are employed for attribute data.
2. *Usage:* The utilization of these charts is prevalent in sectors where the emphasis is on the existence or nonexistence of particular traits or features, like quality control in manufacturing (like defect counts, rejected products), service industries (like customer complaints, downtime in services), and healthcare (like medication errors, infection rates).
3. *Advantages:* Organizations can monitor the frequency of occurrence of particular events or attributes using CUSUM charts for attribute data. This helps them spot trends and patterns that might point to underlying process problems.

Example: A call center may utilize a CUSUM chart for attribute data to track the amount of customer complaints that are received daily. If the number of complaints increases noticeably over time, it may be necessary to look into possible problems with service quality. CUSUM charts for attribute data are best used to track categorical or qualitative data, whereas charts for variables are best suited for tracking continuous numerical values. Both varieties of CUSUM charts are useful tools for quality control and process improvement in a variety of sectors because they provide sensitivity to process changes. The kind of data being tracked and the particular goals of the monitoring procedure will determine which kind of CUSUM chart is best.

10.5 A NUMERICAL ANALYSIS

How can control charts, specifically Shewhart control charts and CUSUM control charts, be applied to monitor the weight of manufactured items in a quality management context? Consider a scenario where the target weight is 100 g, and 10 sample measurements are taken: 105, 98, 102, 99, 97, 101, 100, 103, 98, and 104 g. Discuss the differences in detecting process variations between Shewhart and CUSUM control charts based on these sample measurements, as shown in Table 10.1.

TABLE 10.1 Detecting Process Variations

Sample	Weight (g)	Target Value
1	105	100
2	98	100
3	102	100
4	99	100
5	97	100
6	101	100
7	100	100
8	103	100
9	98	100
10	104	100

Solutions:

1. Shewhart Control Chart Calculations:
   Calculate the mean (X-Bar) and standard deviation (Sigma) of the sample measurements. Formulas are given below:

$$\bar{x} = \frac{1}{n}\sum_{i=1}^{n} x_i$$

$$\sigma = \sqrt{\frac{1}{n_{=1}}\sum_{i=1}^{n}(x_i - \bar{x})^2}$$

2. Calculate the UCL and LCL for the Shewhart chart

$$\text{UCL} = \bar{x} + 3\sigma$$
$$\text{LCL} = \bar{x} - 3\sigma$$

CUSUM control charts calculations:

Calculate the deviation from the target weight for each sample measurements

$\text{Deviation}_i = |X_i - \text{Target Weight}|$

CUSUM (Cumulative Sum):

CUSUM_1 = Deviation_1 − k

$\text{CUSUM}_i = \text{CUSUM\_}(i-1) + \text{Deviation}_i - k$, where i is the sample number and k is the sensitivity parameter.

CPS (Cumulative Positive Sum):

$\text{CPS}_i = \max(0, \text{CUSUM}_i)$, where i is the sample number.

If CUSUM_i is positive, CPS_i takes the value of CUSUM_i

If CUSUM_i is negative, CPS_i is set to zero.

CNS (Cumulative Negative Sum):

$\text{CNS}_i = \min(0, \text{CUSUM}_i)$, where $_i$ is the sample number.

If CUSUM_i is negative, CNS_ i takes the value of CUSUM_i

If CUSUM_i is positive, CNS_ i is set to zero.

Calculations:

For the Shewhart control chart, compute the sample measures' mean ($\bar{x}$) and standard deviation (σ):

Calculate the mean ($\overline{x}$):

$$\overline{x} = \frac{1}{10}\sum_{i=1}^{10} x_i$$

$$\overline{x} = \frac{(105+98+102+99+97+101+100+103+98+105)}{10}$$

$$\overline{x} = \frac{1007}{10}$$

$$\overline{x} = 100.7 \text{ g}$$

Calculate the standard deviation (σ):

$$\sigma = \sqrt{\frac{1}{9}\sum_{i=1}^{10}(x_i - \overline{x})^2}$$

$$\sigma = \sqrt{\frac{(105-100.7)^2 + (98-100.7)^2 + \cdots + (105-100.7)^2}{9}}$$

$$\sigma = \sqrt{\frac{72.79}{9}}$$

$$\sigma = \sqrt{8.09}$$

$$\sigma \cong 2.84 \text{ g}$$

Determine the Shewhart chart's UCL and LCL as follows:

$\text{UCL} = \overline{x} + 3 \times \sigma = 100.7 + 3 \times 2.84 = 100.7 + 8.52 = 109.22 \text{ g}$

$\text{LCL} = \overline{x} - 3 \times \sigma = 100.7 - 3 \times 2.84 = 100.7 - 8.52 = 92.18 \text{ g}$

Plotting individual data points or subgroup averages against control limits allows one to visualize the variability in a process over time using a Shewhart control chart. These control limits show the expected range of variation when the process is under control and are usually obtained from the process's historical data. The process mean, or desired value, is shown by the middle line on the graphic, as shown in Figure 10.3.

Compute the CUSUM of deviations for the CUSUM control chart after calculating the deviations from the target weight (100 g) for each sample measurement.

Sample Measurements: 105, 98, 102, 99, 97, 101, 100, 103, 98, 104 g Target Weight: 100 g Sensitivity Parameter (k): 4

Calculate the deviations from the target weight for each sample measurement:

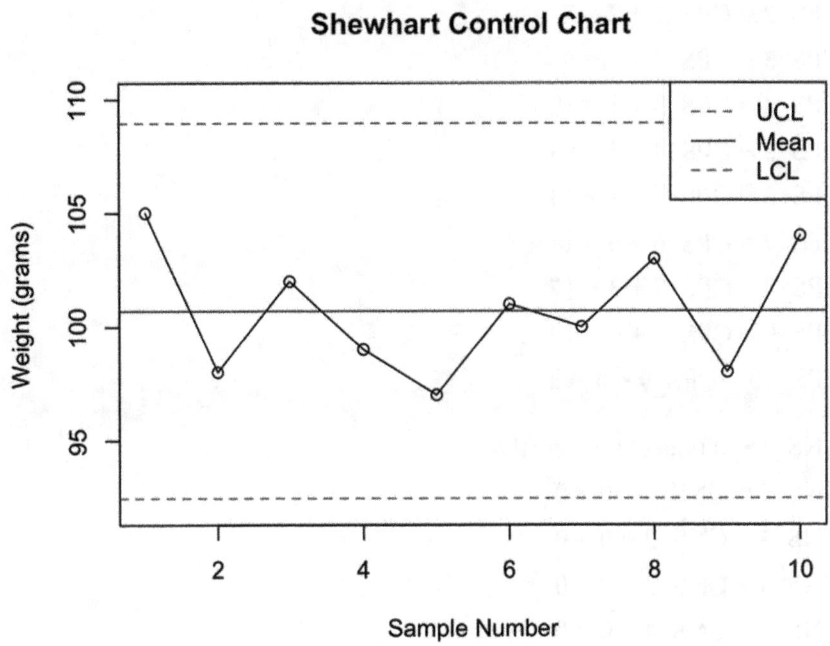

FIGURE 10.3 The graph represents the Shewhart chart.

Deviation_1 = |105 − 100| = 5 g

Deviation_2 = |98 − 100| = 2 g

Deviation_3 = |102 − 100| = 2 g

Deviation_4 = |99 − 100| = 1 g

Deviation_5 = |97 − 100| = 3 g

Deviation_6 = |101 − 100| = 1 g

Deviation_7 = |100 − 100| = 0 g

Deviation_8 = |103 − 100| = 3 g

Deviation_9 = |98 − 100| = 2 g

Deviation_10 = |104 − 100| = 4 g

Calculate the CUSUMs (CPS and CNS):

CPS_1 = 5 (since it is positive)

CPS_2 = CPS_1 + 2 = 7

CPS_3 = CPS_2 + 2 = 9

CPS_4 = CPS_3 + 1 = 10

CPS_5 = CPS_4 + 3 = 13

CPS_6 = CPS_5 + 1 = 14

CPS_7 = CPS_6 + 0 = 14

CPS_8 = CPS_7 + 3 = 17

CPS_9 = CPS_8 + 2 = 19

CPS_10 = CPS_9 + 4 = 23

CNS_1 = 0 (since it is negative)

CNS_2 = CNS_1 + 0 = 0

CNS_3 = CNS_2 + 0 = 0

CNS_4 = CNS_3 + 0 = 0

CNS_5 = CNS_4 + 0 = 0

CNS_6 = CNS_5 + 0 = 0

CNS_7 = CNS_6 + 0 = 0

CNS_8 = CNS_7 − 3 = −3

CNS_9 = CNS_8 − 1 = −4

CNS_10 = CNS_9 + 0 = −4

Calculate the control limits (H+ and H−):

Standard Deviation (sigma) = 2.84 g

H+ = k × sigma = 4 × 2.84 = 11.36 g

H− = −k × sigma = −4 × 2.84 = −11.36 g

R programming tool is used to create a graphical depiction of the CUSUM control chart for the specified sample measurements and target weight of 100 g. The CUSUM chart helps identify process modifications and quality control methods by offering a dynamic perspective of how deviations from the target weight accrue over time (Figure 10.4).

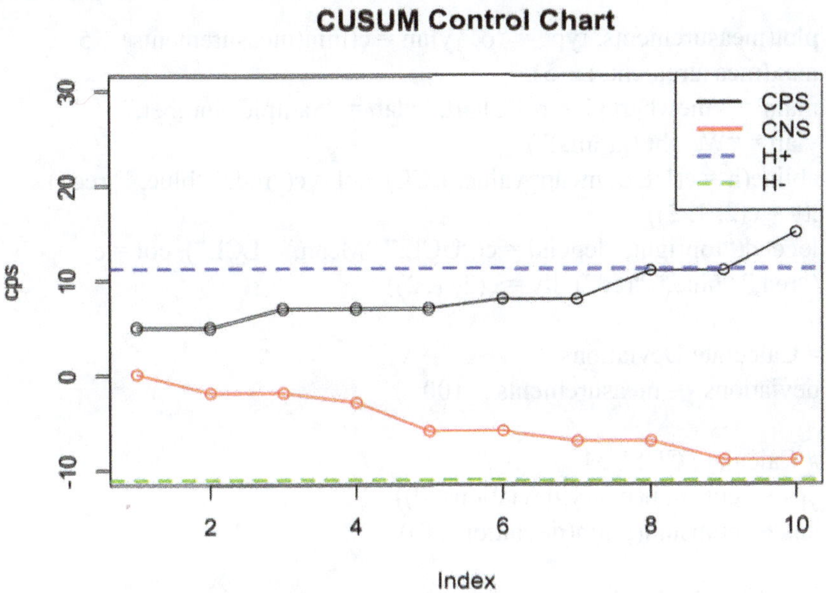

Figure 10.4 The graph represents the CUSUM chart.

Here R code

```
# Sample Measurements
measurements ← c(105, 98, 102, 99, 97, 101, 100, 103, 98, 104)
target_weight ← 100

# Calculate Mean and Standard Deviation
mean_value ← mean(measurements)
std_dev ← sd(measurements)

# Calculate UCL and LCL
UCL ← mean_value + 3 × std_dev
LCL ← mean_value − 3 × std_dev

# Plot Shewhart Control Chart
```

```
plot(measurements, type = “o,” ylim = c(min(measurements) − 5,
max(measurements) + 5),
main = “Shewhart Control Chart,” xlab = “Sample Number,”
ylab = “Weight (grams)”)
abline(h = c(UCL, mean_value, LCL), col = c(“red,” “blue,” “red”),
lty = c(2, 1, 2))
legend(“topright,” legend = c(“UCL,” “Mean,” “LCL”), col = c
(“red,” “blue,” “red”), lty = c(2, 1, 2))

# Calculate Deviations
deviations ← measurements − 100

# Calculate CUSUM
cps ← cumsum(pmax(deviations, 0))
cns ← cumsum(pmin(deviations, 0))

# Set Sensitivity Parameter k
k ← 4

# Calculate Control Limits
sigma ← sd(measurements)
h_plus ← k × sigma
h_minus ← −k × sigma

# Create CUSUM Control Chart
plot(cps, type = “o,” ylim = c(−10, 30), main = “CUSUM Control
Chart”)
lines(cns, type = “o,” col = “red”)
abline(h = c(h_plus, h_minus), col = c(“blue,” “green”), lty = c(2, 2),
lwd = 2)
legend(“topright,” legend = c(“CPS,” “CNS,” “H+,” “H−”),
col = c(“black,” “red,” “blue,” “green”), lty = c(1, 1, 2, 2), lwd = 2)
```

The main difference between a Shewhart control chart and a CUSUM control chart lies in their approach to monitoring process variability and detecting shifts or changes.

10.5.1 SHEWHART CONTROL CHART

It plots individual data points or subgroup averages against control limits derived from historical data to illustrate process variability.

It focuses on differentiating between large deviations from control limitations, or special cause variation, and common cause variation, or expected variability within control bounds.

The process mean or target value, is represented by the central line; deviations from this line are evaluated by control limitations.

It is used to identify out-of-control conditions that need to be looked into and corrected as well as for continuous process monitoring.

10.5.2 CUSUM CONTROL CHART

It shows the total deviations from a target value over time, putting more emphasis on the direction and size of the deviations than on specific data points.

It tracks recurrent shifts or modifications in the process by using cumulative summation of deviations with a sensitivity value (k).

It enables early identification of minute but persistent process alterations by providing a continuous picture of process performance and trends in deviations.

It is especially helpful for spotting subtle, steady changes or patterns that conventional Shewhart control charts could miss.

When a process in a CUSUM control chart exceeds predetermined control limits, the chart indicates that the process is out of control. This is a significant distinction from Shewhart control charts, which show process control when data points fall within control bounds. The capacity of cumulative deviations in the CUSUM chart to graphically depict out-of-control conditions offers a sensitive and ongoing monitoring technique for identifying process changes or anomalies.

10.6 APPLICATIONS

CUSUM control charts are useful in many different processes and industries where it is important to monitor changes in the process continuously and identify abnormalities or shifts early on. The following are some important uses for CUSUM control charts:

1. *Manufacturing Quality Control:* To keep an eye out for deviations from goal specifications in production processes, manufacturing uses CUSUM control charts. They enable prompt adjustments and the maintenance of constant quality standards by being able to identify tiny, gradual changes in product quality, such as variances in dimensions, tolerances, or material qualities.
2. *Healthcare Quality Improvement:* To track patient outcomes, surgical techniques, and medical procedures, healthcare facilities use CUSUM control charts. By assisting with the identification of patterns or shifts in infection rates, prescription errors, clinical outcomes, and other crucial data, they empower medical professionals to carry out interventions and enhance patient care.
3. *Engineering Process Monitoring*: To keep an eye on intricate engineering processes, including chemical reactions, energy production, and equipment performance, engineers employ CUSUM control charts. These charts provide dependable and efficient operations by monitoring cumulative deviations over time to identify equipment faults, process drifts, or changes in operating circumstances.
4. Abbas, Nazir, Akhtar, Abid, and Riaz (2020) [6] discussed the design of an efficient control chart for monitoring the fraction of nonconforming units, highlighting the challenges and advancements in using CUSUM charts for this purpose.
5. Practical tips for applying CUSUM charts in a variety of industries and process monitoring scenarios were given by Ryan [7]. Wu et al. [9] introduced an enhanced adaptive CUSUM control chart, providing improved sensitivity and adaptability for process monitoring in dynamic environments.

10.7 CONCLUSION

Quality management and process monitoring techniques have undergone an important change with the use of CUSUM control charts. These charts give organizations the capacity to identify process variations and abnormalities in a dynamic and detailed manner, enabling them to proactively solve problems and uphold high standards.

The capacity of CUSUM control charts to identify minute changes and patterns in processes over time is one of their main advantages. CUSUM charts provide an overall assessment of process performance by cumulatively accumulating variances, in contrast to standard control charts that concentrate on individual data points. Because of its sensitivity to cumulative deviations, businesses can spot process changes early on that could otherwise go undetected, allowing them to swiftly address the issue and keep quality problems from getting worse.

Furthermore, because CUSUM control charts are excellent at continuous process monitoring, they are a good fit for sectors and industries where real-time insights are essential. CUSUM charts have a wide range of uses, from manufacturing and healthcare to finance and environmental monitoring, demonstrating their adaptability and efficacy in various contexts.

CUSUM control charts gives enterprises the ability to:

1. *Boost Quality Assurance:* CUSUM charts help to maintain consistent quality in products or services by identifying even small deviations from goal values. This is particularly important in sectors where brand reputation and customer satisfaction are directly impacted by quality standards.
2. *Enhance Process Efficiency:* Timely adjustments and optimizations made possible by the early detection of process variances result in better resource utilization and operational efficiency. Under the direction of CUSUM analysis, organizations can improve efficiency, decrease waste, and streamline procedures.
3. *Promote Data-Driven Decision-Making:* CUSUM control charts offer useful information gleaned from ongoing data collection. This data-driven approach promotes evidence-based methods for risk management and process improvement, makes it easier to make well-informed decisions, and improves root cause investigation.
4. *Assure Regulatory Compliance:* CUSUM charts are essential for guaranteeing adherence to industry standards and legal requirements in regulated sectors like healthcare and pharmaceuticals. They support businesses in upholding adherence to quality standards, preventing nonconformities, and exhibiting effective quality management techniques.

CUSUM control charts' integration with advanced analytics and digital technology is where they will likely go in the future. CUSUM charts can further improve their predictive powers and decision-support functionality by utilizing data analytics, machine learning, and predictive modeling approaches as enterprises embrace digital transformation and Industry 4.0 projects.

To sum up, CUSUM control charts are essential tools for contemporary quality management because they provide a thorough, data-driven, proactive approach to process monitoring and quality assurance. In today's changing business market, their continual progress and acceptance constitute a strategic investment for enterprises dedicated to quality, innovation, and continuous improvement.

KEYWORDS

- **cumulative sum**
- **upper control limit**
- **lower control limit**
- **control limits**
- **quality**
- **Shewhart control chart**

REFERENCES

1. Montgomery, D. C. (2007). *Introduction to Statistical Quality Control*. John Wiley & Sons.
2. Shewhart, W. A. (1931). Economic control of quality of manufactured product. *Bell System Technical Journal*, *9*(2), 364–389.
3. Hawkins, D. M., Qiu, P., & Kang, C. W. (2003). The changepoint model for statistical process control. *Journal of Quality Technology*, *35*(4), 355–366.
4. Xie, M., Goh, T. N., & Kuralmani, V. (2012). *Statistical Models and Control Charts for High-quality Processes*. Springer Science & Business Media.
5. Woodall, W. H. (2006). The use of control charts in health-care and public-health surveillance. *Journal of Quality Technology*, *38*(2), 89–104.
6. Abbas, Z., Nazir, H. Z., Akhtar, N., Abid, M., & Riaz, M. (2020). On designing an efficient control chart to monitor fraction nonconforming. *Quality and Reliability Engineering International*, *36*(2), 547–564.
7. Ryan, T. P. (1998). Statistical control by monitoring and feedback adjustment. *Journal of Quality Technology*, *30*(4), 409–413.

8. Mesnil, B., & Petitgas, P. (2009). Detection of changes in time-series of indicators using CUSUM control charts. *Aquatic Living Resources*, *22*(2), 187–192.
9. Wu, Z., Jiao, J., Yang, M., Liu, Y., & Wang, Z. (2009). An enhanced adaptive CUSUM control chart. *IIE Transactions*, *41*(7), 642–653
10. MacCarthy, B. L., & Wasusri, T. (2002). A review of non-standard applications of statistical process control (SPC) charts. *International Journal of Quality & Reliability Management*, *19*(3), 295–320.

CHAPTER 11

Premium Precision: A Bayesian Approach Using Poisson and Exponential Models in Insurance Risk Assessment

AVNEET KAUR CHAHAL[1], RAKESH KUMAR[1*], and OLAYAN ALBALAWI[2]

[1]*School of Chemical Science and Engineering, Lovely Professional University, Phagwara, Punjab, India*

[2]*Department of Statistics, University of Tabuk, Saudi Arabia*

*Corresponding author

ABSTRACT

The study examines the utilization of credibility theory, specifically Bayesian techniques, to improve the accuracy of estimating insurance premiums. This study examines the Poisson and Exponential models by analyzing real-world insurance data, intending to determine their predictive accuracy in estimating premiums. In the insurance industry, precise premium prediction is critical for financial sustainability and equitable pricing. Bayesian approaches further enhance the robust framework of credibility theory, which combines individual and aggregate data. These methods combine previous knowledge and observed data to enable detailed risk assessment and pricing. The Poisson/Poisson model uses the Poisson distribution to predict claim frequency and severity. It utilizes Bayesian inference, specifically Markov Chain Monte Carlo simulation. Conversely, the exponential model proposes an exponential distribution of claim severity, seamlessly integrated into the Bayesian framework. We evaluated the effectiveness of these models in estimating insurance premiums by analyzing real-world insurance data, which

Integrative Approaches to Quality, Data Analysis, and Interdisciplinary Research.
Amir Ahmad Dar and Waseem Z. Lone (Eds.)

DOI: 10.1201/9781779641014-14

includes information about policyholder demographics and claim history. We will compare using metrics like mean squared error and mean absolute error. The study seeks to provide valuable insights into the capabilities and constraints of these models, assisting insurers in making well-informed choices for risk management and pricing. Ultimately, this will enhance the financial stability and competitiveness of the insurance business.

11.1 INTRODUCTION

The insurance industry operates at the intersection of financial stability and socioeconomic equity, where the accurate evaluation of premiums is vital for both insurance companies and policyholders. Several factors, ranging from individual actions to macroeconomic patterns, influence the inherent complexity of insurance risk, underscoring the need for sophisticated methods in determining premium rates.

Traditional approaches to calculating insurance rates, while important, are sometimes unable to account for the complex nature of insurance risk. Occasionally, these procedures, rooted in actuarial science, rely on simplified assumptions and statistical distributions that may not fully capture the range of variability and uncertainty found in actual insurance scenarios. Insurers face challenges in accurately assessing risk, leading to variations in pricing and financial uncertainty.

To tackle these issues, recent advancements in statistical modeling have presented innovative techniques aimed at enhancing the precision and reliability of premium estimation. The ability of Alomair's Statistical Model for Count Data Study and Population Size Estimation to address overdispersion in the analysis of count data sets it apart. Alomair's model presents a novel mixed Poisson distribution that incorporates zero truncation. This approach efficiently mitigates the influence of overdispersion and yields dependable estimates of population size. Accurate evaluation of occurrence frequency is particularly crucial in industries such as healthcare [1–3].

Najafabadi's work introduces an innovative approach to calculating insurance premiums that surpasses the limitations of current approaches and challenges the accepted principles of credibility theory. Najafabadi suggests a credibility formula that estimates credibility by minimizing the mean square error (MSE). This formula provides insurers with a flexible and responsive framework, enabling them to effectively manage different scenarios and types of losses. This departure from traditional approaches signifies a significant shift in the process of premium estimation. Insurers can enhance their decision-making process by leveraging both existing information and observed data [4–7].

Kristofer Mansson's research adds better estimators for the Poisson regression model that are designed to deal with problems like multicollinearity. This makes the number of premium estimation methods available larger. Mansson's methodology employs shrinkage estimators to enhance forecast precision and offer significant insights for fine-tuning model parameters. This allows insurers to enhance their premium estimation processes [8].

However, among these technological advancements, insurance businesses view the integration of Bayesian approaches into the credibility theory framework as a highly promising strategy. Bayesian methodologies, renowned for their ability to integrate previous knowledge and observed data into a coherent probabilistic framework, offer insurers a complete strategy to assess risk and establish pricing. Previous research has focused on analyzing Bayesian models, such as Poisson and Exponential, individually. However, there is a notable absence of direct comparisons between these models in terms of their predictive capabilities for premium calculation in a specific context.

The objective of this study is to examine the efficacy of Bayesian methodologies in calculating insurance premiums. More precisely, it examines and contrasts the Poisson and Exponential models within the framework of insurance risk evaluation. Our goal in conducting a comprehensive comparative analysis is to highlight the advantages and disadvantages of these models. Providing insurers with important data will improve their ability to refine their premium estimating procedures, ensuring financial stability and fairness in policyholder pricing.

11.1.1 OBJECTIVES OF THE STUDY

The primary purpose of this research is to evaluate the Poisson and exponential models' predictive abilities for premium estimation in a Bayesian context. To achieve this goal, we have:

1. Assess how well Bayesian methods—such as the simulation of Markov Chain Monte Carlo (MCMC)—work when calculating premiums using actual insurance data [1, 2, 9].

2. Evaluate the Poisson/Poisson model's and the exponential model's predictive accuracy in estimating the frequency and seriousness of claims.
3. Use quantitative measures like mean absolute error (MAE) and MSE to compare how well various models perform.
4. Provide insights into the strengths and limitations of each model and offer recommendations for insurers seeking to enhance their premium estimation processes [7].

11.2 LITERATURE REVIEW

Alomair's Statistical Model for Count Data Analysis and Population Size Estimation: Mixing Poisson–Lindley Distributions with Zero Truncation addresses overdispersion in count data analysis with the Poisson-improved second-degree Lindley distribution, a one-parameter mixed Poisson distribution. Direct application of this distribution is difficult when the unobserved event frequency is unknown. To solve this, a tractable zero-truncated distribution with varied dispersion values is proposed. Due to unobserved event frequency, a Horvitz–Thompson-like estimator using the truncated distribution is created to estimate population size. The estimators and population size estimates of truncated and untruncated distributions are asymptotically unbiased and consistent. In medical datasets, dicentric chromosome counts postradiation and Salmonella positive counts are used to validate these distributions and the population size estimation. In overdispersion and uncertain event frequency circumstances, the literature study shows that the proposed count data analysis method is suitable and reliable [1–3].

Najafabadi's paper "A new approach to the credibility formula" discusses the limitations of the traditional credibility formula in cases where certain conditions are not met, such as when the claim size distribution does not belong to the exponential family; the prior distribution does not conjugate with the claim size distribution, or when a different loss function is considered. To address these limitations, the chapter proposes a new approach based on minimizing MSE. This approach aims to approximate the Bayes estimator under a general loss function and prior distribution by using a convex combination of the observed mean and the prior mean, resulting in what is termed an approximate credibility formula. The chapter further explores adjustments to this approximate credibility formula for various scenarios and provides its formulation for significant loss functions. This literature review highlights the chapter's contribution in developing a more flexible and practical approach to credibility theory that accommodates diverse conditions and loss functions beyond the scope of traditional methods [4–6].

Kristofer Mansson's study on Improved Liu Estimators for the Poisson Regression Model talks about a new shrinkage estimator for the Poisson model. This method builds on Liu's estimator, which was first made for the linear regression model. It will be used instead of the usual maximum likelihood (ML) method when there is multicollinearity, because ML's MSE goes up when that happens. This chapter also finds the best value for the shrinkage parameter and suggests ways to predict it based on that value. By running a Monte Carlo simulation and finding the MSE and MAE, it can be seen that the Liu estimators work better than the ML when used with these suggested shrinkage parameter estimators [8].

11.3 CONCEPTUAL FRAMEWORK

11.3.1 TRADITIONAL CREDIBILITY THEORY

Conventional credibility theory has been a cornerstone of insurance risk assessment for many years, offering a systematic approach to integrating individual and group data for premium computation. This mid-1900s theory by Bühlmann and Bühlmann–Straub emphasizes the significance of experience rating, wherein premiums are modified depending on policyholder-specific data and historical loss history. The fundamental foundation of traditional credibility theory is its ability to strike a balance between the individual policyholder experiences and the group risk variables. This makes it possible for insurers to set rates that fairly reflect the risk profiles of each policyholder individually as well as the group as a whole. Classical credibility theory employs statistical techniques such as credibility equations and weighted averages to assist insurers in making educated risk assessments [9, 10–12].

However, there are situations when classic credibility theory may not work well when dealing with complex risk profiles or scant data. A lack of individual policyholder data may lead to a higher reliance on group data and perhaps less accurate risk estimates since individual experience may not be given the weight it deserves. In addition, the conventional credibility theory may have trouble explaining the variation in policyholders' risk profiles, particularly in companies with a broad variety of risk characteristics. These drawbacks emphasize the necessity for different approaches, such as Bayesian inference, which provide more adaptability and resilience when addressing uncertainty and incorporating previous information.

11.3.2 BAYESIAN INFERENCE IN INSURANCE ANALYTICS

The discipline of insurance analytics has completely changed since the introduction of Bayesian inference, which provides a strong and adaptable framework for fusing previous understanding with observed data. Insurance companies may make better judgments on risk evaluation and pricing by using Bayesian inference, which is based on the Bayes' theorem and offers a methodical way to update beliefs about unresolved variables based on fresh data. In contrast to conventional statistical techniques, which frequently depend only on observable data, Bayesian inference enables insurers to include expert judgments, personal beliefs, and past data in the modeling procedure, thereby producing risk forecasts that are more accurate and trustworthy [13, 14].

The capacity of Bayesian inference to quantify uncertainty using the posterior distribution of parameters is one of its main advantages. Insurance companies may estimate posterior distributions and define uncertainty intervals by utilizing methods like MCMC simulation, which gives them a more thorough grasp of the underlying risk variables. Additionally, Bayesian inference makes model comparison and sensitivity analysis easier, enabling insurers to evaluate how resilient outcomes are to various modeling assumptions and priors. The insurance industry's decision-making procedures could be strengthened, risk management techniques could be supported more successfully, and premium prediction accuracy might increase with the use of Bayesian inference in analytics [8, 13–15].

11.3.3 POISSON MODEL FOR INSURANCE PREMIUM ESTIMATION

The Poisson model represents a fundamental tool in insurance premium estimation, particularly for predicting claim frequency within a specified period. Rooted in the Poisson distribution, this model assumes that claim occurrences follow a stochastic process characterized by a single parameter representing the mean claim frequency. In practice, the Poisson model offers a straightforward and intuitive approach to modeling claim frequency, making it well-suited for applications such as automobile insurance and property insurance. By estimating the Poisson parameter from historical claim data, insurers can make informed decisions in setting premiums that accurately reflect the underlying risk of claim occurrence [16, 17].

But in some cases, especially when handling overdispersion or heterogeneity in claim frequencies, the Poisson model might not work as intended. When the Poisson model is applied in situations where the constant mean claim frequency assumption is broken, biased or inefficient parameter estimations may result, producing forecasts of premiums that are not ideal. In addition, the Poisson model could have trouble identifying intricate patterns or nonlinear correlations in claim frequency data, which might restrict its use in sectors with a range of risk profiles. The aforementioned constraints highlight the need to examine substitute modeling methodologies, including generalized linear models or Bayesian methods, which provide increased adaptability and resilience in representing intricate risk dynamics [12, 18–20].

11.3.4 EXPONENTIAL MODEL FOR INSURANCE PREMIUM ESTIMATION

An alternate method for estimating insurance premiums is provided by the exponential model, which emphasizes modeling claim severity above claim frequency. Based on an exponential distribution, this model postulates that claim amounts are established by a stochastic process with a single parameter that represents the mean claim severity. In situations when an exponential distribution may fairly approach the claim severity distributions, the Exponential model is a compelling option due to its simplicity and ease of comprehension [5, 21].

One of the key advantages of the Exponential model lies in its straightforward parameterization, with a single parameter governing the mean claim severity. This simplicity facilitates model estimation and interpretation, allowing insurers to obtain quick insights into the average size of insurance claims within a given portfolio. Moreover, the Exponential model lends itself well to analytical calculations, enabling insurers to compute expected claim amounts and assess the financial implications of different risk scenarios.

On the other hand, complicated patterns or nonexponential behavior in claim severity distributions may be difficult for the exponential model to capture. In real-world scenarios, claim severity data could show skewness, heterogeneity, or heavy-tailed distributions that do not follow the exponential model. Under such circumstances, the Exponential model can produce skewed or ineffective parameter estimations, which could result in imprecise premium projections. Furthermore, the simplicity of the exponential model could restrict its ability to incorporate factors that affect claim severity or accommodate a range of risk profiles. To account for more complicated claim severity dynamics, insurers may thus need to carefully evaluate whether the exponential model is appropriate for their particular risk setting and take into consideration alternate modeling methodologies, such as extended linear models or Bayesian approaches [22].

11.4 METHODOLOGY

In this section, I outline the methodological approach employed in this research, detailing the implementation of Bayesian inference techniques and the specific modeling methodologies utilized for premium estimation in insurance risk assessment.

11.4.1 BAYESIAN INFERENCE BASICS

The underlying model for this study is Bayesian inference, which allows for the integration of prior information and observed data to estimate parameters and quantify uncertainty. The process begins with the specification of prior distributions, denoted as $P(\phi)$, which indicate opinions about the parameters under consideration. These priors are then updated by Bayes' theorem to generate posterior distributions, denoted as $P(\phi|X)$, that reflect the new opinions about the parameters based on the observed data (X):

$$P(\phi|X) = \frac{P(X|\phi) \times P(\phi)}{P(X)} \tag{11.1}$$

where:

- $P(\phi|X)$ is the posterior distribution of parameters given the observed data,
- $P(X|\phi)$ is the likelihood function representing the probability of observing the data given the parameters,
- $P(\phi)$ is the prior distribution representing beliefs about the parameters,
- $P(X)$ is the marginal likelihood or evidence.

MCMC simulation techniques, such as Gibbs sampling and Metropolis–Hastings's algorithms, are used to sample from posterior distributions and estimate parameter values. The resultant posterior samples enable the generation of summary statistics such as posterior means and credible intervals, which provide information about parameter estimations and uncertainty.

11.4.2 CREDIBILITY THEORY

Conventional credibility theory, pioneered by Bühlmann and Bühlmann–Straub in the mid-1900s, has been a cornerstone of insurance risk assessment. It provides a systematic approach to integrating individual and group data for premium computation. At its core, traditional credibility theory emphasizes experience rating, wherein premiums are adjusted based on policyholder-specific data and historical loss history [23].

The fundamental principle of traditional credibility theory lies in its ability to balance individual policyholder experiences with group risk variables. This allows insurers to set rates that fairly reflect the risk profiles of each policyholder individually as well as the group as a whole. The theory employs statistical techniques such as credibility equations and weighted averages to assist insurers in making educated risk assessments [6, 24].

$$\zeta = \frac{\delta^2}{\delta^2 + \frac{\delta_0^2}{n}} \tag{11.2}$$

where:

- ζ is the credibility factor,
- δ^2 is the variance of the individual experience,
- δ_0^2 is the variance of the group experience, and
- n is the number of observations.

11.4.3 POISSON MODEL IMPLEMENTATION

The Poisson model holds significant importance in the estimation of insurance premiums, specifically in the prediction of claim frequency over a designated period. Implementing a model requires the following steps:

- *Likelihood Function:* The likelihood function, represented as $P(Y|\varphi)$, represents the probability of observing the data Y given the parameter φ, the Poisson parameter.
  The likelihood function for the Poisson model is given by

$$P(Y|\varphi) = \frac{e^{-\varphi}\varphi^{Y}}{Y!} \tag{11.3}$$

  where:

  - Y: number of claims that have been seen
  - φ: the average frequency at which claims occur

- *Prior Distribution:* Prior distribution determines suitable prior distributions for the Poisson parameter φ in consideration of historical data on the frequency of claims. Priors frequently selected for implementation consist of conjugate priors, including the Gamma prior.
- *Posterior Inference:* Posterior inference involves the application of Bayesian methods, including MCMC simulation, to sample parameters from the joint posterior distribution. This process entails applying Bayes' theorem to the prior distribution to derive the posterior distribution, which represents the revised assumptions regarding the parameters in light of the observed data.
- *Parameter Estimation:* Parameter estimation involves the computation of posterior summaries, including credible intervals and posterior means, using posterior samples acquired via MCMC simulation. The insights offered by these summaries pertain to parameter estimations and uncertainty.

11.4.4 EXPONENTIAL MODEL IMPLEMENTATION

The Exponential model is another method for estimating insurance premiums, focusing on modeling claim severity rather than claim frequency [25, 26]. Model implementation follows similar steps as the Poisson model:

- *Likelihood Function:* Specify the likelihood function, denoted as $P(A|\beta)$, represents the probability of observing the data A given the parameter β,the Exponential parameter. The likelihood function for the Exponential model is given by [3, 5, 22]

$$P(A|\beta) = \beta \times e^{-\beta A} \tag{11.4}$$

  where:
    - A represents the observed claim amount, and
    - β represents the mean claim severity.

- *Prior Distribution:* Select appropriate prior distributions for the Exponential parameter β based on historical claim severity data. Common choices for priors include Gamma distributions or conjugate priors such as the Gamma prior.
- *Posterior Inference:* Utilize Bayesian inference techniques, such as MCMC simulation, to sample from the joint posterior distribution of parameters. Update the prior distribution using Bayes' theorem to obtain the posterior distribution, reflecting updated beliefs about the parameters given the observed data.
- *Parameter Estimation:* Compute posterior summaries such as posterior means and credible intervals from the posterior samples obtained through MCMC simulation. These summaries provide insights into parameter estimations and uncertainty.

11.4.5 MODEL EVALUATION METRICS

To assess the effectiveness of the Poisson and Exponential models in premium estimates, different model evaluation criteria are used. These include MSE, MAE, and root mean squared error, which measure the difference between expected and observed values. Furthermore, model fit metrics such as the Bayesian Information Criterion and Deviance Information Criterion are used to evaluate goodness of fit and compare the relative performance of the Poisson and Exponential models. Sensitivity analysis is used to assess resilience under various modeling assumptions and parameter settings. Overall, these model assessment measures give useful information on the correctness and dependability of the Poisson and Exponential models in premium estimation using the Bayesian framework. The flowchart of the methodology is given in Figure 11.1.

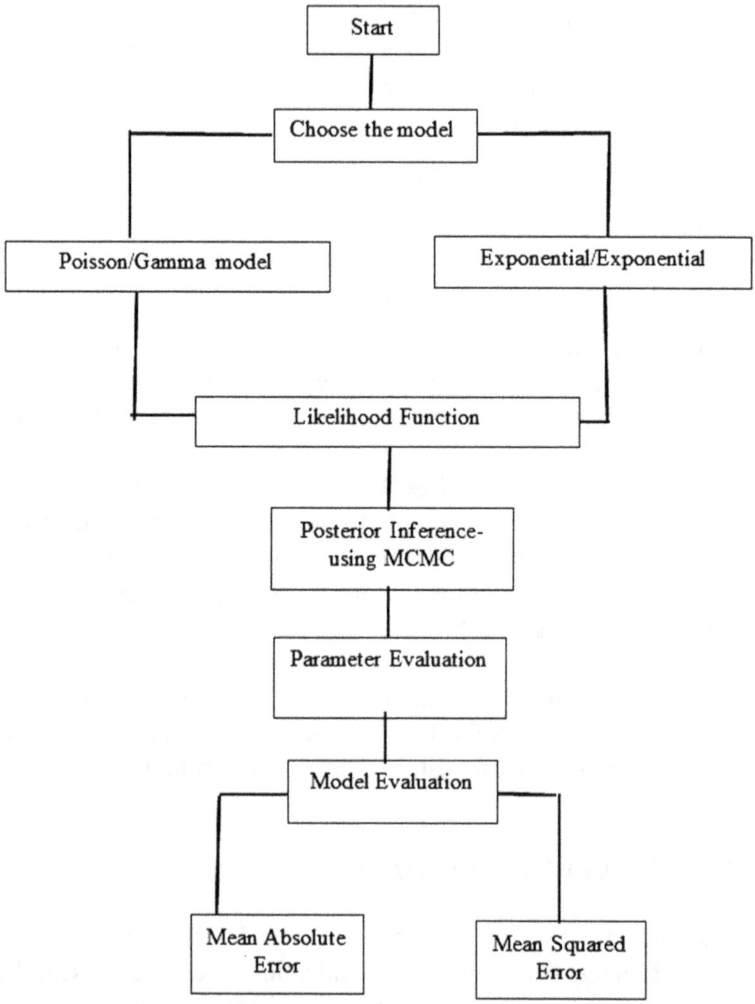

FIGURE 11.1 Flowchart of the process.

11.5 EXPERIMENTAL RESULT

11.5.1 DATA

The data is acquired From the Insurance Regulatory and Development Authority of India (https:/irdai.gov.in/.). This data consists the information about various companies and their claims amount. After preprocessing the data, I have taken columns that are crucial for analysis, including variables such as policy details, claim amounts, incident types, and other relevant factors.

11.5.2 DATA PREPROCESSING AND MODEL IMPLEMENTATION

Data preprocessing included things like cleaning up the data, dealing with missing numbers, and changing variables as needed. For instance, we might have gotten rid of any records that were missing or did not belong and made sure that all the variables were in the same style.

Bayesian inference methods, especially MCMC sampling, were used to build the chosen models. When we used the Poisson model, we gave the claim frequency parameter its likelihood function and previous distribution. In the same way, we set up the probability function and prior distribution for the rate parameter in the exponential model. I have an RStudio Software for the implementation and the MCMCpack package was used for performing MCMC simulations to estimate parameters in Bayesian models [14].

11.5.3 EVALUATION METRICS

To assess the performance of the models, we calculated key evaluation metrics such as MSE and MAE. These metrics provide quantitative measures of predictive accuracy and help compare the performance of different models.

Interpretation and Conclusion: Based on experimental results obtained using the MCMCpack library in R, several key conclusions can be made.

11.5.4 MODEL ESTIMATION

For the Poisson model, the posterior mean estimate of the claim frequency parameter is approximately 2.61, with a 95% credible interval ranging from 1.60 to 3.37. In contrast, the exponential model estimates the rate parameter theta claim amount parameter with a posterior mean estimate of approximately 56,103,257, and a 95% credible interval ranging from 26,706.25 to 155,280,992. The model estimation results for both the Poisson and exponential models are summarized in Table 11.1.

TABLE 11.1 Model Estimation

Model	Mean Estimate of Parameter	Confidence Interval
Poisson	2.61	1.60–3.37
Exponential	56,103,257	26,706.25 to 155,280,992

MSE and MAE were computed for both the Poisson and exponential models to evaluate their predictive performance.

The Poisson model achieved an MSE of 3.15e+15 and an MAE of 56,103,254, while the exponential model had an MSE of 3.14e+15 and an MAE of 56,074,027. The model evaluation results for both the Poisson and exponential models are summarized in Table 11.2.

TABLE 11.2 Model Evaluation

Model	MAE	MSE
Poisson/Gamma	56,103,254	3.15e+15
Exponential/Exponential	56,074,027	3.14e+15

The MSE and MAE comparison between the Poisson and exponential models suggests that both models perform similarly in terms of predictive accuracy.

The Poisson model focuses on modeling claim frequency, whereas the exponential model emphasizes claim amounts.

11.5.5 VISUALIZATION

Separate plots were created to compare the MSE and MAE values for both models. The comparison for MAE is visualized in Figure 11.2, and the comparison for MSE is visualized in Figure 11.3.

11.6 DISCUSSION

The results show that the Exponential model is better at figuring out the Premium risk than the Poison model. This is because it has a lower MSE and MAE, with an MSE of 3.14e+15 and an MAE of 56,074,027, respectively. Even though there is not much change between the two models.

The Poisson model and the Exponential models are both useful for understanding different parts of figuring out how risky an insurance policy is. It shows how important it is to pick the right model based on the study goals and the type of insurance claims data.

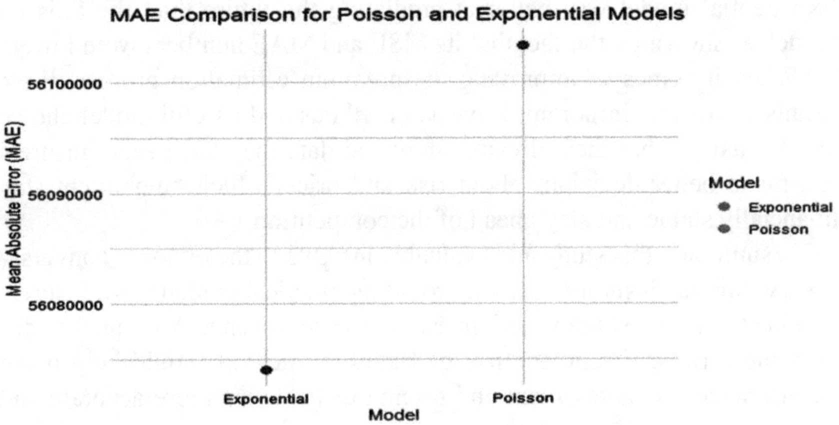

FIGURE 11.2 Comparing MAE for both Poison and Exponential models.

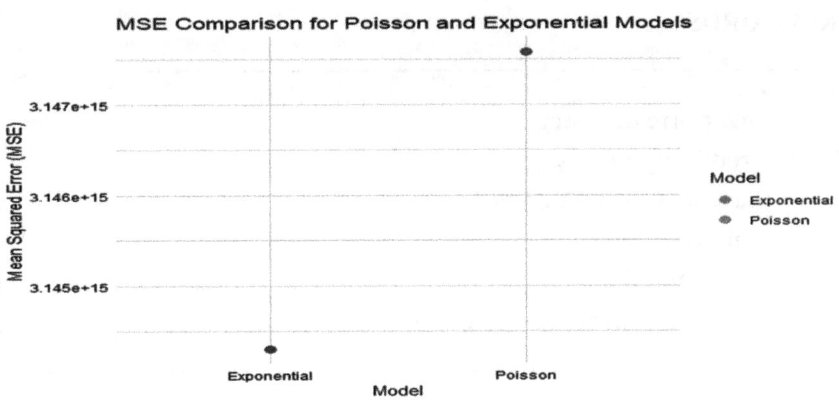

FIGURE 11.3 Comparing MSE for both Poison and Exponential models.

11.7 CONCLUSION

In conclusion, this study gives a thorough look at how Bayesian reasoning and credibility theory can be used in the insurance industry, mainly when estimating premiums. The study tries to improve the accuracy of premium assessments by looking closely at the Poisson and Exponential models along with Bayesian methods.

The study was very helpful because it looked at real insurance data and used numbers like MSE and MAE to measure errors. Notably, the Exponential model was better at predicting the future than the Poisson model, as shown by the fact that its MSE and MAE numbers were lower.

When it comes to improving the premium estimation process, these results show how important Bayesian methods and careful model choice are. By using what they already know and data they have seen, insurers can make better decisions about risk and price, which helps them stay financially stable and stay ahead of the competition.

In summary, this study adds valuable insights to the ongoing conversations within the insurance sector, providing practical guidance for insurers looking to improve their premium estimation approaches. Moving forward with more research and the use of Bayesian methods could help make an insurance risk assessment and pricing tactics even more accurate and useful.

KEYWORDS

- **insurance industry**
- **credibility theory**
- **Bayesian methodologies**
- **Poisson model**
- **exponential model**
- **premium estimation accuracy**

REFERENCES

1. Alomair, G., Ridzuan, R., Tajuddin, M., Bakouch, H. S., & Almohisen, A. (2024). A statistical model for count data analysis and population size a statistical model for count data analysis and population size estimation: introducing a mixed Poisson–Lindley distribution and its zero truncation. *Axioms, 13*, 125. https://doi.org/10.3390/axioms

2. Goulet, V. (1998). Journal of Actuarial Practice 1993–2006 Finance department 1998 principles and application of credibility theory. *Journal of Actuarial Practice, 6.* http://digitalcommons.unl.edu/joaphttp://digitalcommons.unl.edu/joap/93
3. Gulia, P., Kumar, R., Kaur, A., & Dhiman, G. (2022). A comparative study of fuzzy linear and multi-objective optimization. https://doi.org/10.4018/978-1-6684-4405-4.ch007
4. Gong, Y. M., Li, Z., Milazzo, M., Moore, K., & Provencher, M. (2018). Credibility methods for individual life insurance. *Risks*, *6*(4), 144. https://doi.org/10.3390/RISKS6040144
5. Payandeh Najafabadi, A. T. (2010). A new approach to the credibility formula. *Insurance: Mathematics and Economics*, *46*(2), 334–338.
6. Sobel, J. (1985). *Source: The Review of Economic Studies* (Vol. 52, Issue 4). https://about.jstor.org/terms
7. Wang, W., Wen, L., Yang, Z., & Yuan, Q. (2020). Quantile credibility models with common effects. *Risks*, *8*(4), 1–10. https://doi.org/10.3390/risks8040100
8. Mansson, K., Kibria, B. M. G., Sjolander, P., & Shukur, G. (2012). Improved liu estimators for the Poisson regression model. *International Journal of Statistics and Probability*, *1*(1). https://doi.org/10.5539/ijsp.v1n1p2
9. Gómez-Déniz, E., & Calderín-Ojeda, E. (2018). Multivariate credibility in bonus-malus systems distinguishing between different types of claims. *Risks*, *6*(2), 34. https://doi.org/10.3390/risks6020034
10. A Course in Credibility Theory and its Applications. (2005). In: *A Course in Credibility Theory and its Applications*. https://doi.org/10.1007/3-540-29273-x
11. Atkinson, D. B. (2019). *Credibility Methods Applied to Life, Health, and Pensions*. https://www.soa.org/globalassets/assets/files/resources/tables-calcs-tools/credibility-methods-life-health-pensions.pdf
12. Sangwan, P., Kumar, R., Sharma, Y., Bhosale, D. G., & Prasad, C. D. (2023). Application of computing in recognition of input design factors for vapour-grown carbon nanofibers through fuzzy cluster analysis. *International Journal on Interactive Design and Manufacturing*, *18*, 6225–6235. https://doi.org/10.1007/s12008-023-01547-7
13. Arellano-Valle, R. B., Castro, L. M., Genton, M. G., & Gómez, H. W. (2008). Bayesian inference for shape mixtures of skewed distributions, with application to regression analysis. *Bayesian Analysis*, *3*(3). https://doi.org/10.1214/08-BA320
14. Beeley, C. (2012). Applied Bayesian hierarchical methods. *Journal of Applied Statistics*, *39*(8), 1845–1845. https://doi.org/10.1080/02664763.2012.657788
15. Hadj-Amar, B., Jewson, J., & Fiecas, M. (2023). Bayesian approximations to hidden semi-Markov models for telemetric monitoring of physical activity. *Bayesian Analysis*, *18*(2), 547–577. https://doi.org/10.1214/22-BA1318
16. Delong, Ł., Lindholm, M., & Wüthrich, M. V. (2021). Making Tweedie's compound Poisson model more accessible. *European Actuarial Journal*, *11*(1), 185–226. https://doi.org/10.1007/s13385-021-00264-3
17. Forthmann, B., & Doebler, P. (2021). Reliability of researcher capacity estimates and count data dispersion: A comparison of Poisson, negative binomial, and Conway-Maxwell-Poisson models. *Scientometrics*, *126*(4), 3337–3354. https://doi.org/10.1007/s11192-021-03864-8

18. Kumar, R., Chandrawat, R. K., Garg, B. P., & Joshi, V. (2017). Comparison of optimized algorithms in facility location allocation problems with different distance measures. *AIP Conference Proceedings*, *1860*, 020041. https://doi.org/10.1063/1.4990340
19. Slathia, S., Kumar, R., Lone, M., Viriyasitavat, W., Kaur, A., & Dhiman, G. (2023). A performance evaluation of situational-based fuzzy linear programming problem for job assessment. In: *Lecture Notes in Networks and Systems* (Vol. 612). https://doi.org/10.1007/978-981-19-9228-5_56
20. Zhang, C., Shahbaba, B., & Zhao, H. (2018). Variational Hamiltonian Monte Carlo via score matching. *Bayesian Analysis*, *13*(2), 485–506. https://doi.org/10.1214/17-BA1060
21. Chandrawat, R. K., Kumar, R., Makkar, V., Yadav, M., & Kumari, P. (2019). A comparative fuzzy cluster analysis of the Binder's performance grades using fuzzy equivalence relation via different distance measures. In: *Communications in Computer and Information Science* (p. 955). https://doi.org/10.1007/978-981-13-3140-4_11
22. Trivellato, B. (2023). Sub-exponentiality in statistical exponential models. *Journal of Theoretical Probability*. *37*, 2076–2096. https://doi.org/10.1007/s10959-023-01281-6
23. Kakar, G. (2007). A course in credibility theory and its applications. In: Bühlmann, H. & Gisler, A. (Eds.), *Annals of Actuarial Science* 2(2), (Springer, 2005). https://doi.org/10.1017/s1748499500000415
24. Senthilkumar, R. (2015). Clustering of fuzzy data set using credibility theory,_*Chapter 2 Shodhganga* http://hdl.handle.net/10603/258477
25. Chang, H., Wu, Q., Gan, Z., & Shen, F. (2023). Study on thermo-mechanical properties of energy piles based on the improved exponential model. *Case Studies in Thermal Engineering*, *52*. https://doi.org/10.1016/j.csite.2023.103679
26. Manu, S. L., & Shikaa, S. (2023). Mathematical modeling of Taraba State population growth using exponential and logistic models. *Results in Control and Optimization*, *12*, 100265. https://doi.org/10.1016/j.rico.2023.100265

CHAPTER 12

Optimizing Supply Chain Efficiency with Mathematica Mathematical and Statistical Methods for Finite Planning Horizons

RANU[1], NITIN KUMAR MISHRA[2*], RENUKA S. NAMWAD[2*], JATOTH HEERAMAN[3], and PRERNA JAIN[2]

[1]*Department of Mathematics, NIILM University, Kaithal, Haryana, India*

[2]*Department of Mathematics, Lovely Professional University, Phagwara, Punjab, India*

[3]*Department of Mechanical Engineering, Sridevi Women's Engineering College, Jawaharlal Nehru Technological University (JNTUH), Hyderabad, Telangana, India*

*Corresponding author

ABSTRACT

Data-driven decision-making is increasingly recognized as a critical success factor in supply chain management. This study explores how integrating statistical analysis and mathematical models, facilitated by Wolfram Research's Mathematica, can revolutionize supply chain management. By leveraging Mathematica's sophisticated mathematical models, precise computations, and extensive statistical capabilities, enterprises can extract valuable insights from large volumes of supply chain data. This chapter investigates specific methods and approaches for optimizing supply chain operations, enhancing productivity, gaining competitive advantages, and

Integrative Approaches to Quality, Data Analysis, and Interdisciplinary Research.
Amir Ahmad Dar and Waseem Z. Lone (Eds.)

DOI: 10.1201/9781779641014-15

achieving long-term success. Through case studies and practical examples, we demonstrate how businesses can use Mathematica to make informed, data-driven decisions that improve overall supply chain efficiency within a finite planning horizon.

12.1 INTRODUCTION

In today's competitive landscape, effective supply chain management hinges on the ability to extract actionable insights from vast amounts of data. These data encompass everything from customer demand patterns to supplier performance metrics. To navigate this complexity and make informed decisions, businesses increasingly rely on sophisticated mathematical models and rigorous statistical analysis.

Supply chain operations are characterized by dynamic interactions and dependencies across various stages, from procurement to distribution. The challenge lies in optimizing these processes to enhance efficiency, reduce costs, and improve overall performance. Mathematical models provide a structured framework to analyze these complexities, while statistical analysis offers empirical validation and predictive capabilities.

This study explores the pivotal role of statistical analysis and mathematical models in transforming supply chain management. Specifically, it delves into how these methodologies enable businesses to forecast demand accurately, optimize inventory levels, evaluate supplier reliability, and streamline logistics operations. By leveraging advanced tools such as Mathematica from Wolfram Research, organizations can harness the power of data to drive strategic decisions and gain a competitive edge in today's global marketplace.

The remainder of this research study is structured into various sections. Section 12.2 provides a comprehensive review of the existing literature. In Section 12.3, the notations and assumptions employed are outlined. Section 12.4 outlines the mathematical model and its calculations, while Section 12.5 focuses on algorithms and techniques. Section 12.6 elaborates on numerical simulations, while Section 12.7 presents sensitivity analysis in both tabular and graphical formats. Section 12.8 discusses academic and management implications. Additionally, Section 12.9 offers conclusions, and Section 12.10 provides suggestions for future research.

12.2 LITERATURE REVIEW

Data from supply chain activities are produced in large quantities, ranging from purchase histories to patterns of client demand. To glean valuable insights from this mountain of data and empower firms to make well-informed decisions about a range of supply chain activities, mathematical models and statistical analysis are essential. Statistical methods combined with mathematical models, including regression analysis and exponential smoothing, are essential for projecting future demand from past sales data. Precise demand projections enable enterprises to maximize stock levels, minimize stockouts, and improve client contentment [1–3]. Supported by statistical analysis, mathematical models such as reorder point computations and economic order quantity (EOQ) help to optimize stock levels and spot patterns in inventory. Organizations can manage stockout risks and inventory carrying costs by using methodologies such as ABC analysis [4–6]. To provide quantitative insights into supplier performance, mathematical computations, such defect rate and lead time analysis, are used in conjunction with statistical measurements. Organizations may negotiate better terms, eliminate supply chain interruptions, and identify failing suppliers by doing mathematical analysis on supplier data [7–9]. Statistical analysis combined with mathematical optimization approaches, such network analysis and linear programming, helps firms save expenses associated with shipping, expedite transit times, and optimize transportation routes [10–12], and other scholars have noted that logistics processes may be optimized for greater efficiency by doing mathematical calculations on historical transportation data.

Mathematica equips supply chain experts with an extensive collection of mathematical functions, models, and statistical tools designed to handle the complexities of supply chain data analysis. Calculating measurements of central tendency, dispersion, and distributional properties is made easier by Mathematica's built-in functions [10–14] and state that mathematical computations like regression analysis and optimization models supplement statistical insights to provide a comprehensive picture of supply chain dynamics. Users of Mathematica may verify assumptions and make data-driven decisions by using hypothesis testing. To give solid decision-making based on statistical data, statistical functions and mathematical computations collaborate [13–16]. Regression analysis features in Mathematica allow users to model connections between variables and provide forecasts. Regression analysis is enhanced by mathematical modeling approaches like queuing theory and simulation, which provide a deeper understanding of supply chain dynamics [13–18]. Organizations may resolve challenging supply chain optimization issues with the use of statistical analysis and mathematical optimization approaches. Mathematical algorithms and statistical analysis generate efficiency and cost savings in supply chain operations, from inventory optimization to production scheduling [13–20].

From the above literature review, it is evident that very few publications in existing research have addressed the problem of supply chain management by using statistical methodology and the Mathematica tool. Moreover, there are no authors who have considered both statistical methodology and the Mathematica tool under a finite planning horizon. Therefore, this chapter aims to fill this gap by considering these parameters comprehensively.

12.2.1 PURPOSE OF THE STUDY

The main purpose of this chapter is to lower carbon emissions and reduce the total cost by enhancing coordination in supply chain operations. Specifically, this study investigates the supply chain with statistical methodology under a finite planning horizon. By incorporating these parameters, the research aims to provide more sustainable and cost-effective supply chain management solutions. This study investigates how integrating these advanced statistical and mathematical methods with Mathematica can revolutionize supply chain management practices. We illustrate the transformative impact of data-driven decision-making on operational efficiency, cost-effectiveness, and overall business performance in today's dynamic market environment.

12.3 ASSUMPTIONS AND NOTATIONS

12.3.1 ASSUMPTIONS

1. Demand consistency: The demand rate (D) for the product remains constant over the planned horizon.
2. No stockouts: The model assumes there are no shortages or stockouts within the planning period.

3. Instantaneous replenishment: Inventory replenishment is immediate, with no lead time.
4. Fixed setup costs: The setup or ordering cost (S) is constant for each order placed.
5. Constant holding cost: The holding or carrying cost per unit (H) is consistent throughout the planning horizon.
6. Finite planning horizon: The study considers a finite planning horizon (T) for the total cost calculation.

12.3.2 *NOTATIONS*

1. D: Demand rate (units per period).
2. S: Ordering or setup cost per order.
3. H: Holding or carrying cost per unit per period.
4. EOQ: Economic order quantity.
5. T: Total planning horizon (time intervals such as months or years).
6. TC: Total cost function.

12.4 MATHEMATICAL MODEL: EOQ

The EOQ model is a classical inventory management model that determines the optimal order quantity that minimizes total inventory costs. The costs of ordering inventory and setting it up are compared to the costs of maintaining inventory in the EOQ model. The formula for EOQ is as follows:

$$\text{EOQ} = \sqrt{\frac{2DS}{H}}.$$

12.4.1 *TOTAL COST CALCULATION*

For a finite planning horizon, over the entire time horizon T, the ordering and holding charges are included in the overall cost:

$$\text{Total cost} = \frac{\text{D T}}{\text{EOQ}}\, S + \frac{\text{EOQ}}{2}\, H \times T,$$

where T is the total planning horizon (expressed in terms of time intervals, like months or years), D is the rate of demand (units per period), S is the ordering or setup fees per order, H is the cost of holding or carrying per unit for a given length of time, and EOQ is the economic order quantity.

The EOQ model anticipates constant demand, nonexistent shortages, and prompt inventory replenishment. Using Mathematica to calculate the EOQ and then analyzing the resulting inventory policies can help organizations make data-driven decisions to optimize inventory levels and save costs.

- Demand rate (D): This represents the average demand for the product over a specific time, such as a month or a year. It is typically based on historical sales data or market forecasts.
- Setup cost per order (S): The expense incurred each time a product order is placed is referred to as this. It covers expenditures related to placing an order, including order processing, documentation, and delivery charges.
- Holding cost per unit (H): This is the total cost of keeping or transporting one inventory unit for a certain amount of time. It includes expenses such as storage costs, insurance, obsolescence, and the opportunity cost of tying up capital in inventory.
- EOQ: By keeping holding and setup expenses equal, The optimal order quantity that lessens total expenditures on inventory is the minimum order quantity. The square root of the product of twice the yearly demand (D), the setup cost per order (S), and the holding cost per unit (H) are used to compute it.

12.5 ALGORITHM FOR COMPUTING EOQ

1. The demand rate (D), holding or carrying cost per unit per time period (H), and setup or ordering cost per order (S) should be
2. Compute the EOQ using the formula: $\text{EOQ} = \sqrt{\frac{2DS}{H}}$.
3. Output the calculated EOQ as the optimal order quantity.

12.5.1 OPTIMIZED TECHNIQUE TO SOLVE THE MATHEMATIC PROBLEM

An enhanced method for calculating the EOQ entails looking for the ideal order quantity using sophisticated optimization techniques like gradient descent or genetic algorithms. Even in intricate supply chain systems with numerous restrictions and variables, these algorithms may effectively explore the solution space and converge to the ideal EOQ.

Theorem: Optimal value of total cost

The following is the definition of the total cost function (TC) given a restricted planning horizon (T), demand rate (D), setup or purchasing cost per order (S), and maintenance or carrying cost per unit over time (H):

$$\mathrm{TC} = \frac{\mathrm{D\,T}}{\mathrm{EOQ}} S + \frac{\mathrm{EOQ}}{2} H \times T,$$

Proof:

To find the optimal value of the total cost function TC, we first differentiate it with respect to EOQ and set the derivative equal to zero to find the critical points:

$$\frac{\mathrm{D\,T}}{\mathrm{EOQ}} S + \frac{\mathrm{EOQ}}{2} H \times T.$$

Solving for EOQ, we get the following:

$$\mathrm{EOQ} = \sqrt{\frac{2DS}{H}}.$$

This is the overall cost function's crucial point. We may apply the second derivative test to verify if this point belongs to a minimusm, maximum, or saddle point. Calculating TC's second derivative in relation to EOQ, we get the following:

$$\frac{d^2\mathrm{TC}}{d\mathrm{EOQ}^2} = \frac{\mathrm{D\,T}}{\mathrm{EOQ}} S + \frac{\mathrm{EOQ}}{2} H \times T.$$

The second derivative is positive, suggesting that the critical point is in fact a minimum because S and D are both positive and EOQ is always positive. As a result, the following scenario represents the best overall cost value: the EOQ:

$$\mathrm{EOQ} = \sqrt{\frac{2DS}{H}}.$$

This optimal order quantity minimizes the total inventory costs by balancing the setup costs and the holding costs over the entire planning horizon.

12.5.2 NUMERICAL EXAMPLE AND ILLUSTRATION

Let us consider an example where:
Annual demand (D) = 10,000 units
Setup cost per order (S) = \$100
Holding cost per unit per year (H) = \$5

$$\text{EOQ} = \sqrt{\frac{2 \times 10,000 \times 100}{5}}$$

$$\text{EOQ} = \sqrt{\frac{2,000,000}{5}}$$

$$\text{EOQ} = \sqrt{400,000}$$

$$\text{EOQ} \approx 632.46.$$

Approximately 632.46 units is the optimal order quantity (EOQ) in this scenario. This amount of inventory will ensure that there is enough on hand to satisfy client demand while also reducing overall inventory expenditures for the company.

12.6 MATHEMATICA SOLUTION FOR SENSITIVITY ANALYSIS AND VISUALIZATION

12.6.1 GRAPHICAL REPRESENTATION AND INTERPRETATION

To support the analysis further, we need to examine Figures 12.1–12.7, which likely illustrate how EOQ and total cost change with variations in D, S, H, and T. These graphs would provide visual insights into the relationships and help more accurately measure the consequences described in Table 12.1.

Demand rate (D):

- As the demand rate increases from 8000 to 12,000, the EOQ also increases from approximately 565.685 to 692.82.
- As a result, the total cost rises to 41,569.2 from around 33,941.1.
- This implies that greater order volumes and overall costs are a result of increased demand rates.

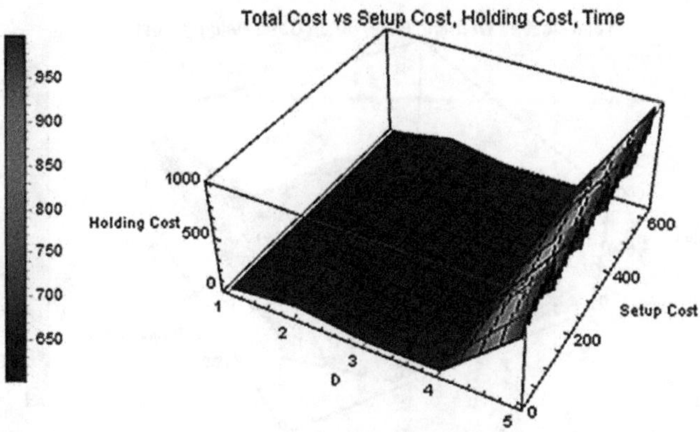

FIGURE 12.1 Sensitivity analysis for total cost with *S*, *H*, and *T*.

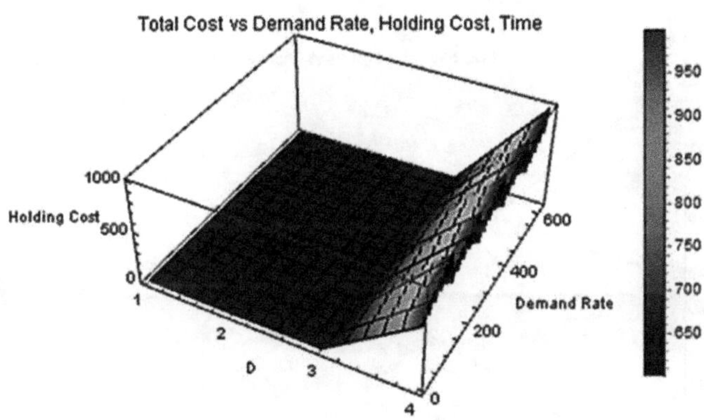

FIGURE 12.2 Sensitivity analysis for total cost with *D*, *H*, and *T*.

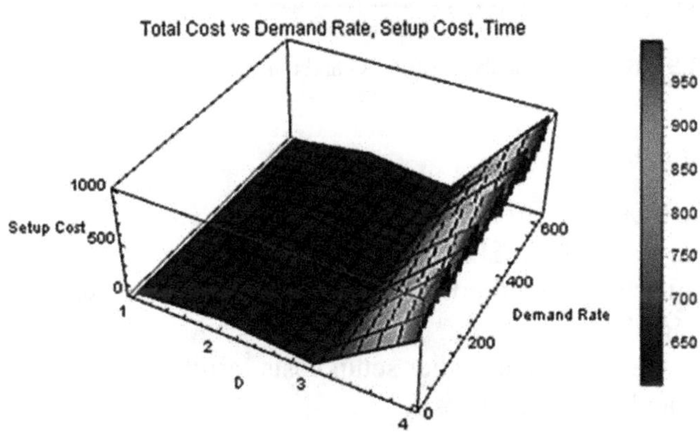

FIGURE 12.3 Sensitivity analysis for total cost with *D*, *S*, and *T*.

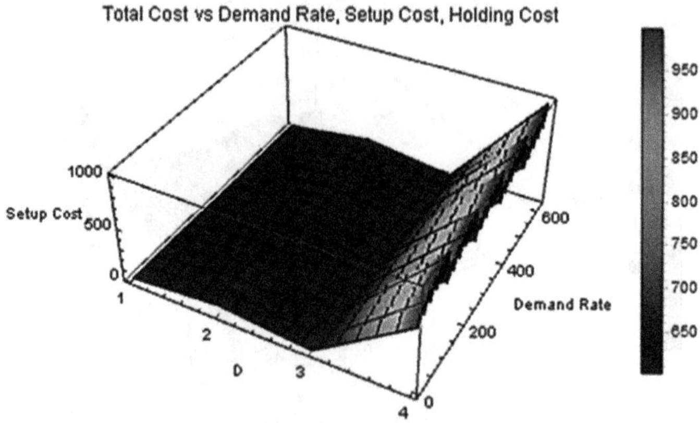

FIGURE 12.4 Sensitivity analysis for total cost with *D*, *S*, and *H*.

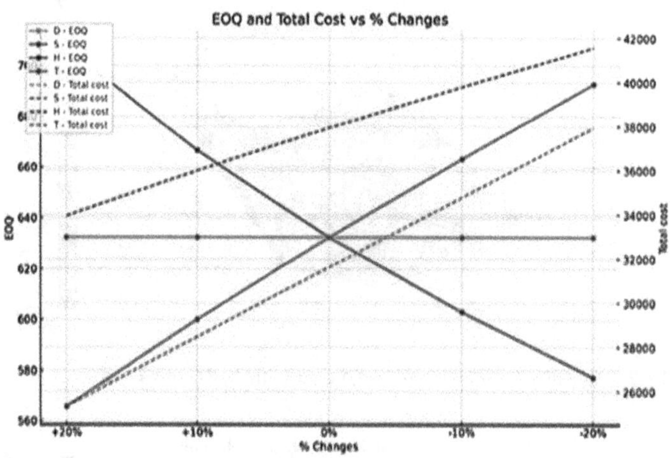

FIGURE 12.5 Sensitivity analysis for EOQ and total cost.

Setup cost (S):

- The EOQ rises from around 565.685 to 692.82 when the setup cost rises from \$80 to \$120.
- Similarly, the total cost increases from approximately 33,941.1 to 41,569.2.
- This indicates that higher setup costs result in larger order quantities and higher total costs.

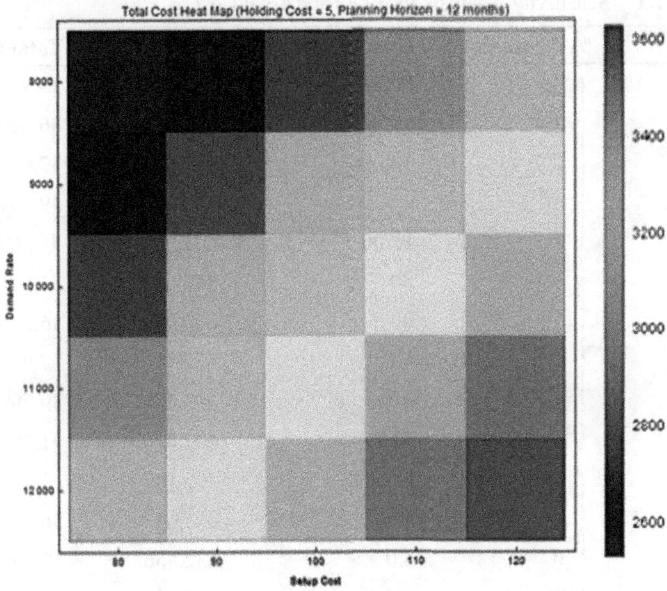

FIGURE 12.6 Sensitivity analysis by heat diagram.

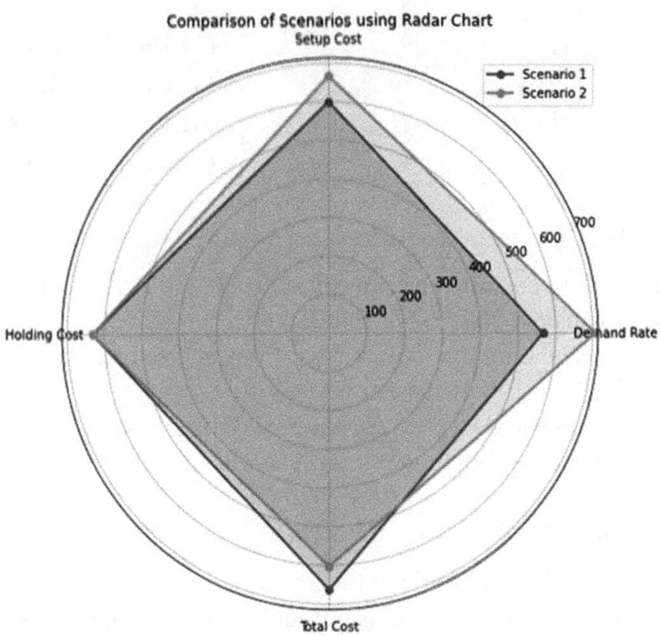

FIGURE 12.7 Sensitivity analysis by radar diagram.

TABLE 12.1 Sensitivity Analysis for EOQ and Total Cost

Parameters	% Changes	Changes' Values	EOQ	Total Cost
	+20	8000	565.685	33,941.1
	+10	9000	600.000	36,000
D	0	10,000	632.456	37,947.3
	−10	11,000	663.325	39,799.5
	−20	12,000	692.82	41,569.2
	+20	80	565.685	33,941.1
	+10	90	600.000	36,000
S	0	100	632.456	37,947.3
	−10	110	663.325	39,799.5
	−20	120	692.82	41,569.2
	+20	4	707.107	33,941.1
	+10	4.5	666.667	36,000
H	0	5.0	632.456	37,947.3
	−10	5.5	603.023	39,799.5
	−20	6.0	577.35	41,569.2
	+20	8	632.456	25,298.2
	+10	9	632.456	28,460.5
T	0	10	632.456	31,622.8
	−10	11	632.456	34,785.1
	−20	12	632.456	37,947.3

Holding cost (H):

- As holding cost increases from $4 to $6, the EOQ decreases from approximately 707.107 to 577.35.
- However, the total cost increases from approximately 33,941.1 to 41,569.2.
- This demonstrates how increased holding costs result in lower order quantities but higher total costs due to higher holding charges.

Total planning horizon (T):

- The total planning horizon ranges from 8 to 12 periods.
- However, the EOQ remains constant at approximately 632.456 for all values of *T*.

- In a similar vein, the total cost changes linearly as the planning horizon changes.
- This suggests that although the overall cost rises linearly over the course of the planning horizon, the EOQ is independent of it.

12.6.2 EXPLANATION OF THE CODE

1. EOQ and total cost functions: Specifies how the EOQ and total cost calculations work.
2. Parameter ranges: Defines the bounds on holding expenses, setup charges, and demand rates.
3. Calculate total costs: Determines the overall expense for every set of parameters
4. Heat map: To show how sensitive the overall cost is to variations in the setup and demand rates, a heat map with a given holding cost is created.
5. Radar chart: To compare EOQ and total cost under various situations, generate a radar chart.

Below is a sample Mathematica code snippet to perform sensitivity analysis and generate a heat map and radar chart.

12.6.3 HEAT MAP

The heat map shows how the overall cost fluctuates in response to different setup and demand rates. Lighter colors denote lower overall prices, whereas darker hues suggest greater total expenditures. This makes it possible for supply chain managers to find the setup costs and demand rates combinations that save overall costs rapidly.

12.6.4 IMPLICATION OF THE HEAT MAP

Supply chain experts may make better judgments regarding inventory policy and cost control by using this heat map to see how sensitive total inventory costs are to variations in setup costs and demand rates. Red markings draw attention to certain combinations of setup cost and demand rate, which aids in keeping focus on crucial parameter combinations.

- The demand rate, setup cost, holding cost, and total cost are only a few of the criteria that the radar map uses to evaluate various situations. A polygon with vertices matching the parameter values represents each scenario.
- The average value of each parameter across all situations shown in the radar map may be referred to as the mean in this context. This average aids in comprehending the typical value or central tendency of each parameter under various conditions.

12.7 SUMMARY STATISTICS

- The order quantity that often reduces the overall expenses of inventory is shown by the EOQ values. Consistent ordering patterns are shown by the near closeness of the mean and median, which points to a somewhat symmetrical distribution of EOQ values. There is moderate fluctuation around the mean EOQ, as indicated by the standard deviation of 50.2386 in Table 12.2.
- The total cost is the result of adding holding and ordering charges together. It is possible that the cost distribution is reasonably symmetrical since the mean and median total costs are similarly near. A standard deviation of 3014.32 in Table 12.2 suggests some variation in the overall expenses, which may be brought about by changes in the holding costs, setup costs, planning horizon, or demand rate.

TABLE 12.2 Statistics Analysis for EOQ and Total Cost

Parameter	Mean	Median	Standard Deviation
EOQ	630.857	632.456	50.2386
Total Cost	37,851.4	37,947.3	3014.32

12.8 PRACTICAL APPLICATION

There are several useful benefits when supply chain management incorporates sustainability. First, there is a definite financial gain as better resource management and reduced operating expenses are two benefits of logistics optimization that support long-term financial viability.

Second, by lowering regulatory risks and guaranteeing supply chain continuity, sustainable integration improves risk management. Furthermore, it functions as a tactical instrument for distinguishing brands in the market, augmenting their prestige and edge over competitors by showcasing their dedication to ethical business conduct. Finally, this strategy protects corporate expansion and profitability by anticipating and responding to potential legislative changes as well as changing customer preferences.

12.9 CONCLUSION

For EOQ and total cost, the above summary statistics provide typical values and variations. Comprehending the ways in which the criteria impact these figures enables enterprises to make knowledgeable choices regarding inventory control and minimize expenses. A more thorough and quantitative knowledge of these linkages may be obtained by looking at certain numbers and data trends in greater depth.

To conclude, statistical analysis and mathematical models are crucial for data-driven supply chain management decision-making.

With its vast mathematical and statistical capabilities, Mathematica software helps businesses to become more competitive in today's ever-changing business landscape, enhance supply chain operations, and obtain insightful information. Through the utilization of data-driven solutions, Mathematica enables enterprises to effectively handle intricate circumstances, satisfy the increasing need for flexibility and productivity, and promote sustainable growth in supply chain management.

12.10 FUTURE STUDIES

It is recommended that future research concentrate on improving analytical machine learning methods, such as benchmark data analytics or real-life data, in supply chain optimization settings. Global supply chains can benefit from enhanced operational efficiency and improved decision-making processes thanks to these technologies. Further investigation is required on how sustainability practices may be fully integrated into the dynamics of global supply chains.

KEYWORDS

- **economic order quantity**
- **total cost calculation**
- **inventory optimization**
- **finite planning horizon**
- **setup cost**
- **holding cost**

REFERENCES

1. Armstrong, J. S. (Ed.). (2001). *Principles of Forecasting: A Handbook for Researchers and Practitioners* (pp. 1–2, Vol. 30). Kluwer Academic: Boston, MA, USA.
2. Chopra, S., & Meindl, P. (2010). *Supply Chain Management, Strategy, Planning and Operation.* Pearson: Upper Saddle River, NJ, USA.
3. Makridakis, S., Wheelwright, S. C., & Hyndman, R. J. (1998). *Forecasting: Methods and Applications*. John Wiley & Sons.
4. Hadley, G., & Whitin, T. M. (1963). *Analysis of Inventory Systems*. Prentice-Hall.
5. Harris, F. W. (1913). How many parts to make at once. *Factory, The Magazine of Management*, *10*(2), 135–136.
6. Silver, E. A., Pyke, D. F., & Peterson, R. (1998). *Inventory Management and Production Planning and Scheduling*. Wiley.
7. Wu, Y., & Blackhurst, J. (2007). Evaluating supply chain disruption: The importance of vulnerability, threats, and risk management. *International Journal of Production Economics*, *111*(2), 291–301
8. Talluri, S., & Sarkis, J. (2002). A model for performance monitoring of suppliers. *International Journal of Production Research*, *40*(16), 4257–4269.
9. Ho, W., Xu, X., & Dey, P. K. (2010). Multi-criteria decision-making approaches for supplier evaluation and selection: A literature review. *European Journal of Operational Research*, *202*(1), 16–24.
10. Levine, D. M., Stephan, D. F., Szabat, K. A., & Baroudi, B. (2014). *Business Statistics: A First Course*. Pearson: Upper Saddle River, NJ, USA.
11. Dantzig, G. B. (1963). *Linear Programming and Extensions*. Princeton University Press.
12. Krajewski, L. J., & Ritzman, L. P. (2002). *Operations Management: Strategy and Analysis*. Addison-Wesley.
13. Wolfram Research. (2020). Wolfram mathematica. Retrieved from https://www.wolfram.com/mathematica/
14. Hogg, R. V., McKean, J., & Craig, A. T. (2005). *Introduction to Mathematical Statistics*. Pearson: Upper Saddle River, NJ, USA.

15. Montgomery, D. C. (2017). *Design and Analysis of Experiments*. John Wiley & Sons.
16. Devore, J. L. (2011). *Probability and Statistics for Engineering and the Sciences*. Cengage Learning.
17. Draper, N. R., & Smith, H. (1998). *Applied Regression Analysis*. John Wiley & Sons.
18. Law, A. M. (2014). *Simulation Modeling and Analysis*. McGraw-Hill.
19. Hillier, F. S., & Lieberman, G. J. (2015). *Introduction to Operations Research*. McGraw-Hill.
20. Bazaraa, M. S., Jarvis, J. J., & Sherali, H. D. (2010). *Linear Programming and Network Flows*, 4th edn., Wiley.

Index

Note: Page numbers followed by 'f' and 't' indicate figures and tables, respectively.

B

C

L

M

X

www.ingramcontent.com/pod-product-compliance
Lightning Source LLC
LaVergne TN
LVHW020626300926
849161LV00004B/627
* 9 7 8 1 7 7 9 6 4 1 0 0 7 *